The Last Hippy Poet
of the
Woodstock Generation

C. Steven Blue

Sunset West Publishing Group

The Last Hippy Poet
of the
Woodstock Generation

Copyright © 2023 C. Steven Blue
(C. Steven Blue is the pen name for Steven C. Schreiner)

All rights reserved. No part of this book may be reproduced in any form or by any electronic or mechanical means, including information storage and retrieval systems, without the written permission of the publisher, except by reviewers, who may quote brief passages in a review.

First Edition

ISBN 978-0-9979975-0-7

Printed in the U.S.A.

Sunset West Publishing Group

The Last Hippy Poet
of the
Woodstock Generation

Contents

Part 1: Heartbreak Kid—on the streets of Hollywood in the 1960s 1

1950 – 1962: Arizona, Pasadena, The Rose Parade, and Surfing 3

1963 – 1965: Finally a Teenager, The Beatles and a Family Goodbye 13

1966: American Bandstand, Katie and The Sunset Strip 23

1967: The Summer of Love, Tahquitz Falls, and Arizona 35

1968 – October, 1969: High School Marriage and Arthur 49

1969, November-December: Kidnapped and Robbed, Topanga Beach 67

1970, January-April: Sandy and Lady, My Teens Are Over 85

1970, April-June: The Beatles Break Up, From Inglewood Back to Hollywood 99

1970, July-October: The Manson Family, Birth of Shane 113

1970, October-December: Jessie Returns, Jimi & Janis 131

1971: Kids, Love-Ins, and the Earthquake 163

Original Artwork by C. Steven Blue 1966-1972 189

1972 – 1973: A New Beginning Behind the Orange Curtain and Celeste 215

1974, January-September: California Jam, Leaving Gourmet Collective 231

1974, October – 1975: Soul Mates and the Black Forest Deli 253

1976 – 1977: Breakdown, The Road There & The Road Back 267

1978 – 1979, March: Back From the Road, Return to Hollywood, and Stage Production 289

1979, April-December: Back With Shelly 317

Part 2: Bat's Ass Blues 343

Set #1: self-perception and temporal contemplation 345

Set #2: paid my dues for the retrospective blues 365

Set #3: resounding ramifications of political instigations 391

Set #4: introspective reflections and peripheral articulations 427

Set #5: inner observations and nature's illuminations 451

Set #6: fantasy ballads and human frailties 463

Set #7: artistic declarations, religiosity, and amphigory moments . . . 501

Part 3: Butterflies On Lavender 517

Set #1: incidental observation: awakenings of love 519

Set #2: passionate articulation: intricacies of love 543

Set #3: reflective contemplation: movements of love 567

Set #4: singular declaration: futures of love 591

Set #5: enduring revelation: resolutions of love 609

About the Author 631

Credits & Acknowledgements 632

Appendix A: Part 1 633

Appendix B: Part 2 634

Appendix C: Part 3 638

Contact information 641

Other Books 642

The Last Hippy Poet of the Woodstock Generation

— A Triad —

Part 1: *Heartbreak Kid—on the streets of Hollywood in the 1960s*
A psychedelic memoir—chronicles of my teens and twenties growing up in Hollywood during the turbulent 1960s and beyond.

Part 2: *Bat's Ass Blues*
A section of narrative verse on the nature of perception—introspection, fantasy and dreams, political, social and spiritual/religious commentary.

Part 3: *Butterflies On Lavender*
A section of narrative verse on the nature of love—unveiling the many facets of love—and the feelings thereof.

— This work is my magnum opus —

the culmination of over 50 years as a poet, author, artist, and musician

Besides being a triad book consisting of three interrelated parts, *The Last Hippy Poet of the Woodstock Generation* is also a hybrid book, containing prose, verse, artwork, and links to performances.

*Special note for this paperback edition:
The artwork and photos in this book are all in black and white. The full color artwork and photos can be seen in both the Hardcover and eBook editions of this book.

For content review, please visit my website, www.wordsongs.com

May my words encourage and entertain you.

— *C. Steven Blue,* 2023

Part 1:

Heartbreak Kid—on the streets of Hollywood in the 1960s

— a psychedelic memoir —

chronicles of my teens and twenties growing up in Hollywood during the turbulent 1960s and beyond.

Written during the pandemic lockdown, March-June, 2020

Preface

Part 1: *Heartbreak Kid—on the streets of Hollywood in the 1960s,* is, in and of itself, a complete book. It is a psychedelic memoir, combining the adventures of my youth with historical elements of the times. It is the story of my teenage years through my twenties, growing up on the streets of Hollywood during the turbulent 1960s and beyond. My generation had a saying—*never trust anyone over 30*. This book covers my life right up to that point—my 30th birthday—the sad day I had to leave my teens and twenties behind. 90% truth with a smidgen of fiction. Or, is it merely a figment . . . of my psychedelic mind?

In all honesty, this book probably could be termed an autobiographical novel, since names have been changed and a few of the circumstances have been altered—to protect the innocent . . . and the guilty—including me. If you think you are one of the guilty, you may remember things differently. Nevertheless, this is my story, remembered my way—from my memories, flashbacks and psychedelic experiences. I have done my best to make this book tell a truthful story and not harm anyone—but it is a story, after all. I regret any unintentional harm resulting from this book.

If you are a teenager growing up in these times, I hope these stories, poems, and works of art will speak out to you—of the universal feelings of youth, no matter what country or century you find yourself in. Because my own time as a teenager was during the 1960s, many of my stories reflect the hippy idealism of those days.[1] I was a true *flower child*, and I am still, as some have called me, one of the last hippy poets of the Woodstock Generation.

If you are a grownup reading this book, I hope it will spark your reminiscence about the wild rollercoaster ride of your own youth.

— *C. Steven Blue,* 2023

---

1. Hippy: in the 21st century, some people say that hippy is an incorrect spelling, when describing the members of the counter-culture of the 1960s. The true fact is that both hippie and hippy are correct spellings, and both were in use during those days. As one of the original hippies on the Sunset Strip, my fellow rebels and I usually referred to ourselves as: hippy—singular, and hippies—plural.

1950 – 1962:

Arizona, Pasadena, The Rose Parade, and Surfing

It was the end of high school and summer was here. To celebrate, I wanted to drop LSD and watch the sunset on the beach. My wife, Jenny, agreed to be my designated driver. It was late afternoon as we headed west out of Hollywood, to Santa Monica. I was already coming on strong to the acid. My whole body tingled. I gazed out the front window. Everything I saw had trails, like rainbow-colored comet tails—the traffic lights, the cars, even the people walking.

By the time we arrived at the beach, I was so stoned that I couldn't talk or even get out of the car. All I could do was curl up in a fetal position in the back seat. Jenny said, "You probably took too strong a dose!" She was so scared! Not knowing what to do, she drove us back to Hollywood and pulled up in front of the police station, ran inside and asked for help.

The next thing I knew, I was flat on my back on an observation table, with bright lights shining down on me. At least six people were leaning over me looking straight into my eyes, and some of them were in uniform! Oddly, I wasn't instantly paranoid. When they told me they had shot me with Thorazine, I realized why. They said I had had a bad drug experience, then proceeded to ask me a bunch of questions, none of which I remember.

I never found out what their questions were, but from then on, I knew I was on their radar. My long hair and love beads surely had marked me as one of the hippies they loved to hassle on the Sunset Strip.

I was lucky they didn't arrest me right then. They let my wife take me home, where I discovered I actually felt great! I think the Thorazine gave me one of the best acid trips I would ever have.

I took out my drawing pad and a pencil. Images of wonder and excitement displayed themselves right on the blank page, as if by magic. I couldn't draw them as fast as I could see them, but I did end up with two pretty weird drawings. Looking at them later, though, I actually thought they were pretty cool.

With all the drugs and alcohol I was ingesting, how did I ever survive to get clean and sober in my 30s? I guess I was one of the lucky ones . . . but more about that later.

↯

My name is Steven. I was born right smack dab in the middle of the 20th century, on January 20th, the day that is Inauguration Day. Since 1986, it is also, sometimes, Martin Luther King Jr. Day.

My birthday always follows the years: I was 10 in 1960 and 20 in 1970. I would be a half-century old at the turn of the new millennium.

My birthplace was Phoenix, Arizona, but my family moved to Pasadena, California when I was only 2 years old. We would often drive back to Phoenix to visit Nini. She was Mom's mother, but for some reason we never called her Grandma. To my sister, brother and I, she would always be Nini.

My sister, Kathy, is a year older than I am. We were both born at the 7th Street hospital, only a few blocks from Nini's house. My brother, Bob, who is two years younger than me, was born in Pasadena after we moved there. I would live in the L. A. area throughout my childhood, my teens and my adulthood, right up until the time I retired from work—over 50 years in all. I may have been born in Arizona, but I was a Southern California boy through and through!

My earliest recallable memories are from Nini's house on Thanksgiving Day, 1953 . . .

It was my own private underworld, and fascination was the driving force of all I could see and hear. All the giggling voices were above me as I crawled out from beneath the dining room table to see what all the commotion was. Nini, Mom and Dad were still spiking the fruitcake. It would be many years before I would understand what that meant.

Later that day, while all the grownups were busy, this little 3 year old went wandering off down the street on my own first adventure alone. Mom spotted me, and she was frantic! By the time she finally caught up to me on the north corner of the block, I was smiling mischievously, with a look of wonder in my eyes. Much to her relief, I had not yet attempted to cross the street.

I loved growing up in Pasadena. In the late '50s, Mom would let us three kids spend New Year's Eve camped out in our sleeping bags on Colorado Boulevard, saving places for our family to watch The Rose Parade the next morning. Our house was roughly three blocks north of the parade route, so Mom could check on us if she needed to.

All along the parade route, campers were having an all-night party. Hot rods and custom cars cruised up and down the boulevard. People huddled in their own little areas, clutching hot chocolate or coffee, trying to fend off the winter night chill. Giant bonfire parties raged on the front lawn of Pasadena City College, where throngs of students gathered to celebrate.

Pasadena was a busy hub for its youth back then, with soda shops, record stores, the Boys and Girls clubs, Friday night school dances and the Saturday night dance at the Pasadena Civic Auditorium.

Bob's Big Boy Restaurants played a big part in Pasadena's culture. Big Bobs and Little Bobs were both on Colorado Blvd. about 3 miles apart. Big Bobs had carhop service, while Little Bobs was only an indoor restaurant. On the weekends, people would wait in a line several blocks long to get into Big Bobs—Greasers and surfers, all the teenagers in their hot rods, trying to get into the carhop service to order burgers, fries and Cokes served right in their cars. The scene was right out of the movie *American Graffiti*! It even inspired a song by Jan & Dean, "The Little Old Lady From Pasadena."

⚡

When I was 9 years old, I became interested in science, particularly electricity. Mom, who was always supportive of whatever interests we kids developed, waited until Christmas and then surprised me with an electrical set, a crystal radio kit and a set of different kinds of magnets.

Experimenting with the electrical set, I learned how to build simple electric circuits that actually worked. I learned the difference between AC and DC currents, which came in handy later in life when I became an electrician in Hollywood, creating the stage lighting behind the scenes in television and live theatre.

I built the crystal radio, but even when I was finished, I couldn't understand how a rock crystal could actually make a radio work without any other power. To me it was like magic. This fascinated me and sparked my lifelong interest in metaphysical things.

The magnets were also fascinating. I played with them for weeks, attracting anything metal lying around the house, yard or garage. I used them at school, pretending to my friends that they were magic. I used them to tease the girls by grabbing bobby pins right out of their hair. I learned that if you put the same poles of two magnets together (either north or south) they would repel away from each other. I dreamed of someday finding a way to use magnetism to actually repel a space ship right off the earth and out of our atmosphere, without any kind of fuel. Maybe I wasn't so far off. Maybe someday we will do just that.

I had a paper route when I was nine. I delivered both the Pasadena Independent and the Star News to people in our neighborhood. I loved riding my bike early in the morning, when people were not awake yet and the streets were deserted and quiet. I had the paper route for several years, and I'd also solicit subscriptions door to door when I went around each month to collect the money from the subscribers on my route.

Something else that was extremely cool happened just before Christmas. Dad would drive up to Victorville and return home with the back seat of his car packed with branches of mistletoe. We always thought he had bought it really cheap somewhere, but years later we found out he had simply knocked it out of trees along the highway with a broomstick.

He brought it home each year, for us kids to sell around the neighborhood, for each of us to earn some spending money for Christmas gifts for the rest of the family. Mom would help us break up the mistletoe into little bunches, then pack it into baggies, tying each with a ribbon into a bow.

Then Dad would give us instructions, "Knock on peoples' doors and when they answer, tell them you are selling mistletoe to earn spending money for Christmas. When they ask you how much it is, tell them it is whatever they want to give you, whatever they feel it's worth." This was ingenious, because we made so much more money that way than if we had done a set price. Of course, some people would give us a mere quarter or 50 cents, but most people would give us $1.00, $2.00, sometimes even up to $5.00. People knew the Christmas tree lots were selling a little teeny sprig of mistletoe, with a tiny ribbon, for around $1.49, but we were offering them a baggy chock full of mistletoe—and fresh! So Dad's plan worked really well.

My brother and I loved selling the mistletoe, and we looked forward to it each year. But my sister was not really into it. She didn't want to knock on people's doors. She was pretty shy about that kind of stuff. I don't know what she did for Christmas spending money (I think Mom would give her some), but Bob and I always scored big and had a great time.

Just as I turned 10, the '60s began. That year our babysitter, Beverly, taught Kathy and me how to dance the California Swing as we watched *American Bandstand* on Saturday afternoons, broadcast live on TV from Philadelphia. Boy, did I love to dance!

Bob and I used to ride our bikes downtown to the Pasadena Bowling Alley at the corner of Lake and Colorado behind the Thrifty Drug Store. While we were bowling, we'd order extra crispy french fries with blue cheese dressing for dipping instead of ketchup. The dressing was from Bob's Big Boy. It was the best blue cheese dressing in the world! Bob's was famous for it, and they bottled it for sale. You could even get it at the local supermarket, and Mom used to bring it home.

I belonged to the Pasadena Boys Club. I loved going there because there were so many interesting projects and skills to do and learn. I'd swim, play pool, and create stuff in their machine shops. There were volunteer counselors who taught me how to use a lathe, drill press, table saw, metal bender and other tools. One of them taught me how to make a multicolored teardrop, which was certainly popular in those days amongst young boys, and it was a lot of fun to make. Here's how:

- Cut out several small squares of 1/4" thick plastic.
- Glue the squares together with glue dyed in different colors.
- Draw a teardrop shape on top.
- Cut the shape out with a band saw.
- Use an electric sander to shape the whole thing into a round, teardrop shape.
- Sand the teardrop with rough and then fine sandpaper until super smooth.
- Buff it out with a buffing wheel until crystal clear like glass.

When I was done, I had what looked like a multicolored gemstone in the shape of a tear. It was so cool! I drilled a hole in it and wore it around my neck.

The Boys Club also had a summer camp, Camp Norris, which I went to for two weeks every summer. We swam in the lake, rode horses and explored the forest. On one exploration I found a small stick of wood with a round, gnarled hunk at one end, which made it look like a cave man's club. I painted it red, to look like there was blood on it. Then I'd walk around pretending to be a cave man—Ug! Ug! (I still have it).

At night around the campfire, we would roast marshmallows and sing, "skin-a-merink-a-dink-e-dink, skin-a-merink-e-doo, I love you . . . Camp Norris!"

We would all bunk together by age group in large bunkhouses, and we would be served pancakes for breakfast every morning—bad pancakes! Although I had loved pancakes, I became so sick of them that I wouldn't eat pancakes again until I was an adult.

My first year at camp, when we were riding horses through the forest, I fell off mine. It scared me so bad, I would not get back on. The next year, however, they made me get back on a horse, and I was fine after that.

The Boys Club celebrated Tom Sawyer/Sadie Hawkins Day every summer at a park adjacent to the club. Our families came, and we'd all barbecue hot dogs and hamburgers and play games. The kids had a treasure hunt. Then, the parents joined in for a gunny sack race and tug-of-war in the mud: There was a long rope, with a pool of mud in the middle, and families on each side trying to pull the other side into the mud. It was all great fun!

They also had a contest called 'Mr. Full Pockets.' They would count everything the boys had in their pockets, and whoever had the most stuff won. When I was 11, I won the contest and my picture appeared in the local newspaper, along with an article describing the event. There was also an article about my win in the monthly newsletter of the company my dad worked for. Here it is:

HONEST ANSWERS

The job application blank asked, "Have you ever been arrested?" The sweet young applicant put down, "No". The next question was, "Why"— meant for those who had been arrested. But the would-be secretary simply wrote, "Never got caught."

SPEAKERS' DILEMMAS

Two great public speakers were comparing experiences.

"Nothing makes me madder," said Mr. Stassi, "than to see a salesman glance at his watch during one of my training sessions."

"Even worse," said Mr. Sentman, "is to see the clock-watchers in my audience hold their watches up to their ears to make sure they haven't stopped."

IN A DOCTOR'S OFFICE

As his wife helped him into the doctor's waiting room, the middle-aged man was limping badly, all bent over at the waist. A woman seated in the office viewed the scene with sympathy. "Arthritis with complications?" she asked.

The wife shook her head. "Do-it-yourself," she explained, "with concrete blocks."

CHILDHOOD ESSAY

Asked to write a brief essay on the life of Benjamin Franklin, one little girl wrote, "He was born in Boston, travelled to Philadelphia, met a lady on the street, she laughed at him, he married her, and discovered electricity."

Rep's Son Elected "MR. FULL POCKETS"

Steven Schreiner, 11-year-old son of California representative C. H. Schreiner, recently won the title of "Mr. Full Pockets" in a Pasadena boy's club contest.

Twenty man-minutes were needed to count the valuable bottle caps, rubber bands, floor tiles, match boxes, paper clips, checkers, sea shells, string, dice, pencils, nails, thread, crayons, even soap in Steven's pockets. That's a Polynesian tiki around his neck.

Steven lives in Pasadena with his parents and their two other children, Kathy and Bob. His golf-loving father didn't seem particularly surprised to see what Steven had in his pockets.

"It's nothing at all," he shrugged. "You should see what my wife Phyllis keeps in her **purse**."

Tangley Topics

Published twice a month for Tangley Oaks Representatives and their families.

Editor . . . . . . Jerry Hofeld

⚡

During the summer, Mom would often give the three of us each a quarter to go to the Saturday movie matinee at the Washington theatre at the corner of Lake and Washington. A quarter was enough money for the movies and treats. I would get popcorn and Coke, along with Milk Duds, Flicks or Ice Cream Bon Bons. While I stuffed my face, I could see the latest Commander Cody episode, a cartoon and two movies. My favorite movies we saw there were *House on Haunted Hill* and *The Mask*, which was in 3D—and I could keep the glasses we wore to watch it.

Like every other kid, summertime was my favorite time. School was out and Mom would pack a big picnic lunch and take us to the beach at Belmont Shore. There, we would spend the day body surfing, hunting sand crabs, building sand castles and, of course, eating.

Summer was also a great time to play hide-n-seek with everyone in the neighborhood. When we played hide-n-seek, my favorite place to hide was in the top of a tree right across the street from our house. I would climb the tree and perch on a branch where I could see everything that was going on but no one could see me. It seemed like I was almost always able to get away with it.

Mom would also set up a sprinkler in the front yard for us and our neighborhood friends to run through in our bathing suits to cool off. Then she'd set up a table on the front driveway and cut up a bunch of watermelons for us all to eat, so we could spit seeds outside and make as big a mess as we wanted, then run through the sprinkler again to wash off all the sticky juice. When we were finished, we'd take our watermelon rinds out into the middle of the street and skip them down the road, like skimming flat stones on a lake, to see who could get them the farthest. Even though the rinds ended up all over the neighborhood, nobody complained.

Mom also made the best homemade hard-shell tacos in the world (her mom's Southwest recipe). The secret is in the making of the shells. Whenever she would make them, all my friends wanted to come over to our house for dinner. She passed the recipe and the know-how down to me, and I've been making them for years. Now my kids make them too.

⚡

Kathy and I loved to go to the dance at Dewald's Ballroom every Saturday night at the Civic Auditorium. Her boyfriend, Mick, was a surfer, and one of his surfer buddies had a '49 Cadillac Hearse, with purple velvet interior. He painted it bright orange and turned it into a surf wagon. Mick and his buddy would show up at the Civic after the dance ended to pick up Kathy, me and other friends. We'd all pile into the back, cruise Colorado Boulevard and end up at Big Bob's, where we'd wait in line with the rest of the cruisers until it was our turn to get into the carhop service. We'd all order burgers, fries and Cokes. They would let you add extra flavors in your Coke if you wanted, and I always had them add cherry and chocolate syrups. Cherry-chocolate Cokes were my favorite!

Sometimes Bob and I were given permission by Mom to go to the beach in the hearse with my sister and Mick. They would always go to County Line (the L.A./Ventura county line) on Pacific Coast Highway, which was one of the best surfing spots in SoCal. We would watch the surfers catch waves all day while we'd swim and play and lie in the sun.

In the summer of 1962, Mom let me and Bob spend a couple of weekends there with Kathy, Mick and all the surfers. Mick taught me how to surf, and I finally stood up on a surfboard for the first time, riding a wave into the shore. What a blast!

Each evening, the surfers would build a big bonfire on the beach. They put all their surfboards around it in a big circle, stuck on edge into the sand to create a wind block. Then, we put our sleeping bags just inside the circle, so the boards blocked us from the wind. We fell asleep on the dark beach, watching the bonfire and the bright stars.

Across the highway from the beach was a little restaurant called Mother's. We'd go over there in the morning for breakfast. They had a pinball machine that I loved to play. So did Bob. I became an expert on it and would often win game after game for free. I'd spend hours at Mother's playing pinball.

1963 – 1965:

Finally a Teenager, The Beatles and a Family Goodbye

The days of *mischief* were ending and my teens were drawing near. *Mischief* is the term my neighbor buddies and I called our excursions through the backyards of our neighborhood. Beginning when I was 5 years old up until I turned 12, we would get together and climb our own back fences, then hop onto other neighbors' garages and climb their trees or walk their fence lines up and down the block. We'd pick fruit and practice our jumping and climbing skills, while looking in peoples' backyards to see what kind of new and interesting stuff they had, generally looking for anything new or exciting to do or see.

We had a little pomegranate bush in the corner of our backyard that gave us only 10-12 pomegranates every year. My brother and I would have wars with the seeds, spitting them at each other and leaving our mouths, hands and everything we touched lipstick ruby. Mom would be so pissed trying to get the stains out of our clothes. We also had an apricot tree and two fig trees. I loved apricots but hated figs.

We had three old, huge avocado trees in our backyard—so big, I had a treehouse in one of them. All my buddies were allowed in my 'sky fort.' But girls, no! With one exception, Faye, who lived down the block. Faye and I were great friends. We talked to each other about anything and everything: school, crushes, family, movies, everything.

In the fort, I always kept salt and pepper along with spoons and a knife to eat avocados with. When they were ripe, Faye and I would stick our hands out the treehouse window and pluck them right off the tree, cut them in half, sprinkle them with salt and pepper, and eat 'em right out of the shell. Yum!

One day as I was climbing up the tree to my hideaway, one of the ladder planks that I had nailed into the tree trunk gave way. I fell backward, crashing onto a chain-link fence and landing on my back—on a pile of bricks! It knocked the wind out of me! Faye ran screaming to Mom, and she came rushing out of the house. She leaned down and held me until I finally caught my breath, then told me everything was fine. If Mom said it, you could believe it. I stood up, and we carried on with our playing as though nothing had happened.

That was 1962. My days at Longfellow Elementary School had ended. After that summer, I would finally be a teenager going to John Marshall Junior High School. All my teenage years would play out during the '60s— a most exciting and turbulent time in the U.S. and around the world.

⁂

At 13, in my first year at Marshall, I had become a southpaw pitcher in the Pasadena Little League. I used to practice my pitching in the backyard. Mom was always my catcher and coach since Dad seemed always to be away selling Collier's Encyclopedias. Traveling salesmen are rarely home.

One time when we were practicing, one of my pitches went wild and whacked Mom in the knee! She sustained a knot on it that lasted for years. I don't think it ever went away, actually, but that didn't stop her from being my catcher. She was always encouraging me to do whatever I loved.

I was also 2nd trumpet in our school orchestra. I started playing in elementary school, where I learned on a rented trumpet while Mom tried to decide if I was serious enough about it to continue. When I started junior high, Mom and Dad bought me my own trumpet. They used to make me practice in my bedroom closet so I wouldn't drive everyone else crazy with the noise.

In school, I was an avid learner, full of optimism and excitement. I was a natural in math; it came easily to me. I hardly had to study at all to ace my tests.

At our school, there were the usual cliques—rich kids, preppies and so forth—but the kids were mainly divided up into two groups: greasers and surfers. My sister, Kathy, my brother, Bob, and I were greasers, mostly because Kathy's new boyfriend, Kenny, was such an influence on us. Kenny's brother, Jessie, was in my class, and we hung out a bit. He turned me on to my first cigarette. When Mom found out I was smoking, she insisted I stop. But I figured, hey, if she smoked, why couldn't I? It couldn't be so bad. She smoked Parliament brand cigarettes, which had these long, white filters. They tasted awful, but that didn't stop me from sneaking one from her pack when I could.

In my first year at Marshall, I met another Jessie, one who would become my best friend during junior high. Jessie was part of the surfer crowd, which might have stopped him from being best friends with a greaser. However, we had something in common: We both loved music. He was a drummer and I was a trumpet player. And we both loved to dance. Our school had a Friday night canteen dance, where I could practice my dancing chops with girls from my class. Jessie and I hung out on Fridays at the dances and at the Allen drugstore down the street almost every day after school. Allen's had a soda fountain and jukebox, so lots of kids liked to hang there after school let out.

⚡

Dad gave me my first alcohol in 1963. In summertime, our family loved to barbecue and eat outside in our back yard. Dad would cook something on our Weber charcoal grill while the rest of the family played ping-pong. One day that summer, Dad was teaching me how to barbecue ribs and he let me taste a sip of his beer. I instantly took to it!

After that, I would try to get beer whenever I could. Jessie and I would hang out in front of a liquor store on the weekends, trying to get someone to buy it for us. When that didn't work, we'd try another source. Down the street from my house lived a man named Fay, who was the neighborhood drunk and a hoarder. When Jesse and I walked into his house, newspapers and junk were piled as high as we were tall. We had to walk down narrow aisles between the junk to get to his kitchen, where he was usually hanging out smoking filterless Camel cigarettes—everybody knew this was the hardcore brand. We'd offer to buy Fay cigarettes if he'd buy us some beer.

We would hide the beer at my house, in the garage, and then sneak in there to drink whenever we could. One time, we got sooooo... drunk and walked downtown to Little Bob's, where a lot of college students hung out. Jessie grew belligerent with one guy, who then threatened to beat the shit out of us. We had to sneak out of there on our hands and knees, and then we ran down the street until we were safe.

Later on, in high school, we'd score some cherry brandy and drink it under the bleachers during football games. So alcohol became a familiar friend to me at a pretty young age.

⚡

I had my first crush at 13. California beach movies were all the rage for teens at the time, like *Beach Party* and its sequels starring Frankie Avalon and Annette Funicello, who were sunny, wholesome, wholly California. And then there was Sandra Dee, the *Queen of Teens*, in *Gidget*—surfing, singing and dancing on Southern California beaches, all on the big screen!

That summer, Ann Margret burst onto the movie screen in *Bye Bye Birdie*! The opening and closing scenes, with her singing and wiggling her breasts practically out of that low cut dress while shaking her long red hair . . . all that on a bright blue background—Wow! Ann Margret was totally breathtaking, the be-all-and-end-all for me. The way she looked. The way she sang. Especially the way she danced! I think every teenage boy must have had a crush on her that year. In the summer of '63, as I said, I was 13. And I saw *Bye Bye Birdie* 13 times!

⚡

Everything looked rosy at age 13, but as it turned out, my teenage years were destined to be like the '60s themselves—tumultuous!

One day, I was sitting in science class waiting for the teacher to show up. He suddenly burst into the room and called the whole class to order. "President Kennedy has just been killed," he said, and then he actually broke down in tears. It was the first time I had ever seen a grown man cry. I could not believe it because he was such a stern teacher, always serious and never seemingly showing any emotion. To this day, I am amazed by his vulnerability, which you rarely saw from men in my dad's generation.

That day, November 22, 1963, is the day I became politically aware—much sooner than I should have. I believe it was the day that marked the end of my childhood. Our whole country mourned the man who said, "Ask not what your country can do for you; ask what you can do for your country."

Only three months later, on February 9th, 1964, the Beatles burst on the scene, performing in the U.S. for the very first time—on *The Ed Sullivan Show*. It was history in the making, and a new optimism seemed to take hold!

It seemed as though every teenager in the country had their eyes glued to their TVs that night. *Beatlemania* swept through America like a whirlwind. With that one TV appearance, The Beatles changed everything. They woke us up! Their arrival on the scene completely changed the musical landscape for my generation, and they definitely inspired me in the years to come.

Our family always watched *The Ed Sullivan Show*. Every week we would all sit together in our living room in front of the TV and watch the many performers and original acts presented. We never knew what was coming next, but it was always exciting.

From that first moment when The Beatles appeared on our TV screen, with their clean-cut suits and mop-top hair, Kathy and I fell in love with them and their music. Bob, at 12, was disinterested, but to a 15-year-old girl and a 14-year-old boy, the world seemed to open up. And we were transfixed.

Later that year, we found out that The Beatles would be playing at the Hollywood Bowl. We had to go. We bought tickets, and in August of 1964 Mom drove Kathy and me to see them in concert.

There was an energy in the air, and I was exhilarated, intoxicated. All those screaming girls in the audience, many crying and some even fainting, screaming so loud you couldn't even hear the music. That music! The Beatle's music was a precursor to the music happenings of our generation.

⚡

For me, right then at age 14, it was all about dancing to the music—especially at Dewald's Ballroom on Saturday nights at the Civic. All the boys had to wear coats and ties. If you didn't have the proper attire, you could rent it at the coat-check area before you went in. Girls had to wear skirts or dresses, and we loved to see them twirling on the dance floor. Grey felt skirts with embroidered poodles were all the rage.

A girl named Liz looked absolutely incredible as she swiveled in one of those skirts. The first time I saw Liz dancing, I couldn't take my eyes off her big blue eyes and natural, long blond hair. She looked like Hayley Mills. I asked her to dance. We danced so well together, and it felt so right, that we became dance partners. We went to different schools, but we would meet at the Civic every Saturday night.

We danced to some of the most famous bands of the day: The Kingsmen, The Ike and Tina Turner Revue, Dick & Dee Dee, The Righteous Brothers, and many more. We especially loved dancing slow to the song, "Bubbles," an original by the house band, The Diaboliques. Whenever that song began, the ballroom lights would go down and a giant mirror ball on the ceiling would spin, creating the dreamiest atmosphere for slow dancing—stars spinning all over the floor, walls and ceiling.

Then there were the long line dances, where couples would dance down the middle of the line, doing the *Slauson*, the *Pony* and the *Jerk*. We knew all the latest dances and loved doing them.

The ballroom at the Civic was huge. It had a large stage on the east side, big enough for a small orchestra, with a dance floor that looked as big as the skating rink it would many years later be converted into. On the south side, there were big, double doors that led to an outside balcony, where we would go to cool off after dancing amid hundreds of teens. The balcony was also the smoking area, and there was always billowing smoke from so many teens smoking.

It was out on that balcony that I asked Liz to go steady, and I knew she accepted when she wrapped her arms around me and accepted the St. Christopher on a chain that I handed her. It was our symbol of going steady in 1964 in Pasadena. Dancing together, and loving it, had led to us going steady and feeling in love—puppy love!

I didn't know it then, but found out soon after, that Liz's family was wealthy. They lived in one of the rich parts of town, up Linda Vista Ave., in the hills above the Rose Bowl. That was six miles from my house and up and down steep hills, a trek I simply could not make on foot, or on my bike, as often as I wanted to see her. So I discovered what it was like to hitchhike.

Liz's family had a swimming pool, and we spent many fun afternoons after school swimming and hanging out together with our school friends. Our time together would be short lived though, because she informed me that soon her family would be moving to Mill Valley in Northern California. To this 14 year old, it might as well have been China. I didn't ever want Liz to leave.

My family lived on Michigan Ave., a little north of Villa Ave., in a typical working class neighborhood, nowhere near Liz or the richer kids from school, who mostly lived where she did or in Hastings Ranch. Mom and Dad rented our house. They never owned one. I remember we lived in four different houses in Pasadena while I was growing up. I guess you could call us lower middle class.

Mom had a college education, from USC. But Dad did not go to college, and somehow we could tell he resented Mom's higher education. She had studied to be a fashion designer and Dad used to belittle her about it. I saw some of her designs and drawings, and I thought they were wonderful—full of style and beauty. As I said earlier, Dad was a traveling salesman—a door-to-door salesman. Mom worked in a local hearing aid store on Colorado Blvd. Even though they both worked, they struggled to make ends meet. But I do remember that Dad bought a new car once, because he needed it for travel for his work.

Kathy, Bob and I often had to make our own lunches in the mornings and take care of ourselves after school until Mom came home from work.

Mom and Dad loved to go out dancing and drinking with their friends, leaving us with the babysitter. Dad would often get drunk, and when he did, he was a mean drunk, taking it out on Mom or on us. When I couldn't take his drunkenness or hangover behavior, I would run down the street to Jefferson Park on Villa St., where I'd climb up the giant metal rocket ship, which had monkey bars and a slide. I would climb all the way up to the tiptop, and then just sit there. It was my place to hide from the world. There was a song that year by The Beatles, "There's A Place." Whenever I heard that song, I thought of my secret place where I could go to get away.

Dad would withhold our allowance when we didn't do what he wanted. Or, worse, he would make us pull down our pants and lean over his knees while he whacked us with his belt on our bare bottoms. If we didn't remove our clothing fast enough, or if we resisted, he would hit us harder and longer. One time, he had told me to clean up all the old fruit fallen from the apricot tree in the back yard—but I hadn't done it. He became so angry that he full-fisted slugged me—right in the face! I'll never forget it, and I never felt the same about him after that. I felt as if he didn't care about me and had no idea who I was.

⚡

My whole family loved music, and from an early age I loved all the arts—music, painting, drawing, writing, and of course dancing. As far back as I can remember, I always had big dreams. Teachers used to catch me staring out the window, daydreaming. Yes, I was a dreamer with a vivid imagination, which encouraged me in my desires, but often got me scolded.

On reflection, 4th grade seems to have been a milestone in my early creative development. I had gone to Longfellow Elementary School, named after the poet, Henry Wadsworth Longfellow. My 4th grade teacher, Mrs. Kime, had read an epic poem to us, written by our school's namesake, titled, "The Song of Hiawatha." I loved the poem so much that I read it over and over . . . *"By the shore of Gitche Gumee / By the shining Big-Sea-Water / At the doorway of his wigwam / In the pleasant Summer morning / Hiawatha stood and waited."*

I wrote my first poems in Mrs. Kime's class when I was 9 and 10 years old. She encouraged reading and writing, and she convinced me to join the book club at the library across the street from school, which also had a poetry club. My favorite book was *King Arthur and the Knights of the Round Table*. At home, I would build forts out of the huge cardboard boxes my brother and I found behind the local appliance store. I would sit in my cardboard fort and pretend I was Sir Galahad. I created a little handmade book of poems in Mrs. Kime's class and drew a picture of Sir Galahad on the cover. Because of her encouragement, I won my first poetry award at age 12.

By junior high, I was drawing, painting, and writing poetry in a journal that I kept under my bed. I was also playing the trumpet, and of course playing baseball. I was the star southpaw pitcher in Pasadena Little League. I still have my trophy.

My friend, Max, was on my baseball team, The Cubs. His family lived on the next block over from us. They were of Mexican and Dutch descent, and everyone in their family was distinctly good looking. Max was in my class at school, and his sister, Maria, was in the class one year behind us. I had a huge crush on Maria before I met Liz. I used to go swimming at the Pasadena community pool downtown, and I would often run into Maria there. I loved watching her swim and she looked great in a bikini. She liked me too, and once kissed me deeply in the pool. Nothing else ever came of it, but we remained friends throughout junior high. The Beatles song, "Do You Want To Know A Secret," always reminded me of that kiss.

⚡

Flash forward to the summer of 1965. Little did I know it would be the last innocent summer of my life.

I had just graduated from junior high school—9th grade was done! It was the first week of summer vacation. Mom let me take a backpack and sleeping bag and hitchhike to the beach with my friend, Gary, from school. We were planning to be on the beach for at least a month. Why did Mom let me go, without even an argument? After all, I was only 15. I would not find out until fall that when I left she was already gearing up to divorce my father.

Many families of the richer kids from school had summer rental homes on the beaches of Southern California: Laguna, Balboa and Newport. Our plan was to hitchhike down to the beach and party with our friends up and down the coast all summer.

First, we hitched down to Laguna Beach, where Liz's family had a vacation home. We stayed there for a few nights. Liz and I hung on the beach all day. Then on the second day, I fell asleep on the beach and received a severe sunburn with large sun blisters on the back of both legs. Liz's mom gave her some cocoa butter, which she rubbed on my legs. It may have helped, but the sunburn took days to heal, and then my skin peeled off my legs in big patches. It actually seemed pretty cool to see how big the pieces were that I could peel off.

After leaving Laguna Beach, Gary and I worked our way north, staying with other friends and their families. Sometimes we would even sleep on the beach in our sleeping bags, which you could do in those days.

Our friends' families would often feed us lunch and dinner. Sometimes, to get some breakfast, we would wash dishes in a local restaurant at the beach or on Pacific Coast Highway.

During that summer, one song echoed along all the beaches: "Like A Rolling Stone," by Bob Dylan. It was his first electric rock-n-roll song and the biggest hit of 1965. It became an anthem of our generation, and some still say it is the greatest rock-n-roll song of all time. What a glorious summer it was!

In the previous month, right before summer break, I had been given a fantastic opportunity because of my dancing. At our school's Friday night Canteen Dance, there was an announcement that our school would have an opportunity to be represented as part of a forthcoming live TV concert to be held in Hollywood in July (a month after school let out). I was one of the best dancers at school, so I was invited to try out to be in the dance contest at the *1st Annual POP TV Music and Dance Festival*. I was accepted and my friend, Beverly, who was in my class and also one of the best dancers at our school, was accepted to be my partner. We were both extremely excited. The 1st, 2nd & 3rd place winners of the dance contest would get to appear on live TV, as part of the show. We couldn't wait for summer!

Gary and I returned from our hitchhiking excursion right in time for the show. I was more excited than I had ever been—about anything. Even Liz announcing that her family was moving could not distract me from the opportunity to be a real dancer on TV.

The concert was to be held at the Hollywood Palladium and was to be broadcast live on TV in July. Besides the dance contest, there was to be a 'Battle of the Bands.' The winners of both contests would appear on TV along with famous Rock-n-Roll and Pop performers, including Donovan, Sonny & Cher, Bobby Vee and The Dixie Cups. The star of the show, however, was to be Chuck Berry.

Bev and I came in third place in the dance contest. The first and second place winners, along with Bev and I, got to experience being on stage dancing on live TV, as Chuck Berry played to hundreds of enthusiastic teens crowding below the stage, and thousands more on television. It was the most spectacular thing that had ever happened to me. I was dancing on the stage, twirling my partner, while Chuck Berry was doing his famous *duck walk* a mere couple of feet away.

The Hollywood Palladium was also the site of the annual Teenage Fair, which I would start attending in 1966. It had a dance contest as well, one that I would win in 1968.

A little before summer ended, Liz announced that her family was moving before school would start. I was certainly sad, but I knew it was coming, so I was not that surprised. Smokey Robinson & The Miracles' new song, "Ooh Baby Baby," a soul searching heartbreak ballad, now reminded me of Liz every time I heard it. It made me cry and became my dedication to her. To this day, whenever I hear it, I think of Liz.

⚡

In September, I started high school at a brand new school, Blair High School. I had been looking forward to going to Pasadena High with most of my junior high school friends, but because it was 1965, we became part of the first school busing experiments of the Civil Rights Movement, designed to integrate schools.

You see, Pasadena was split in half, almost down the middle, basically at Los Robles Blvd. White people lived mostly on the east side of town, and their kids went to Pasadena High. Black people lived mostly on the west, and their kids went to Muir High.

As the Civil Rights Movement began, a third high school, Blair High, was built near the southwest end of town and sophomore students were bused there from both the other high schools. My sister was in the actual first class at Blair High School, and I was in the second. There was no freshman class in high school because, in those days, your last year in junior high was the 9th grade, and 10th grade was the first year of high school.

I loved Blair High. We kids, or at least those I hung around with, had never felt the color barrier the way our parents did. Growing up, I had many Black friends, as well as Mexican friends, and I loved having us all in it together at Blair. The color of our skin did not matter to us. We didn't think about it much. We all just hung out together and did our thing.

21

My first semester was also our first football year, with only juniors on the team, since there was no senior class yet. We won the city championship, anyway. We also won it the following year—two years in a row. Go Vikings! I took a drafting class and it became a new obsession for me. It was like art drawing, but not my freehand drawing—more technical. I could imagine myself an architect in the future.

I made new friends at school that year. One of them, Paul Van der Puil, was a regular dancer on *American Bandstand*. We were the two most popular boy dancers at school. One day, Paul asked me if I would like to go on the show and I said, "Yeah, for sure!" He took me with him to one of the tapings, where I experienced dancing on the show that had first started me dancing.

High school was shaping up to be a lot of fun, but just as it started, Mom kicked Dad out of the house and everything changed—she had had enough of his abuse.

Dad rented his own place in the south of town, and I would have to go over there to see him. He was teaching me how to drive his car so I could get my driver's license as soon as I turned 16. When I went over to his house for a driving lesson, I saw that he already had a new girlfriend. I did not even want to know about it. I ignored her as much as I could. Dad had given me our old '54 Ford coupe, which was not running. I had plans to fix it up. It would be my first car. But that was never to be.

1966:

American Bandstand, Katie and The Sunset Strip

1965 was my last innocent summer. It was the last year of going to school with the same kids I had known since kindergarten, as well as hanging out with the same friends from my earliest years—dancing, surfing, pining for girls from school and at the dances, living what I thought was a happy existence with my family. My life would never again be the same.

It was interesting that this happened to me when I was 15 years old, because I now know that in the U.S., 15 is often the end of childhood, the end of adolescence, maybe even the end of innocence. I know that 15 was the age of change for me, as it is for many—both boys and girls.

It is the age of limbo—you are old enough yet too young. You are no longer a child, but not yet an adult. You think you are smart and independent, and often think you know more than your parents do. This is when so many lose their way. Unless you have someone who can help and guide you, someone to lean on, a mentor or someone else like that to help you find your way—chances are that you can lose it. This is when so many go astray.

I know it now that I'm older, as I witnessed it in my own life, and I have witnessed it in my own children, and in the children of others—so many young people needing someone to listen—just listen, and needing some wisdom and understanding to help guide them. Otherwise, they will think they know better and simply go their own way, often to dismay.

As for me, beginning at 15 I had no one to guide me—not really. I would have to think for myself and go my own way—make my own mistakes the hard way.

1966 would be life changing for me. In January—right after I turned 16, Mom told me we were moving to Hollywood, just the two of us. My sister was pregnant by her boyfriend. They were getting married and she would be moving in with him. Mom and Dad agreed that I would go with Mom and Bob would go with Dad. Our family was disintegrating.

I had barely started high school, but now I had to leave everything and everyone I knew and start over in a new, unfamiliar city. I didn't have my driver's license yet, and the Ford that Dad had given me was still not fixed. Mom said I had to get rid of it, since there was no way to take it with us, and no parking at the apartment building where we would be living. To make matters even worse, she told me she had a new boyfriend, and he would be living with us. I was angry at her, at the changes, at everything, but more than that, I felt betrayed. I didn't try to express any of that—because I didn't know how. So I stuffed it.

When you are young, a year can seem like an eternity. But this year felt like a whirlwind of change. I suppose it was fitting that I moved with Mom to Hollywood, merely one year before the *Summer of Love*, at the birth of the psychedelic revolution.

With no one to talk to or confide in, I withdrew into a fantasy world of my own. The only outlet I had for my feelings was my poetry journal, which stayed hidden under my bed. Mom was too busy with her new boyfriend, and I didn't want to confide in her anyway at this point.

I did make the best of it, though. During the day, I went to my new high school, Hollywood High, but at night I roamed the famous Sunset

Strip. For a 16 year old like me, the Sunset Strip was magical—a place of wonder. On the weekends, cars lined both sides of the street, packed with teenagers cruising Sunset Boulevard, trying to catch a glimpse of the scene. Hundreds of teenagers paraded up and down the sidewalk in front of the Strip's most famous nightclubs: The Whiskey A-Go-Go, Gazzarris, The Galaxy, London Fog, The Trip, The Sea Witch, It's Boss—just to name a few.

Groups of teens would linger in front of the various clubs, hanging out and talking, hoping to catch a glimpse or earful of the local bands whose music emanated from inside the clubs. These were the up-and-coming L.A. bands who would become the minstrels of our generation. Bands like The Doors, Buffalo Springfield, Love, The Byrds, Sonny & Cher, Iron Butterfly, Johnny Rivers, The Mamas & Papas, Strawberry Alarm Clock, The Bobby Fuller Four, and, of course, The Beach Boys. Many of the clubs were teenage nightclubs where the admission age was set at 15, which was perfect for someone like me who loved to dance.

I managed to get a job at one of the teenage clubs—It's Boss, as a doorman and DJ, spinning my 45s on the turntable in the audio booth between sets of the house band, The Regents. Yes, at 16, here I was already working in a teenage nightclub on the Sunset Strip!

Many of the bands I mentioned played at It's Boss. I also met other soon-to-be famous people. For example, the year before Steppenwolf recorded their first album, John Kay used to bum cigarettes off me at the door, while I was letting people into the club.

I met a new group of friends at It's Boss: Sherman, Marnell, Sunny and Sheila. Except for Sunny, they were all older, over 21. Even so, they would invite me to drink with them. We would go out back, behind the club, and chug Colt 45 malt liquor. It was stronger than regular 3.2 beer. It went down easy and sure did help with my churned-up feelings.

Speaking of friends, Jessie also came to Hollywood—as a runaway from juvie, and I found him a place to crash for a while. More on that later . . .

⚡

Shortly after Mom and I moved, I met Katie. She was 16, like me, and my first true love—a real, honest-to-goodness, sensual, heart-throbbing love. She wasn't my first steady; that, of course, had been my puppy love, Liz, who was my girlfriend until she'd moved away to Mill Valley and I never saw her again. We had kissed; we had danced; we had held hands—but never anything more.

Katie and I met at It's Boss one night while I was working. She often came there with her best friend, Karen. They lived in the San Fernando Valley but would come over the hill to Hollywood because they both loved dancing, and It's Boss was one of the best teenage dance clubs on the Strip.

I had seen Katie a couple of times before, but I was too shy to approach her. However, thanks to my friend Sherman and his Colt 45, I found the courage to ask her to dance—and she accepted. We ended up dancing together all night long.

She was this gorgeous, petite Italian girl, almost pixie-like at five foot two, slim, with piercing brown eyes and slightly teased, brown bobbed hair that curled to a point on each side of her face. We were great together, and we both loved dancing. We became inseparable.

One Friday night, on our way home from Casey Kasem's Drop-In dance in Hawthorne, we were in the very back of my friend, Manuel's, '56 Chevy Nomad wagon (with a Vibrasonic sound stereo system). The car was full, so Katie and I had to curl up in the area behind the back seat. We were cruising on the freeway, the music was blaring—and we were kissing passionately! I slipped my hand under her blouse to feel her bare skin. She moaned and kissed me deeper. We were both super excited. I slipped my hand up her skirt and she moaned even more, as we continued kissing deeply, hardly stopping to breathe. It was the most exciting sensual time I had ever experienced with a girlfriend.

After that, every opportunity we had to make out, we did. We were aching to actually make love. Neither one of us was technically a virgin. My first time had been an awkward, drunken experience at a party after I was egged on by some friends, and it was with a girl I didn't even know who merely wanted it. All I felt after was shame and shyness.

Katie, likewise, had done it only once, with the boy she dated before me, but she also said it was awkward and she did not really enjoy it. So we were, in actuality, each other's first love, and we were aching to make love and be together totally.

Believe it or not, our first time was under the pool table in her parents' game room. She had invited me over to her house for dinner, and afterwards we were watching TV in the living room with her parents. She told them we were going to go into the game room and play pool.

So there we were, playing pool, and of course we started making out—and then we could not contain ourselves. We did it! We crawled under the pool table and did it. We were scared someone would come in, but we couldn't help ourselves. We wanted each other so bad—we just could not wait anymore. Luckily, we were not caught.

After that, we looked for every opportunity to make love. We would do it most often at my apartment when Mom was gone, but every so often there would be an opportunity to do it at her house, even though it was harder because she also had a younger sister who was around. We even did it in a swimming pool once when we were visiting a friend from my school who had invited us over to go swimming in his backyard pool.

It wasn't all sex, though. Katie and I talked about everything that was important to us, as teenagers do. We talked about our dreams and just loved being together.

I would often take Katie to dance with me on *American Bandstand*, where I had become a regular dancer, and on other TV dance shows that were popular then.

She went to North Hollywood High School, so often I would ditch 6th period at school and hitchhike through Laurel Canyon to meet up with her after school, to hang out and listen to our favorite songs. "Light My Fire," the first smash hit by local band, The Doors, was one of our favorites. It would usually be playing on a car radio or at full blast on a radio in a house I would be passing by whenever I hitchhiked through the canyon. If it came on when we were riding in a car with friends, everyone in the car would sing along—*yes, baby, our fire was surely lit!* Katie and I were blissfully happy and it seemed like it would always be that way.

Then, one fateful night, we had been having so much fun at the clubs that we didn't even notice that the hour had gotten late. Katie could not go home at that hour without getting into deep trouble, so she called her parents and told them she was staying overnight at Karen's house. We were still in Hollywood, however, and there was no way for her to get to Karen's. We were not going to hitchhike over the hill to the San Fernando Valley that late at night. She couldn't stay at my place, 'cause Mom would never allow it. So we asked Jessie if she could stay where he was temporarily crashing, and he said, "Sure!"

And then he slept with her! Jessie slept with Katie. My best friend and my first love betrayed me. I could not believe it happened. I could not even comprehend how either of them could do that. I mean, holy crap! Did you even think about me at all?

Shortly after that, Katie broke up with me. Her betrayal was my first, deep heartbreak, and my little high school heart was crushed. I would never be the same, and life would never look the same again.

And then I smoked the 'devil weed.' When I was younger, I believed what they said about pot in *Reefer Madness* and the other public service announcement films they showed us in health class at school, where they said marijuana was the 'devil weed' that would drive you insane. With Katie's betrayal, however, I no longer cared whether I lived, died or went mad.

I smoked my first joint under the Santa Monica pier . . .

6/19/1966

you were my first love
it was me and you

my best friend
walked with us too

then one night
we stayed too late

you couldn't go home
we were too young

you stayed with him
the damage was done

now I walk the beach alone

⚡

what do you do
when you're 16
and your best friend
sleeps with your first love

they no longer
are the best friends
you can confide in

wish there was someone
to talk to

lost in the struggle
of the tumble
. . . alone again

just a heartbreak kid
with nowhere to turn
because of what she did
there's no way to return

⚡

Katie had betrayed me, and the whole world weighed heavy on me. I was arguing with Mom and I hated her boyfriend, so I decided to run away from home. I hitchhiked to San Francisco, where I had heard about the hippies in Haight Ashbury. When I arrived there, I was filled with wonder at the boys with long hair, the girls with no bras, bell-bottom jeans, pot and incense everywhere, and the ideals the hippies professed—*Peace, Love, and the Brotherhood of Man*. They were against the war in Vietnam. They believed in women's equality, and they believed all people were equal, no matter what race, creed or color.

I needed a place to stay, and someone suggested I talk with The Diggers, who were part of a local *free clinic*. The Diggers directed me to a place with a bunch of cots in a large room, where I could crash for a few nights along with about a dozen other kids.

That night in my sleeping bag, I began thinking about the other time I had run away, at age 11. Like I said before, Dad was a mean drunk. He would sometimes take it out on us kids, but he would mostly malign or beat Mom sometimes.

I remembered one morning that had started peacefully enough. My sister, my brother, and I had been watching cartoons on TV in the living room, at around 6:00 a.m., before school. Suddenly, Dad came storming out of his bedroom—stark naked. "You kids stop making so much damned noise!" he screamed, angry in his hangover. He came towards us—and then stepped right into a pile of cat poo. He was so mad that he chased the cat around the living room and tried to kick it. But he kicked the edge of the rug instead and broke his big toe. Jumping around, furious, he yelled, "Get that damn cat out of this house!" We were all laughing under our breath (so he couldn't tell), and as soon as there was an escape route, we hightailed it out of there and hid in our bedrooms.

Dad's drunken antics were rarely that funny. One day, after a particularly bad night with him screaming at Mom and hitting her, my sister said to me, "If he does it again, we're gonna run away." I said, "Okay!" So when it happened again, my sister crept into my room and said, "Let's go. Let's run away and teach them a lesson." We hopped out my bedroom window and ran down the street.

Now, in Pasadena in those days, there were only a couple of police officers, so everyone knew them by name. We knew my brother would tell Mom we were gone and they'd both be out looking for us. We went downtown and watched from behind the corner of a building near the police station to see what would happen. Soon enough, Mom and Dad showed up and talked with the police officers. Then they all set out to find us. We kept hiding so that no one would, first behind some trees across from the police station, then on the side of the nearby Episcopalian church, where we would go on Sundays sometimes with Mom. Finally, we let the police find us.

The officers took us to the station and asked us some questions about what was going on. Kathy told them honestly about what happened, and we both expressed how upset and scared we were. They called our parents back to the station and had a long talk with them. We never found out what was said. However, our lives did get better after that—but only for a little while.

By the time I was 15, Mom had had enough of Dad. Early one morning, after a night he belittled her, screamed at her, hit her and yelled at us kids, she threw up her hands and said, "That's it!" She pushed Dad out the front door and out into the front yard. She told him to leave and never come back.

Remembering it all was a bummer. I felt as though there was no home for me anywhere anymore.

I stayed in the Haight for a few days, then started feeling desperate, as I had no money. I finally broke down and called Mom. She was so relieved and immediately drove up to San Francisco to get me. On the way home, I felt better and promised her I would try to do better in school and never run away again.

The scene in Haight Ashbury had affected me profoundly. I was now beginning to feel like a *flower child*, and I became one of the original hippies on the Sunset Strip. We all believed in the hippy ideals of *Peace, Love, and the Brotherhood of Man,* and we would profess and practice our beliefs on the Strip, as well as at the love-ins in Griffith Park on Sundays. Like most of my counterculture tribe, I took to the streets and demonstrated against the Vietnam war and other atrocities that our government was perpetrating on us. I did so even when it meant confronting police brutality.

The next year, 1967, there was this one particularly violent Vietnam war protest I was involved in. President Johnson had flown in to L.A. to give a speech in Century City. Thousands of us marched in the streets chanting, "No more war." The mostly violent L.A.P.D—by now we were calling them *the pigs*—pushed into the crowd and hit us with their billy clubs. I saw one woman, who was sitting on top of a school bus with a baby in her arms, being dragged off the bus and beaten by a pig. Her head was bleeding, and the baby was on the ground crying. She was not the only one. There was a lot of beating and a lot of blood that day. The pigs had a heyday!

As time went on, I would participate in war protests in Haight Ashbury as well as in Southern California, hitchhiking up and down Pacific Coast Highway to join in. Hippies also thrived midway between the two locations, in Big Sur, so I would often stop there and hang awhile on my way up the coast, or on the trip back.

⚡

I was a changed person. Gone was the boy who loved playing trumpet in orchestra at school. Gone was the southpaw pitcher in little league baseball. Gone were the friends of my youth, all those who I had played hide-n-seek with and gone to school with—and gone was family as I had known it.

Mom's boyfriend was pushy towards me. He tried bossing me around by telling me when to go to bed, what chores to do, etc. This only made me more obstinate. He was not my dad! Mom might have intervened, but she was too caught up with this new man in her life. They spent their time skiing and partying with their friends, leaving me to my own devices. I did my own laundry. I cooked for myself. I cleaned up after myself. All of these living lessons/chores Mom had taught me, probably so they could do what they wanted without her having to worry about me. But after my chores were done, I was roaming the streets of Hollywood.

That is how I began hanging out in the Sunset Strip's famous teenage nightclub scene, where I ended up working with and seeing many of the local L.A. rock bands. It was also where I could dance and forget my troubles. I danced almost every night at It's Boss during and after work. I would also dance at The Whiskey A-Go-Go, The Sea Witch, Gazzarris, The Trip, London Fog, The Galaxy and Pandora's Box (Pandora's Box would become even more famous after an infamous riot later that year—one I would participate in).

Most of the clubs looked pretty much alike. They had a raised stage for the bands to play on and a dance floor in front of it. They had tables and chairs off to the sides, and some had a bar area. It's Boss had a DJ booth behind the stage, where I did my thing. Some of the clubs, like Whiskey A-Go-Go, had disco cages up on the side walls, with disco dancers in them, mostly female, but some male as well.

I loved dancing at the clubs. One of them, The Sea Witch, was only one block west of It's Boss on Sunset, so I would walk over there. I saw The Doors and Canned Heat play there. Besides the live music, they had a jukebox instead of a DJ booth. My favorite song on their jukebox was

"Expressway to Your Heart" by The Soul Survivors. Whenever I was there and the band wasn't playing, I'd play that song and dance my ass off!

Dancing had always been my thing, and dancing on *American Bandstand* even more so. Now, it was easier to get to where they taped the show, as my apartment was less than a mile away from where they taped. Paul had helped me to get on the show again, and I became a regular dancer.

That's where I met Famous, one of the most popular regular dancers. We became great friends almost instantly. Because of his dancing fame, he was able to get me on as a regular dancer on another show, *Shebang*, hosted by Casey Kasem (of *Top 40* fame). Then, through Lauralee, a close friend of mine at Hollywood High, I was able to get both Famous and I on *9th Street West*, with host Sam Riddle. Lauralee's mom was the show's producer. I was also able to get on *The Lloyd Thaxton Show*, because I went to school with his son, Lee Thaxton. Famous and I were both regulars on that show as well. It taped right down the street from where I lived. I won the dance contest on *Lloyd Thaxton*, and I also participated in a skit called 'The Lip Sync,' where Lloyd would invite one of the kids to lip sync on camera to a current hit record. The song I lip synced to was, "Hey Little Girl," by Syndicate of Sound.

These after-school and weekend dance shows were super popular with the kids at school, as well as teenagers nationwide. I was one of the lucky ones who got to dance on several of them during high school.

American Bandstand had originally aired five days a week, when it was broadcast live in Philadelphia; but when it moved to Hollywood, it aired weekly on Saturdays and was pre-taped. We would tape several shows each Saturday at the ABC studios on Vine St, bringing several changes of clothes so it wouldn't look as if we were wearing the same thing on the show week after week.

One of the best girl dancers on *American Bandstand* was Toni. We danced together sometimes and became good friends. We still keep in touch to this day.

Shebang, my favorite of all the dance shows, aired five days a week after school, and both Famous and I would dance on that show several times a week. We would also get together to go to the many popular weekend dance spots around the SoCal area. On Friday nights we would usually hit Casey Kasem's Drop-In dance in Hawthorne or Harmony Park in Anaheim, where Dick Dale and the Deltones were the house band. On Saturday nights it was Dewald's Ballroom at the Pasadena Civic Auditorium or another dance out in Sherman Oaks (can't remember the name). There was even a popular dance on Tuesday nights: Gunn Park in Whittier.

Famous and his mom lived in South Central L.A., on Crenshaw Blvd. He would often invite me over for dinner, and sometimes to stay overnight. His mom always welcomed me into their home and cooked great food. I especially loved her fried chicken. It was just as good as Mom's.

I wish I could say that Mom returned the favor, but Famous wasn't welcome in our apartment because he was Black. Mom said she was worried about what the landlord or the neighbors might think, as she was a single, working mom, raising me alone, and she couldn't take any chances. I was upset that she felt that way. However, I do not think she was racist. I actually think she was liberal, particularly for someone who grew up in Arizona, where diversity was not accepted as much as it was in California. She had always accepted my Black and Mexican friends when I was younger. Mom never said anything or did anything to affect my relationships with kids of other races and cultures. So I think she was merely scared, as she said.

The Civil Rights Movement would help bring about some much-needed racial equality on television beginning in the late 1960s and extending into the '70s with more Black family shows such as *The Bill Cosby Show* and *The Jeffersons*. However, these changes were first reflected on the teenage dance shows we participated in during the '60s. Take *American Bandstand* for example. When it had originally aired in Philadelphia, Black teenagers struggled to have a place on the show. When the show moved to Hollywood it became more integrated, but they still would not let us do integrated dancing. White dancers had to have White dance partners and Black dancers had to have Black dance partners. (The struggle Black dancers had to go through to be on the show in Philadelphia would be portrayed years later in the movie and Broadway show, *Hairspray*.)

It was the same policy on all the TV shows we danced on, but whenever we went to the weekend dances around SoCal, it was anything goes. We could dance with anyone we wanted and no one bothered us or seemed to care. The same was true at It's Boss. Famous often came to dance while I was working there, and his dance partners were not ever limited by race. No one ever said anything at the clubs about who danced with whom.

⚡

After It's Boss closed at 2:00 am, my friends and I would all head for one of the after-hours spots. One night after work, I was sitting in Barney's Beanery around 3:00 a.m., hanging out with friends, drinking coffee and having breakfast. Along with Ben Franks on the Strip itself, and Canter's Deli on Fairfax, Barney's was one of the main hangouts for hippies after-hours—after dancing in the clubs all night.

That night, I saw Jim Morrison—drunk, stagger out the front door of Barney's Beanery with two hippy chicks—one on each arm, and then head across the street to a motel. I thought he was so lucky because he could get any chicks he wanted—it was surely his prowess, his sheer magnetism. The hippy girls surrounded him wherever he went, strutting his stuff in his black leather pants.

When my friends and I were not at one of the clubs dancing, we would be walking the streets of the Strip outside the clubs. Hundreds, sometimes thousands, of teens and older hippies crowded the streets every night. We would walk along looking for friends, maybe trying to score some pot, or we'd hang out in front of one of the clubs—talking and pondering the war, the origin of the universe, or some such hippy ideological topic.

In the summer of '66, a new song, "Summer In The City" by the Lovin' Spoonful, was resonating on the Sunset Strip. It seemed to be everywhere—I heard it all the time and loved it so much.

One of my good friends on the Sunset Strip was Lizzy. We went to school together and would inevitably run into each other on the street or in a club. Whenever we did, we'd hang out together. One night, we were hanging out when another friend, Rodney, came up and told us the Rolling Stones were recording at RCA Studios over by Sunset and Vine. A bunch of us went over there to check it out. Sure enough, The Stones came out of the studio, jumped in their limo, and then headed west on Sunset Boulevard. We all followed them to the Beverly Hills Hotel. Several of us snuck around back to where the bungalows were and tried to find which rooms The Stones were staying in. We were still hunting around when a security guard caught several of us. He told us all to sit on the grass, right there, and not to move. Then he left to round up some other troublemakers. While he was gone, we got the hell out of there, quick!

Jim Morrison! The Rolling Stones! Cher—The Goddess of Pop! She was just beginning to get known, not only for her singing but also for the psychedelic hippy clothes she designed. Yes, she herself designed those multi-colored giant bell-bottom pants she often wore.

Cher had her own clothing boutique in Hollywood; at the corner of Crescent Heights and Sunset, where she sold the clothes she designed. One night she showed up at It's Boss and asked if some of us would like to participate in a fashion show she was going to do at our club. I said, "Yeah—*bitchin'!*" When it came time for the show, our girlfriends got to wear outfits designed by Cher, while we all danced as couples, around the dance floor. That was the fashion show. Afterwards, Cher let our girlfriends keep the outfits they had worn. *Far out!*

Many years later, I would have a career in stage production in Hollywood, in television and live theatre. One year, while I was working on the Academy Awards, Cher was one of the presenters. Backstage, I reminded her of that fashion show back in the '60s. She said she remembered it well, then giggled. We had a nice conversation, reminiscing about it and about those times on the Strip.

Kitty-corner from Cher's boutique on the Strip was one of the other teenage nightclubs, Pandora's Box. In November of 1966, it was the site of an infamous riot, epitomized a year later by the counterculture-era exploitation movie *Riot on Sunset Strip*. Local rock-n-roll group, The Standells, performed the title song of the movie (their drummer, Dick Dodd, would figure later in my life when we both would play congas on the stage together in the 1970s).

I was right in the middle of that riot! Initially, it was a bunch of us marching in a hippy protest against a new curfew law that had recently been imposed on us by the L.A. County Sheriff's Metro Squad—a new special pig squad set up to control the hippies on the Strip. Even though the nightclub I worked in, and the other teen clubs like it, allowed teenagers 15 and older admission into their clubs, and even though the clubs were open until 2:00 am, the Metro Squad passed a 10:00 pm curfew on the Strip—on all teens under 18 years old—in an effort to ban us from the clubs and keep us from hanging out on the Sunset Strip itself. It gave them more excuses to use their billy clubs on us, which they loved doing.

Besides the curfew, the powers-that-be in the local business community had threatened to change the admission age of all the teen nightclubs on the Strip, effectively making them all adults-only clubs.

Pandora's Box had already been closed, and was boarded up, slated for demolition. I was with some others right in front of the club when the riot broke out. The pigs started hitting us with their billy clubs and arresting us. Some protesters started rocking a big police bus back and forth. The pigs had brought it in, explicitly to haul us away in. More people joined in, and they actually turned the bus over on its side—then lit it on fire. At that point I was definitely scared, so I lit out of there.

A police bus on fire! That made the news. The burning bus was all over the newspapers and TV the next day. Later, I heard that Stephen Stills, of Buffalo Springfield, was nearby that night, and he wrote a song inspired by the riot titled, "For What It's Worth." It was a huge hit for Buffalo Springfield and became an instant hippy anthem. For all of us—*there was something happening there,* and now with this song—definitely! It became our rallying cry.

⚡

Despite having been betrayed by Katie and Jessie, I remained friends with Jessie. How or why did I forgive him? I don't know, but in those days, boys who grew up together stuck together.

Jessie had turned me on to my first joint. Now, he convinced me to do my first acid. LSD was still legal in 1966, and we bought it over the counter at Psychedelic Conspiracy, a hippy head shop on the Strip. My friend, and Lauralee's boyfriend, Sam, worked there. Sam picked out narrow, thick, pink pills, that he called 'pink barrel' acid, especially for us—telling us it was the best. We were now—both, ready to do our first acid.

The next day, Jessie and I hiked up into the hills of Hollywood, climbing up the huge stairs behind Grohman's Chinese Theater, on the hill where the Yamashiro Hotel is. We sat down on the hillside on the west side of the hotel and dropped the LSD. The view was spectacular. We could see all the way to Santa Monica Beach and the horizon. We lit up a joint while the acid came on and settled in to watch the sunset.

The scene before us turned red and pink, yellow and blue, green and violet—so colorful it was like a hippy Disneyland playing out before our eyes. All my senses were acutely alive. I held a blue carnation in my hand throughout the trip, and whenever I smelled it, it was like magic—it made my senses even more vibrant—its glorious fragrance sending chills throughout my body. For years afterward, I would buy a blue carnation whenever I could, to carry around wherever I went. It was my hippy comfort blanket.

—I know I said earlier that my 16th year would be life changing. As you can see, it truly was!

1967:

The Summer of Love, Tahquitz Falls, and Arizona

I turned 17 in 1967, the year known as *The Summer of Love*. I was right in the heart of the hippy counterculture, spending Sundays at the love-ins in Griffith Park, and hitchhiking up and down Pacific Coast Highway between L.A., Big Sur, and Haight Ashbury. I also started using alcohol and recreational drugs on a more regular basis, including pot, acid, mushrooms and mini-bennies. Drugs, especially pot and psychedelics, were the happening thing, which was very fortunate for me. They kept my mind on the *groovy* parts of life, and away from all my problems.

1967, for me, was all about music, and *The Summer of Love* may have been the best year of rock and roll music ever. There were so many great songs—too many to mention.

My love of dancing would get me involved with a band named Rings of Knight, a local band who played at one of Hollywood's teenage nightclubs, Gazzarris West, located off the Sunset Strip on La Cienega Blvd. I hung out there a lot and found out that Rings of Knight was looking for a new drummer. I told Jessie about it. A great drummer, he was at first reluctant to audition because he was only 17, as well as a runaway from a California Youth Authority detention center (which we referred to as—*juvie*). I finally convinced him to audition, though, and when he did, they hired him on the spot.

Tuesday nights were audition night at Gazzarris West. If there was a new band to audition, Rings of Knight would sit out a set and let the new band try out. One Tuesday night the club auditioned a local band named Spirit. They didn't hire the group because they were 'too out there, too strange.' If they only knew.

Jessie and I started hanging out with two Rings of Knight members, Ted and Spencer. Ted was the rhythm guitarist, and he had a knack for the rhythm-and-blues *chicken-pickin'* style that definitely rocked. Spencer was the lead singer of the band. He strutted and sang like Mick Jagger, shaking his leg while playing his maracas and swaying the microphone and mic stand as he sang. Later in life, Spencer created The Musician's Contact Service in Hollywood, a business that helps other musicians find gigs in town. It was hugely successful, and he still has it online on Facebook.

I became like a roadie to them, helping the band load and unload their equipment, as well as helping them set up on stage. Some of us who were regulars at Gazzarris West started hanging out together more as a group, in support of the band. Often we'd go behind the club in the alley with Ted and Spencer and smoke joints when the band was on break. The people in our core group would often travel wherever the band was playing in support of them.

In our group were Luna and Elena, two beautiful sisters of Spanish heritage, with long, silky black hair. Later on, their brother, Bob, became the keyboard player for Rings of Knight. He was married to renowned folk singer, Jenni Soul. In 1971, Bob would play with Frank Zappa and The Mothers of Invention. He was on two albums as one of their keyboard players: *The Mothers—Fillmore East 1971*, and the John Lennon/Yoko Ono album, *Sometime In New York City*. Parts of both albums were recorded live at the Fillmore East in a concert that featured both bands.

Luna and Elena came from a musical family: Their grandmother had been a famous Spanish recording artist and actress, in New York City and around the world, during the 1920s-1930s.

Elena liked to create things with leather. She made a handmade leather wallet for me that was *far out!* It was so cool of her—I still have it.

The previous year, in the summer of '66, Elena and I had entered a dance contest at the original Gazzarris on the Sunset Strip where the 1st prize was two tickets to see The Beatles at Dodger Stadium. We won the contest! Elena sold her concert ticket to help her buy a Volkswagen, but I went to the concert with mine. It was my second time seeing The Beatles, and it was the first-ever concert at Dodger Stadium, on August 28th, 1966. The 56,000 seat stadium would host many more rock-n-roll concerts in the future, but I was there at the first—The Beatles!

Later in life, Luna and Elena both married musicians who played with some of the most memorable artists of the 1960s-1970s and beyond.

Luna married a renowned trombone player who played with many of the most famous bands of the times, as well as on the recording sessions for their albums. Just a few of the bands/artists he played and recorded with: Count Basie, Woody Herman, Harry James, Frank Sinatra, Rita Coolidge and Kris Kristofferson, Neil Diamond, Donna Summer, The Beach Boys, Supertramp, Madonna. The list goes on and on.

Elena married a renowned trumpet player who played in the Tonight Show band with Doc Severinsen. He was also part of The Wrecking Crew: the session musicians who played on many of the hit records of the '60s and '70s, as well as on the recording sessions for many albums recorded by some of the most renowned artists of those times. Just a few of them: B.B. King, Steely Dan, Miles Davis, Toto, Jackson Browne, George Benson, George Harrison, Elton John, Carole King, The Rolling Stones, Joni Mitchell. His list goes on and on as well.

Also in our Rings of Knight group of followers was Carla, who I went to high school with. We were in art class together at Hollywood High. Carla and I would hang out together at Spencer's apartment, and sometimes at Luna and Elena's house. Carla's sister, Carrie, also hung around with us once and a while. Both sisters were genuinely cute blondes. Carla was taller, so everyone always thought she was the older one, but she was younger than Carrie.

When Rings of Knight was gigging, Carla, Elena and I, along with Luna, would usually be the first ones on the dance floor—and the last to leave it at the end of the night. We loved to dance and always helped to get the crowd going. We had our own special word that we used when we were excited and having a great time, kind of like *bitchin'* or *groovy*. It was—WORK!

⚡

It was early summer, I think June or July when, one day, Jessie told me that he and Ted had recently hiked up to a place called Tahquitz Falls, in a canyon on Indian reservation land, just outside of Palm Springs on the southwest side. He said Ted was going to camp there for a week or so and asked if we wanted to join him.

"There are seven waterfalls in the canyon," Jessie said, "and if you hike to the top of the canyon you will end up in Idyllwild. If you start at the bottom of the canyon in Palm Springs, it'll take you over a week to climb all the way up the canyon and see all seven waterfalls." So of course, we decided to join Ted, at least for a couple of days.

I had a canvas backpack from when I used to go to the Boys Club summer camp, that I had also used when I was in the Cub Scouts for a short period. Jessie found a similar one at the Army Surplus store. We packed some camping items to get us by for a few days: pocket knives, flashlights, Sterno and matches. We packed some food: dried fruit and nuts, chips and crackers, canned fruit, beef stew, candy bars and more; whatever we could fit in. Of course, we packed some pot and rolling papers. Ted told us there was plenty of fresh water up in the canyon, so we didn't need to worry about that. He also said he would bring some beer.

We met up with Ted in Palm Springs and then drove out to the southwest side of town. You had to park and hike in a mile or two in the flat desert area to reach the mouth of the canyon. We did that, and then started up the canyon path along a small stream, which grew larger the further up the canyon we went. Soon, we had to rock-hop on large boulders to continue our hike along the path. There was a fallen tree to use as a bridge to the other side of the water, where it was easier hiking. We crossed and made good time, eventually arriving at the first waterfall. It was breathtaking—at least a 20-foot drop spilling into a pool of water almost the size of a small lake. Several people were already hanging around there and swimming. It must have been deep, because there was a large rock on the south side that you could jump off of, into the center of the pool. It must have been 15 feet high. People were climbing up on it and screaming with joy as they jumped off, making big splashes—cooling off in the summer heat.

At Ted's motion, we continued on and found ourselves rock-climbing up the face of the falls on the south side of the waterfall, so that we could get above it and continue our journey. Once we reached the top, we could still see the people below, and we could also see a river leading farther up the canyon. We followed the river, at one point having to cross it where it was shallow. Right there in front of us, on the north side of the canyon wall, there was a large rock painting of Jesus. Ted told us it was known as Jesus Rock, but he did not know who had painted it.

We kept going. Further along, we came to a rock cave. Wow! Inside it was astonishing, with a solid stone firepit in the middle, surrounded by seats carved out of rocks. Someone had also carved a shelf out of the sheer rock cave wall—and there were sacks of flour and grain that had been left there—I guess for anyone who might come along. Ted told us that Timothy Leary had stayed in this cave while he was on the lam from the law. Wow! This was truly a unique and unforgettable experience.

We continued our trek up the canyon, coming to the second, smaller, waterfall and then a larger one. What a beautiful canyon, full of clear running water and gorgeous waterfalls!

We had been hiking for several hours by the time we arrived at the fourth falls. Ted told us this was where we would be camping. It was almost unbelievable. Over time, the force of the falls spilling down had carved a 15-foot deep, almost completely square, stone pool—carved right out of the rock mountain. Ted said it was known as the Square Pool. The water was crystal clear, reflecting a deep blue sky, and you could see all the way to the bottom. In front of the pool was a small beach-like area with sand, where we set up camp.

Ted grabbed cans of fruit and beers out of his backpack and threw them right into the pool. He said that being on the bottom of the pool would keep everything cold. When you wanted something cool, you could simply swim to the bottom and grab it. Jessie and I laughed, then tossed what we had in there too, everything that needed to be cold.

This was a magical place to camp. I was excited, amazed, and thrilled to be able to actually have this experience. This was nature as I had never experienced it before.

We had barely finished setting up camp when we heard a noise that sounded a lot like crickets, but more scratchy sounding. Ted said they were a natural warning alarm; a special kind of cricket, native to the canyon. Their unique screeching sound was a natural warning signal of people approaching up the canyon from below. We climbed up on a rock where we could see the path below, where we had climbed up to our location, and there, about half a mile below us, we could see people hiking up. Ted said the crickets always sounded off when people were coming up, so we would always know way before anyone came near. Another wow!

Right before dusk, I saw something else amazing. To my right, on the south side, way up high on the face of the canyon's rock wall, hundreds of little birds were flying right into the canyon wall and just—vanishing! They were like a funnel—a huge group of birds, funneling down to just one, and then disappearing into the cliff. It was another surprising/amazing sight in this magical Indian canyon. The next morning, they all came funneling back out of the unseen crack, the same way they had gone in. There were no cell phones in those days to record what I saw, and I wasn't toting a camera. However, it was so memorable that I can still picture it vividly in my mind to this day.

As if that were not enough to boggle my mind, later that night when I was asleep in my sleeping bag, I was suddenly awoken by a noise in the camp area that sounded like something scratching around. I woke Ted and Jessie. Ted shined a flashlight at the sound—and there they were: several small critters about the size of small cats; like house cats, but with extra long tails with rings around them. I had never seen any cats that looked like that. Ted said they were harmless ringtail cats, simply another one of the canyon critters, ones who liked to live near water. My mind was blown! I couldn't help but think more about the fact that we were on Indian reservation land. Everything that had happened so far began to feel magical to me.

The next day, we hung out, swam, then lay on the canyon rocks in the sun to dry off. Ted was brewing some tea. He told us to come and check it out. He said there was a natural weed that grew in the desert valley there, that the Indians would sometimes use for spiritual journey ceremonies. He said he had picked some on the way up. He offered the tea to us. We were game for a spiritual journey, so we drank some.

The experience was like *fryin'* on mushrooms or a mild form of acid. I was *trippin' out* for a long time. At one point, I climbed up and behind the waterfall. There was a little cave behind it, barely big enough for me to crawl into but not big enough to stand up in. I sat there, cross legged, for the longest time. I could see the square pool below me, through the waterfall, and sun rays all around me, that were caused by sunlight peeking through the rocks above me. I felt as though I were at one with the universe, a part of everything. It was like . . . I thought . . . *you are the sender / the mind bender / I am the mender / we are the mind blender.*

I climbed out and sat on a big rock right above the waterfall, enjoying the afternoon sun and listening to the water, while watching the hawks and other birds flying above this magnificent canyon. I felt serene—yes, serenity is what I felt. I pondered the connectedness of all things and my connectedness to my friends below, who were diving to the bottom of the pool for fruit and beer. I felt connected to Mother Earth and the creatures I had seen, as well as to my fellow man. In that moment, I came to the realization that we are all one—a part of everything, and everything is a part of us. I felt it deeply in my soul.

I did not ever want to leave Tahquitz Falls. I wanted to live in the cave where Timothy Leary had slept. Ted told us it was time to move on, climb higher, see the other falls. He planned to hike all the way up to Idyllwild. Neither Jessie nor I wanted to do that, so we decided it was probably time for us to head back down—to the real world we knew—back to the city. The next morning, we packed up and said farewell to Ted as he headed up. We slowly hiked back down the canyon—back to civilization.

I'll never forget Tahquitz. I actually do believe I became one with the universe up there, at age 17. Years later, I heard they fenced off the canyon so you couldn't hike up it any more, since people were trashing it and leaving all kinds of garbage there. It was Indian reservation land, after all, and the tribes wanted it protected. Yep, some people have a tendency to ruin a good thing.

⚡

Jessie and I were back hanging on the Strip one night, and he told me he had gone back to one of the clubs in Pasadena where he had played when we were still living there. He ran into an old friend who was now in the band, Strawberry Alarm Clock, who were also from Pasadena. His friend invited him to come to a recording session the band was doing at Art Laboe's Original Sound Studios on Sunset Blvd. Jessie and I went there and sat in on one of the recording sessions. It was *groovy*, to say the least. Soon after that, Strawberry Alarm Clock had a major hit song, "Incense and Peppermints."

We also hung out sometimes at a head shop on Fairfax, almost right across the street from Canter's Deli. It was called The Infinite Mind. I loved going there, as they had a back room where local musicians would often do acoustic jams. You would go through some curtains into the back room, which had pillows on the floor and assorted percussion instruments strewn around the room.

I met Shaun Phillips there and we would often jam together. He was a famous musician who had a couple of original albums out. He also had worked with Donovan and played on some of his albums. I believe they wrote some songs together. He also hung around with Paul McCartney and his friends when Shaun was in London.

Shaun was a local L.A. musician now, working on his next album. He was well known for his wonderful twelve-string acoustic guitar playing. When we would jam at The Infinite Mind, I would play the bongos that were there in the room. Sometimes we would go across the street to Canter's after, to eat and talk about music and all the happenings in the clubs on the Strip.

↯

It is hard to explain how much music, particularly The Beatles music, meant to me and to my generation. The Beatles would influence all music going forward, and we could see that happening all around us, in real time. We knew we were in the midst of something truly phenomenal.

There had never been anything like The Beatles, and there has not been since. Everybody copied them. Everyone wanted to be like them. Boys grew their hair long, exactly like The Beatles. Girls screamed and giggled and talked about which one they wanted to marry: Paul, the cute one with the sexy voice; John, the smartest and wittiest—the sly jokester; George, the quiet/mysterious one with dreamy eyes; or Ringo, the constantly smiling one with all the rings on his fingers. Kids of every nationality all over the planet waited with bated breath for the next hint of a new Beatles single or album. When one was released, girls just about peed their pants and boys pretended as if they didn't care—but they did! We all did. We all cared a lot.

Then, in 1967, something happened that would change everything . . .

Ted lived with his *old lady*, Maggie, in an apartment in Hollywood. It was the central gathering place for several members of Rings of Knight, along with our core support group. We would often sit in a circle in the front room or around the dining room table, with lit candles and incense; listening to the latest albums by our favorite bands; passing a joint around the circle— each of us taking a long, slow hit before passing it on. We would listen intently to an entire album with no interruptions. It was almost a spiritual thing. We knew this is what hippies all over the country and the world were doing.

Hippies did not sit around watching TV together—that was something you did at home. When we gathered, it was for the ritual of listening to an album of *groovy* music.

I hope you can picture that, because that is the setting where we all first heard *Sgt. Pepper's Lonely Hearts Club Band* in May of 1967. We had never heard anything like it. We realized this was, perhaps, the *grooviest* most *far out* music we might ever hear. It stood miles above anything that had ever come before. Listening to it was like being transported magically to another dimension. We listened to it over and over, from beginning to end—transfixed. The music traveled through you, around you, back and forth, side to side, completely engulfing you. It was incredible. Absolutely mind blowing. *Work!*

So much has been said about *Sgt. Pepper's* through the years. Many believe it was The Beatles' masterpiece and the greatest rock-n-roll record of all time. But instead of offering my opinion or trying to convince you further about its significance in history, I will merely leave it here, with my own personal experience of how it happened into my life. I will never forget it. Like all The Beatles' records before it and after it, I played it repeatedly and never grew tired of it.

A few days later at home, I was listening to *Sgt. Pepper's* on my little portable record player, which Mom had bought me for my bedroom. When the record came to the end of the last song, "A Day in the Life," I heard something that I hadn't heard when we listened to it over and over at Ted & Maggie's. I heard this weird chattering noise—that kept repeating itself, over and over. I looked at the record and saw that the needle had drifted to the center label, while the record simply kept spinning. Evidently, The Beatles had inserted some incredible, unrecognizable chatter after the last song, right at the record's center label. If you had a normal stereo record player, the player's arm/needle would eject after the last song, so you would never hear it. But because I had this little portable record player that did not eject the record, the record arm merely drifted to the label in the center of the record—and there it was—a secret message.

How ingenious! The Beatles had recorded a secret message that you could only hear if your record did not eject. And it played over and over, continuously. It would not stop until you actually took the needle off the record. Wow! This totally blew my mind.

I immediately called some of our group and told them about the secret message I had found on the album that we couldn't hear before. I said if they had a regular stereo record player that ejected the record, they would have to manually place the needle near the center label to prevent the record from being ejected, and then turn the record player on. Then they would be able to hear it. But no one could. No matter how they tried, it wasn't there on their records. They could not understand why, and neither could I.

Then I remembered something. When I had bought my copy of *Sgt. Pepper's*, there were two versions at the store. They both had the same cover, but one cover was shiny, and the other cover had a matte finish. I thought the shiny one was cooler looking, so that was the one I bought. As it turned out, that one was the U.K. version of the record, on Parlophone Records, and the chatter was only on that version, not on the U.S. version, which was on Capitol Records—the one with the matte finish. All my friends had the US version, so I was the only one who could hear the secret message. Later on, we all had fun listening to it together on my little portable, trying to figure out what The Beatles' magical message was.

The Beatles released another album later that year, *Magical Mystery Tour*. It was another spectacular, super psychedelic album for me to get lost in—and I did!

⚡

I think I developed my love of music and dance from Mom and Dad. They loved the big band music of the 1940s and could dance the jitterbug with the best of them. Dad played the bongos and harmonica, and he even wrote a few songs when he was young. He used to sing them to us for fun. Here are some of the lyrics of three of them:

#1
wake up, get dressed,
brush your teeth, eat your breakfast,
go to work, come home,
eat your dinner, go to bed

wake up, get dressed,
brush your teeth, eat your breakfast,
go to work, come home,
eat your dinner, go to bed

#2
If there's a moon above
Would you take it from there
If I put my arm around you
Would you take it from there

If I said I want you
And told you that I really care
If I said that I could
If you only would

Would you take it from there
Would you take it from there

#3
Was a foggy night in Frisco
When my ship found its berth
The crew jumped ashore
To kiss the sweet mother earth

To town they all hurried
Just to catch up with time
While I stayed aboard
To hear the old ship's bell chime

Yeah! I've got the watch
But I've got the Bay City Blues

Now I've been ashore
That's why I know the score
Had a sweet darling chick
Take me for a ride

Slender tender & tall
With personality galore
But she broke my heart
So I sailed off with the tide

San Francisco, the city
The best on the coast
For the liquor and lovin'
You pay the least for the most

The chow and the music's
Really off this earth
But this man's going to stay
Mighty close to his berth

'Cause! I've got the watch
And I've got the Bay City Blues

⚡

When I was growing up, we had a cool Hi-Fi system in our living room. It was mono, as home stereophonic equipment had not come out yet. It was big—a polished oak cabinet with long legs about three feet high. It had a record player on the left side, a multi-band radio on the right, and storage for records in the middle, with two huge built-in speakers. When you turned it up loud, the sound filled the whole house.

Mom would always play her favorite big band music on it. I especially loved the Harry James records. He was the one who made me want to learn how to play trumpet. Mom and Dad used to dance the jitterbug in the living room and show off for us kids.

Mom also loved to play Christmas records all day long during the holiday season, while she cooked, cleaned, and decorated the house. I remember a couple of her favorites, "Little Drummer Boy" by the Harry Simeone Chorale, and the Christmas Carol choir music by the Mormon Tabernacle Choir.

When we moved to Hollywood, Mom bought a newer, bigger stereophonic hi-fi system for our living room. It had two huge, separate floor speakers, one set up on each side of the room. In November of 1967, when *Magical Mystery Tour* came out, I put the record on the big stereo system and turned the volume up loud. I set the speakers in the middle of the room, close to and facing each other. Then I got down on the floor, flat on my back, and put my head directly in between them. I let The Beatles' legendary stereo effects wash over me, traveling right through my head, back and forth. It was *far out*, especially since I had smoked a joint.

When I was 17, The Beatles were my favorite band—by far. My second favorite was Smokey Robinson and The Miracles. Smokey's soulful voice sang the sad laments, giving voice to the deep feelings all teenagers felt. Smokey was one of the founders of Motown Records, and he wrote songs for many of its most popular bands and artists. Heck, even The Beatles did one of his songs, "You've Really Got a Hold on Me," on one of their earlier albums, when they were still recording songs by other artists.

I listened to Smokey on my portable record player when I was in my bedroom. It would play both 45s and LPs, and it was like a small suitcase, with a locking top and handle to carry it, so I could take it with me to a friend's house when I wanted to. Mostly though, I loved to lie on my bed at night, with lit candles and incense and the lights off. I would put on Smokey's, *Going To A-Go-Go* album and listen over and over to that soulful voice singing, "Ooh Baby Baby" and "The Tracks Of My Tears."

4

That summer, Mom sent me to Arizona to spend a couple of weeks with her mom, Nini, who had moved from Phoenix to Seligman, AZ, in the middle of nowhere on Route 66. Nini had moved because she had gotten married again in her golden years. Her new husband, Guy, owned the Standard/Chevron Gas Station in Seligman.

I didn't really want to go, but Mom insisted. I took my portable record player with me and as many of my 45s as I could get inside it, as well as some LPs that I put in my suitcase.

Being a city boy, I had never been to a small town like Seligman before. It had a railroad station, post office, market, one gas station (my stepgrandpa's), one school (kindergarten through 12th grade), a barbershop, and a highway hamburger stand (with a jukebox). That was about it. You could almost hold your breath driving through it on the highway.

Standing at Nini's house, I could see the horizon in almost every direction. I had experienced this vastness before only when I was younger, when we traveled from California to visit Nini in Phoenix. Standing there in the middle of the world—wow! It was breathtaking. To the west, I could see mountains so far away that they were simply a crooked horizon line. In every other direction, it was flat as far as I could see.

Behind Nini's house, there were railroad tracks. If you were to lie down and put an ear to them, you could hear a train coming before you could see it on the horizon. When the train actually approached, the sound was so enormous that it baffled the mind. The silence of a vast desert, then—bam! It was fantabulous.

That year the graduating class from Seligman High was the biggest ever in the school's history—seven.

Some local teenagers around my age hung out at the hamburger stand listening to rock-n-roll on the jukebox. I would go there most afternoons or evenings after dinner to hang out with them and hear music. Believe it or not, several of the teens recognized me from *American Bandstand* and *Shebang*, so I became a local celebrity that summer. They invited me to go with them out into the desert at night to their favorite spot, where they would build a fire and simply hang out together as teenagers. I brought my records and portable player, and we all danced in the desert sand.

In Seligman, if you wanted to go and see a movie, you had to drive to the next town, Ash Fork, which was 30 miles away. One time, Nini let me use her car to actually do that, and I took a couple of the local kids along. It was exciting driving fast through the desert, down the straight, flat line of Route 66. I don't remember what movie we saw, but we had a *bitchin'* time.

There was a clock radio in the room where I slept. Lying in bed at night, I would try to find some rock-n-roll music on it. I could never find any FM stations, but surprisingly, I was able to get Wolfman Jack on AM. He was legendary and seemed to be able to broadcast to anywhere from some secret, giant broadcasting tower nobody could ever find. I could always pick up his station in L.A., but to hear him out in the middle of the desert in Arizona—wow! That blew me away.

One night, lying in bed, I was thinking about you, Katie, and suddenly Wolfman played one of our songs, "I Ain't Gonna Eat Out My Heart Anymore," by The Young Rascals. That night, I dreamed I was drawing a picture of you, but it was when I was younger, so I was using Crayons. Burnt orange was always my favorite Crayon color, and that's what I was using to color in your top. Suddenly I woke up, and for a moment it felt as if you were still around . . . still with me, still mine.

It rained some that summer, and the rain was warm, like shower water. You could see lighting strike all the way to the ground . . . way out in the desert . . . far away.

Mom had let me take the train to Nini's. It was quite an adventure to begin my summer vacation since I had never been on a train before. I wish I could have also taken the train home, but my sister, Kathy, and her husband showed up to visit, and then take me back home with them.

I said my goodbyes to Nini and Guy, telling them what a *groovy* time I had had. When we left, we headed west on Route 66, back towards California. Out in the middle of nowhere, I made my sister stop on the side of the highway, and I unbolted a Route 66 sign off a pole. Luckily for me, my sister's husband, Mick, had a tool box in his trunk. I couldn't have done that if I'd taken the train. Oh—I still have the sign.

⚡

Back home it was time to get ready for my senior year at school. Of course, I *had* to go to the Strip and check out what had happened while I'd been gone. Things had definitely changed. Most of the teenage nightclubs had raised their age limit to 21 for admission, exactly as the Sheriffs and business owners had wanted—so I no longer had my job at It's Boss. What a bummer! However, changing the age at the clubs did not stop the hippies from congregating on the Strip. It was our turf, and no one was taking it from us.

Our hippy idealism would often facilitate long discussions about the differences between our generation and our parents' generation. Hanging out on Sunset Blvd., we often talked about the failures of *The Establishment* and our parents' ideals—based on materialism, consumerism and the acquisition of wealth. Our parents, meanwhile, talked about the *Generation Gap*. They thought the younger generation's long hair looked dirty and unkempt. We liked our hair—it was natural. What could it hurt, except perhaps the barber's income? Our parents said we took no responsibility for anything. That is how they characterized our disinterest in wealth. Their criticism was strong and our treatment by the police was brutal. Nonetheless, we stood up strongly for our ideals and our principles.

The times were changing—for sure—and I did not feel the same about some stuff. I stopped dancing on the TV shows, for example, because the dancers were still clean-cut high schoolers. That certainly wasn't me anymore. I was a hippy now, through and through—not only because of my ideals, but because of my appearance as well. My hair was past my shoulders, I had a moustache, and I wore bell-bottom jeans, a fringed vest and love beads. I didn't want to wear a coat and tie anymore—no way! To me, that was too much like being *the establishment*.

I had fond memories of the dance shows, though, and I was still pining for my job at It's Boss and all the fun I had working there and hanging out on the Sunset Strip, even mixed with all the turmoil of my life. There were so many incredible things I had experienced there and, of course, that's where I had met Katie . . .

1968 – October, 1969:

High School Marriage and Arthur

By 1968, I had become notably rebellious. I felt as if I was doing everything for myself and I was basically on my own, even though I was still living with Mom. She, of course, was still paying all the bills (Dad never gave her any child support for me).

The Sunset Strip, the hippy counterculture, pot, acid and rock-n-roll were my main focus now. Everything else sort of faded into the background.

My long hair caused me much grief at school, where they had strict dress codes. The football coach would sic his players on all the hippy types in school. They would chase us around the campus, harass us, bully us and beat us up. So I cut school a lot. If I could not be who I was, screw them!

To retaliate, a bunch of us did exactly what one did in the '60s: we demonstrated. A bunch of the progressive kids at school organized a sit-down demonstration to protest the ridiculous, archaic dress codes that the L.A. Unified School District forced on both boys and girls. We arranged for a sit-in demonstration on a specific day, at lunch, on the front lawn of school. Word leaked out and hundreds of students showed up to see what was happening. We gave our demands to members of the faculty, and we refused to return to class until our demands were met. Most of the students who had showed up stayed with us.

We disrupted the entire rest of the school day—and we eventually prevailed. We ended the decades long dress codes that had required boys to have short hair—not past their collar, no beards or mustaches, belts no thicker than one inch, no sandals or t-shirts, etc. For girls, the dress code had been skirts or dresses only, below the knee, no pants, must wear bras, no t-shirts or sandals, etc. After our class of '68 was done, there were no more dress codes at Hollywood High. It even eventually helped to end the dress codes in the entire L.A. public school system. We did that!

Take me as I am became my new mantra.

Dress codes were one thing, but the counterculture was focused on more important issues. Ending the war in Vietnam, exposing the harms that materialism was doing to our planet, inequality, and world poverty were all important issues for us.

The Generation Gap was real. We were speaking truth to power and the powers-that-be did not accept our hippy culture at all. We were at odds with the establishment, the police, government and our parents—all of it!

Mom couldn't handle my rebelliousness or my frequent disagreements with her boyfriend, Rick, an ex-Riverside County sheriff. He and I did not get along—no way! We were always butting heads. So the day I turned 18, Mom sat me down and gave me an ultimatum: "Cut your hair and stay in school; get a job; join the army . . . or leave!" I chose the latter—of course!

I went to my room and gathered up some things to take with me. Then Mom said, "Give me your house keys!" I knew that was it, and I never looked back. I was truly on my own from then on. I didn't know it then, but Mom would still be there for me, to see me through many crossroads in my life, but I would never live at home again.

After leaving Mom's, I stayed with Jessie temporarily. He was living in a tiny single apartment above a laundry room, in the back of a large apartment complex on the southeast side of Hollywood. I was still working with Rings of Knight, and Luna and Elena's brother, Bob, was now our keyboard player. It was fortunate that I was staying at Jessie's, because one night I was able to save the lives of Bob and his wife, folksinger Jenni Soul.

Jessie and I were preparing to head up to the Sunset Strip, as we did almost every night. Just as we were ready to go, Bob and Judee knocked on the door. We told them what we were up to, but we invited them in anyway, and we all smoked some pot. When Jessie and I said we were ready to leave, Bob asked if he and Judee could stay in our apartment for a while. We said, "Yeah—sure!" Bob said they needed a place to do it! Well, they did, but little did we know what 'do it' meant.

Jessie and I set out on our usual route to the Strip: walking west from Normandie and Santa Monica, all the way down to Western, then north up to Sunset, then thumbing it west to the Strip.

After walking a few blocks down Santa Monica Blvd., we came upon this trippy looking woman—who approached us. She looked like a gypsy. She looked at us and said . . . "Go back from where you came!" We looked at her like she was crazy, but then she said it again—"Go back from where you came!" We crossed the street to get away from her, and we continued on our way.

Then I stopped. I said to Jessie, "I think we should go back." He said, "No way! We have already walked this far and I want to get to the Strip and maybe score some acid." Now somewhat excited, I replied, "No, I really think we should go back. I'm going back."

I turned around and started walking. Jessie finally turned and relented. Although he was a bit frustrated, he wanted us to stay together. When we got back to the apartment, it was in flames! The only way in was through the laundry room door, and then up some stairs in the back of it. We ran up the stairs. The apartment door was locked. We knocked really loud, but no one answered. We ran back down. Jessie hoisted me up onto the top of the laundry room door, and I climbed in through the window.

We had psychedelic posters covering our walls. They were in flames! They caught fire because a candle had burned all the way down on the small table next to the bed, spilling wax over towards the wall, which caught one of the posters on fire. Many of them were now in flames. I ran to the door and let Jessie in. We ripped all the posters off the walls and stomped on them—putting the fires out.

I looked at Bob and Judee. They were out cold in the bed—they wouldn't wake up! Then I noticed the needle and spoon on the table next to them. Now I knew what 'do it' meant.

We saved them both that night.

I'll never forget that gypsy woman who sent us back.

⚡

I started writing poems about the hippy culture. Almost all of my early poems, the ones I had written from ages 10-17, were gone forever. I had kept them all in that journal hidden under my bed, but I lost them one day while hitchhiking to the Strip. I'd been dropped off at the Sunset Blvd. on-ramp to the Hollywood Freeway. As I stepped out of the car and closed the door, I suddenly noticed I didn't have my journal. I watched as the car entered the freeway on-ramp. My heart dropped as I realized I would never see my poems again. I would eventually incorporate some of them, from memory, into later writings, but I had learned my lesson. From that day forward, I dated everything I wrote and guarded all my work closely.

4/6/1968

we're all here together . . .
we're waitin' to hear

if we wait long enough
it might all disappear

they say we're corrupt
and our morals are wrong

but what they don't know
is together we're strong

so sing it together
let's all sing along

if we keep loving each other
our hang-ups will be gone

the cops . . . they are pigs
they beat us . . . and how

they've pushed us too far
they lie to us now

the government's strong
but their power will fall

we are younger and stronger
and we'll outlive them all

so let's sing it together
yes now . . . sing it again

if we keep making love
then you know we will win

a new world is coming
for you and for me

a world full of beauty
where we all will be free

no more hang-ups
no more hang-ups
no more hang-ups

⚡

Jessie and I were cruising up Sunset one morning on the used motorcycle he had just purchased with money he made from playing with Rings of Knight. He was giving me a ride to school. He passed someone on the right as we were approaching Highland Ave., where he was going to pull over at Hollywood High and drop me off. Suddenly, flashing lights came on behind us.

Jessie handed me a red Marlboro cigarette box and said, "Take this! I can't afford to get busted or they'll send me back to juvie." I took it and stuffed it down the front of my pants. He pulled over in front of the school, and the cop pulled up and stopped behind us. I hopped off Jessie's bike, books in hand, and started walking up the steps of school. The cop said, "Hey, where do you think you're going?" I said, "I'm going to class. He was just dropping me off." The officer then motioned with his forefinger for me to come back down to where he was.

The officer first questioned Jessie, asking him if he knew why he was pulled over. Jessie said he didn't, and the officer proceeded to tell him that passing on the right was illegal. The officer then turned his attention to me and told me to turn around and put my hands on the police car. When I did, he frisked me and found the Marlboro box. He said, "What's this?" I said, "Cigarettes." He told me to open the box. I did, and he saw two joints among the cigarettes. He then asked me, "Whose are those, his or yours?" I guess he had seen me stuff the box down my pants. I looked at Jessie, then replied, "Mine." With that, the officer said, "You're under arrest for possession of marijuana." Even though it was only two joints, possession of pot was still a felony in California in 1968.

He put me in the back of his car, then proceeded to give Jessie a ticket. When he was done, he drove away with me in the back. He took me to the Glass House at Parker Center in downtown L.A., where I was booked and spent three days in jail until my arraignment. They stuck me in the felony tank, which was one big room with about sixty bunk beds in it. All the felony charged criminals stayed in there until their arraignment.

They would feed you twice a day, at 4:00 AM and 4:00 PM. The food was a TV dinner of mystery meat, potatoes, canned veggies and black coffee. For the morning meal, they had powdered eggs instead of the veggies.

When I was allowed my one phone call, I called my brother. He and my brother-in-law raised the money to bail me out. They had to sell my record collection to a local record store to get the money, and I was devastated. My precious records! Fuck!

I did get out on bail, but the money was not enough to pay for a lawyer, so when I had to return to court, I was assigned a public defender. Since it was my first offense, I was sentenced to a $300.00 fine and two years' probation.

Jessie thanked me for taking the rap for him. He promised he would pay for my records and pay the fine, and I believed him. However, he never did pay for either. This was my second betrayal by him; the first, of course, being that he had slept with Katie. As time goes on, you find out who your real friends are.

I went to the store that had bought my record collection, but I had so little money, I could only get a few albums back. It took me years to rebuild my record collection.

5/15/1968

a biker is the carefree one
he's always on the run
he loves it
and he'll never stop
he's having so much fun

he proves his feelings
every day
he has to know he's right
if someone tries to knock him down
he'll end up in a fight

he cares for them
that's close to him
he'll never let them down
they'll never have to run with fear
whenever he's around

he's a criminal
a no good bum
most other people say
but he's happier than they'll ever be
in each and every way

↻

I had other worries that were worse than not having enough money and having a felony on my record. I had a new girlfriend, Jenny, and I had recently found out she was pregnant. Just what I needed!

Jenny and I went to Hollywood High together. We had become friends in 1967, when she was a sophomore and I was a junior. We hung out a lot with her other friend, Deena, so much so that we started calling ourselves The Three Musketeers.

There was a British movie that year that was popular with teenagers, *To Sir With Love*, which starred Sidney Poitier as a teacher who taught troubled teens (how ironic, eh?). British pop singer, Lulu, sang the title song, and it became a huge hit. Jenny and Deena dedicated it to me and used to tease me by singing it to me all the time.

Jenny and Deena were both in the pep squad of cheerleaders, so I started going to our football games to watch them, even though I had barely been into sports at all since my little-league days.

It was funny too, because when I started high school at Blair, they were still building their gymnasium and it was not finished before I left. When I began going to Hollywood High, it was right as they were tearing down their old gym to build a brand new one. So there was no gym for me all through high school.

The Hollywood High School band always marched in the Hollywood Christmas parade, which included the pep squad and cheerleaders, so I was able to watch Jenny and Deena marching down Hollywood Blvd. with Santa Claus that year.

Deena was the first Black girl ever to run for student body president at Hollywood High, and I became her campaign manager. Jenny helped us make some signs and Deena put on a great campaign. She was certainly intelligent and definitely popular. I thought she had a real good chance—but she lost.

When it came time for summer break, Jenny told me that she would not be seeing me anymore because her family was moving away. When I returned to school after the summer, I was approached by this cute girl who said, "Hi Steven! How are you?" I looked at her, puzzled, not knowing who she was. She said, "Don't you recognize me?" I replied, "No. Who are you?" She answered, "It's me, Jenny!" I looked closer and, sure enough, it was Jenny. She said, "I got a nose job over summer. We weren't actually moving away, I was healing for the whole summer and didn't want anybody to know." I was like, "Wow! What a mind blower! I've never heard of a nose job. But you look great!"

Jenny had a big nose before her operation, but it had never bothered me. I thought she was unusually beautiful at five foot four, with long, straight, dark brown hair, sparkly brown eyes and a small, pouty mouth that always looked a little sad. However, I had to admit, she was even more beautiful with a smaller nose.

Because we were good friends, Jenny confided in me why she had never liked her nose. She told me she had been terribly self-conscious about it because she was a first-generation American, half Armenian on her mother's side and half Russian on her father's, who was a political exile from Russia. She had a strong desire to fit in, never mentioned her background, and got that nose job to get rid of the large nose that is typical of many Armenian people. She had even changed her first name to Jenny, from a name I wasn't aware of, so people would not know about her nationality.

In 1968, Jenny was a sophomore and I was a senior. We hung out more and started going steady. I would go over to her house for dinner sometimes. Her mom was a great cook. She made a chicken and rice dish that was to die for. We would hang out in the evenings or sometimes go to The California Stash, a psychedelic headshop near her house. The Stash was upstairs above a business on Western Ave. at Santa Monica. We'd go through some tie-dye curtains at the back of the shop, and step into a black-light room with a jukebox and giant pillows to sit on. The black lights lit up fluorescent, psychedelic hippy posters plastered all over the walls.

When I went to the Stash without Jennie, it was on body-painting nights. Along with other artists, I could paint hippy girls' bodies. The girls would take off all their clothes except their panties. Then, they would lie down on the pillows and we would paint all over their bodies with fluorescent paint. After that, they would dance around to the music of the jukebox with their bodies glowing in the dark from all the *groovy* painting we'd done. It was *bitchin'!*

When Jennie and I went, however, it was all about the music. We would usually smoke a joint before going into the black-light room, where we'd put quarters in the jukebox. We'd sit on the pillows listening to The Stones', "2000 Light Years from Home," Cream's, "Sunshine Of Your Love," and "Summertime Blues" by Blue Cheer. Those were our favorite psychedelic songs of the time. One night, we were unabashedly horny, so we went into the bathroom to make out in private for a few minutes—or so we thought. Once in there, we could not control ourselves. We made out hard and passionate, then ended up doing it! I sat on the toilet seat and she pulled up her skirt and sat on top of me.

Another time, when I was still in the apartment with Mom, we made love in my bedroom while Mom was gone. We must have been high and miscalculated, though, because suddenly Mom walked in on us. She closed the door and left us alone, but I was so embarrassed! I didn't know what to do, but later Mom merely mentioned she hoped we had protection. I told her Jenny was on the pill. All the girls were taking them, as they were the newest form of birth control. She must have missed one, though, because I think that is when she became pregnant.

In April of '68, we went to the Teenage Fair at the Hollywood Palladium, where I was scheduled to be in the dance contest with one of my old partners from Shebang, Sherry. We won the dance contest and I was thrilled! Jenny and I had come to the fair with Linda, who was another friend from school. When I was done with the dance contest, Jenny told me she was not feeling well. She thought her stomach was upset from the ferris wheel or something. She and Linda went into the bathroom, and when they came out, Jenny told me she was pregnant. Linda called her mother, who drove over the hill from her business in Sherman Oaks to drive Jenny home.

When we got married, Jenny was 16, and I was 18. We were one of those teenage high-school pregnancy statistics of the '60s. Mom was upset, but supportive, and she told us she would go along with whatever decision we made—abortion or marriage. Jenny's parents, well, they were not so supportive. Even though they were from a country where marriage was usually the only solution to an unwanted pregnancy, they were worried about what their friends and neighbors would think. We couldn't believe it—they wanted Jenny to get an abortion. Nevertheless, they finally came around when we said we were keeping the baby and getting married. They threw us a formal church wedding and huge reception at the Biltmore Hotel in downtown L.A.—all to impress their friends! On our wedding night, in the honeymoon suite of the Biltmore Hotel, Jenny would not even make love to me. She said she was too drunk and too tired.

So I dropped out of high school, with only two months to go before I would have graduated. I entered the work force as a truck driver in L.A.'s garment industry, working for a clothing manufacturing company, Lanz, Inc. Jenny and I were married in June, and our son, Arthur, was born in November.

Jenny's dad, who was a mechanic at the local Dodge dealership, gave us a used '64 Dodge Dart for a wedding gift, so we could bring the baby to visit and do the errands we needed to do as a young married couple. One good thing for me—it looked like I wouldn't have to hitchhike to work anymore.

School was over for us both now, since Jenny had dropped out of school too, right before her pregnancy started showing. My school dreams of studying for a career in music and art were now gone, perhaps never to return. Still, as I said at the beginning of my story, I wanted to celebrate school being out and the beginning of summer. So I dropped acid, which didn't turn out too well, as we ended up at the Hollywood police station, where I was shot up with Thorazine to bring me down.

In late June, on the day I would have been graduating high school, I attended a large demonstration protesting the assassination of Robert F. Kennedy, who had been gunned down in Los Angeles two weeks before, on June 6th—only two months after Martin Luther King Jr. had been assassinated in Memphis on April 4th. RFK had been the hope of so many in my generation, as MLK had absolutely been the hope of Black people. So many dreams were stolen that year. Two months later, in August, the police riots exploded in Chicago at the Democratic National Convention.

I, like so many others, had been excited about the possibility of Robert Kennedy being our next President. Although his death broke my heart, I was also shocked, because I had gone to school with his killer. In an ironic and strange twist of fate, Sirhan Sirhan, the man who shot RFK, was from Pasadena. He had gone to the same junior high school as me and had been in my sister's class. His brother, Muniur, was in my class and was a casual friend. When I was 13, Muniur and I smoked our first cigarettes together, in an alley behind a local drug store, prompted by the brother of my sister's boyfriend. I even remember the brand, Pall Mall, filterless cigarettes. Sometimes after school, we would hang out and smoke behind Connal's Grinder, a sandwich shop owned by the family of another school friend, Mark. I can't remember if Mark smoked or not, but we often hung out together there.

The streets were on fire in 1968! Hippy riots, anti-war protests, protests over the assassinations of MLK and RFK, the Chicago riots at the DNC—these were all defining political moments in the last years of my teens, and I was directly involved at street level.

Oh, where would we go from here? I wondered what the world would bring after they had murdered our heroes. Everything seemed in turmoil and the dreams of Peace and Love seemed so out of reach now. I could not understand the lack of empathy in the world.

I had no idea what my last teenage year would be like, but given the final months of my 18th year, it felt as if it was going to be a doozy.

⚡

Jenny, Arthur and I lived in a little one-bedroom apartment on Mariposa Ave., one block east of Normandie Ave., and a little south of Santa Monica Blvd. It was actually in that same apartment complex where I had stayed with Jessie over the laundry room. It was a two-story apartment complex that had a common area in the middle with palm trees, and a pond with giant goldfish.

Because Jenny was so young, her mom and her aunt would not leave her alone to raise our son. They were at our apartment every day while I was at work, instructing Jenny on how to do everything. She would complain every night when I came home that she wished they would stop hounding her and leave us alone.

The '60s were all about free love in the hippy culture, especially because the birth control pill had become available. Everyone was sleeping with everyone, with no strings attached, and positive love vibes were everywhere. It was all very *groovy*, as they say. Unfortunately, that did not work well for families with kids. Or at least it did not work well for my little family. I had done my share of lovemaking with hippy chicks at the love-ins before I was married. But it was different now for me. I was married and planned on staying nothing but faithful to my wife.

One day in the summer of '69, Jenny said to me that there was one thing she regretted not doing before we got married—she had never slept with her high-school boyfriend, Kevin. By this time, Kevin was also married, to Jeanine. We knew them both well because we had all gone to school together, and we were hanging around with them because we both had young kids.

Evidently, Jenny and Kevin had already discussed it, and they still literally wanted to do it. So she told me they wanted to do a wife-swap thing. Related to the free love movement, wife-swapping was becoming popular in Hollywood, but mostly in our parents' generation. There were wild stories of wife-swapping, group orgies in the Hollywood Hills—all sorts of things.

Kevin and Jenny somehow talked Jeanine and me into letting it happen. So one day Jeanine came over to our apartment and Jenny went over to their house. All Jeanine could do was cry, so I comforted her and we simply talked. As it turned out, neither of us were comfortable about going through with it, so we didn't—but Jenny got to sleep with her high-school boyfriend!

I guess Jenny had discussed with Kevin how unhappy she was, because of her mom's and aunt's constant interference. She told me about a plan that might work out for us to get away from her family smothering her. Kevin had family in Denver, Colorado, who were in the construction business. They said if we wanted to move out there, I could get a construction job through them, which paid pretty well and had health benefits too.

Jenny and I discussed it and decided it would be great; a new start for us on our own to raise our family and totally be together—just the three of us.

We made a plan, and over the next few weeks we put it into motion. We packed up all of our belongings and stored most of them in her parents' garage where we could get at them later. We gave notice on our apartment, and I gave notice on my job. We were prepared to drive out to Colorado and begin our new life. Everything was looking great.

Meanwhile, my friend Mike had recently returned from Vietnam. He was a year older than I was, and he had joined the Marines at 17, a short time before I moved from Pasadena to Hollywood. He was the only one of my childhood friends who had joined up without being drafted.

He discovered, upon his return, that a soldier in uniform returning from Nam was not popular. Pretty much all of us were against the war and were protesting it, but I didn't judge Mike for joining up. He was my friend. And, anyway, most of the guys who were drafted or joined up were teenagers and did not know what they were actually signing up for or getting into.

When I was growing up in Pasadena, Mike's family had lived on the next block over from us and shared the exact same address number. He used to hop over his backyard fence and cross the street to my house.

His mom was living in Hollywood now, and his little brother, John, was staying with her. Mike stayed there also, while he looked for his own place. So we were hanging around together again. He would come over to our place often, and his little brother would tag along. We would all party together on the weekends, listening to albums and smoking pot. We would usually be at our place because our baby made it harder for us to go other places. We needed to keep to Arthur's schedule for feeding, sleeping, etc.

Jenny and I were all set to leave for Colorado. A few days before our departure date, we had some friends over to celebrate our upcoming move. Mike and John were there, along with my brother and some other neighbor friends from the apartments.

We all proceeded to get high on pot, and a few of us decided to drop acid to do a last spiritual, mind-expanding trip together. After I came on to it and was undoubtedly high, Jenny decided to pick that moment to inform me that she had slept with John. All of my acid trips up to this point had been mostly fun, intuitive and insightful. But this information made me feel nervous and anxious. I wondered why she would tell me this now when she knew I was frying on LSD.

I didn't know what to do. I walked out of the house without saying anything. I was so high that all I could think of to do was walk, so I simply started walking. I didn't know where I was going and didn't care. I walked and walked, and I actually ended up walking all the way up to Griffith Park Observatory, which was probably at least five miles, including a long trek uphill on Fern Dell Drive, all the way up to the Observatory itself.

I looked out over the Hollywood Hills and downtown L.A., then west to the sunset in the distance, which was spreading its colors over Santa Monica and the Pacific Ocean. The sunset was beautiful, but I was feeling overwhelmed. I felt bad, then I felt good. I felt bad because of what had happened with Jenny, but I felt good because of the effects of the acid.

By the time I started back down Western Canyon Road out of the park, it was beginning to get dark. Soon, it was pitch black. There were no cars, no lights, and the quieter it grew, the more scared I became. I was still trippin' hard, and I realized everything was exaggerated—but there might be mountain lions. They were often spotted in the park. I did not want to encounter any of those or any other creatures in the dark, so I walked in the middle of the road until I finally made my way down to Los Feliz Blvd., where I felt much safer.

Then, as I was walking down Western Ave. heading for home, just before I was about to reach Hollywood Blvd., a crow swooped right down on me—right down on my head. Then it did it again. I had never seen anything like that or heard of anything like that. It was freaky. All I could think of was that the crow was somehow in tune to how high I was on acid. That happens sometimes with psychedelics: You think you are in tune with everything, even animals and inanimate things. To me, it was an omen.

Looking back on it, I wonder if it truly happened—I was so high. It did feel real, and even today, I do believe it did happen.

I finally arrived home. The next day my legs were so sore that I could barely walk, so I rested a lot. I was emotionally shattered, in shock from what Jenny had told me. I still thought we were going to go to Colorado, though. At least that is what my heart was hoping for. However, a few days later, when I came home from work, Jenny and Arthur were gone. I called her parents' house. She answered and told me Arthur was sick with a cold, so she was going to stay there for a few days until he was feeling better. But the next day she told me her dad was taking our car back—our wedding gift, to keep us from going to Colorado.

Those few days turned into two weeks. At the end of that time, Jenny told me she had never actually wanted to go to Colorado and leave her family. She told me she was scared to leave and that they had talked her into staying with them.

Now I was extremely depressed! I was having a hard time believing she would actually throw everything away, all the plans we had made. I pleaded with her, saying, "What about our plans? What about our family? You said you wanted to get away from their influence and start out on our own. What happened to that?" But it was no use. She wasn't budging. I could see that our life together no longer truly mattered to her. She'd had a baby so young, and her mother and aunt were the strongest influences in her life. So she stayed with them.

Meanwhile, we had stored all of our stuff and given notice on our apartment, and I had left my job. The landlord, unfortunately, had already rented out our apartment, so I had no place to go. The feeling of having no family again hit me hard. No home for me—anywhere—anymore. What a déjà vu! Luckily, Mike had recently rented a single apartment on Sunset Drive, and he told me I could crash on his couch for a while.

Shortly after I moved in with Mike, Jenny came over with Arthur in his stroller. I tried to convince her to get back together with me, mainly because I did not want to lose Arthur, but it was to no avail. She told me she had left her parents' house and was now staying with John and his mom only a few blocks from where we were. By the time she left, I was visibly angry and sad.

Mike and I walked over to his mom's to see what was up. Everyone was there: Mike's mom, John, Jenny, and Arthur. I confronted Jenny again, telling her she might want to desert me but she could not simply rip my son out of my life. She told me there was no way I could take care of him since I had no place to live and no job, either. She and I argued, and then John shoved me, yelling at me to get out of their house. Without even thinking, I punched him, and the next thing I knew we were on the floor wrestling and pounding on each other. I beat the shit out of him, right in front of his mom, Jenny—everyone! After that, Mike said we should leave. So we did.

I was heartbroken and totally confused. How could this happen to me again? To be cheated on and deserted by the woman I loved, and this time to have my son ripped out of my life as well. I no longer had a family, and I was feeling utterly alone.

But then I kind of figured it out—Jenny had used me to get away from her strict, old-country parents; then she used her parents and John to get away from me. Soon after that, she even deserted Arthur, leaving him to live with her maternal aunt while she disappeared—not to be seen again for years. When she finally did turn up again, she had changed her first name—yet again. I guess she was still trying to become another person, someone other than who she actually was.

what do you do
when you are 19
and someone . . .
sleeps with your wife

they always want the bad boy
not the good boy

sometimes . . .
when you need real love
it still doesn't matter

wish there was someone
to confide in

*lost in the struggle
of the tumble
. . . alone again*

*just a heartbreak kid
with nowhere to turn
because of what she did
there's no way to return . . .*

↯

Heartsick and lonely, not knowing why this was happening to me, I wrote more breakup poems about Jenny . . .

8/15/1969

*we all have had our times
and the memories never die
this is where we get our rhymes
but in the past we do not lie*

*if you think there is no one
you can confide in*

*if you feel there is no one
to care*

*when you are alone
and need someone to talk to
please just remember
I'm there*

*we always have had
a unique understanding
we've lived under one roof
. . . and I know*

*we've gone thru such changes
alone and together
understanding
continues to grow*

*we've always been able
to help one another
it's only
because we both care*

if someone starts using you
just for their own gain
please . . . oh my darling
beware

and don't ever feel
you're alone in the world
please don't think
nobody would care

when everything's wrong
and you're not very strong
remember . . .
there's one who is there

⚡

8/20/1969

some days I'm very happy
some days I am so blue
the days that I am down and out
are when I'm without you

together we were happy
apart—aches to the core
thru trying times we've learned much
but we hardly know the score

we have a lot to go thru yet
we have so much to learn
I'll always care for you
to me you can always turn

so if you're ever down and out
and think it's 'cause of me
remember I won't hold you back
with me you will be free

⚡

9/5/1969

she says her love for me's gone
. . . but she's lied
'cause it's not really gone
she's just makin' it hide

*now we're apart
and she's living her way
I hope we'll be together again
. . . some day*

*our love was strong
in the head and the heart
but our communication
was miles apart*

*for another boy now
she has sexual desire
she no longer wants me
to 'light her fire'*

*she must discover herself
different kinds of emotion
then she'll know what we had
she'll understand my devotion*

*I can't hold her back
she's been held all her life
she needs to be free
man, she needs it from me*

⚡

9/16/1969

*bad days are here
sad eyes staring in the blue
good days are coming near
waiting for me and you*

*so for now and awhile
I'll just live for my work
then maybe I'll find you
where true love lurks*

*the teacher will show
our hearts will know
that we are correct
and we need to reflect*

*with the help of our friends
who give means to our ends
. . . if I could find one*

*it's not a game
love can't be blamed
refuse to get the blues
only to choose
whatever will amuse*

*you're alone in the end
I'm always a friend
stay by me now
we'll make it somehow*

⚡

10/8/1969

*I need you so
why don't you know
it can work now
we can make it somehow*

*it's not only a matter
of right or wrong
it also matters
if the feeling is strong*

*if your feeling is real
then how can you refuse
'cause my feeling's real too
so we've nothing to lose*

*except our grief and woe
and our fears . . . they won't show
'cause the feeling is there
do you know how I care?*

⚡

10/22/1969

*the soft brightening stars
were calling my name
return to the ocean
from whence sprang life's game*

*they kept right on calling
till I finally knew
that I must go down now
or forever be blue*

*got the blues in my body
the blues in my soul
they're quicker than lightning
and hotter than coal*

*if you don't come back darling
you know that I'm crying
you said you don't want me
I feel like I'm dying*

*baby . . . baby . . . baby
if you could see me
you'd know me*

*oh baby . . . baby
if you wanted to
you'd show me*

*but baby
　oh baby
　　you're gone*

*bye baby
　bye baby
　　bye bye*

1969, November-December:

Kidnapped and Robbed, Topanga Beach

I stayed at Mike's for a while. We would hitchhike up to the Strip most nights and hang out. It helped to take my mind off my troubles, and I could usually score some pot, which always helped too.

One day I found a cool suede-fringe jacket at a thrift store. Such a score! It was soft, beige, silk-lined and heavy, and it felt rich when I tried it on. It looked a lot like the one David Crosby always wore. I had never had a jacket this nice before. It was a little big for me, though, so that night Mike and I set out for the Strip. to find one of our female hippy friends who might know how to shorten the sleeves for me.

We started hitching at the corner of Hollywood and Hillhurst. A car stopped. A man in the front passenger side hopped out, held the door open and let Mike in. Another man hopped out of the back passenger door and let me in. We didn't think anything about that, even when it turned out that we were each in the middle of a seat between two other men.

As we drove off, the guy on my left said, "I just got outta jail." I said, "Oh—wow! That's a drag. Say, I happen to have a joint. You wanna get high?" He said, "Sure," so I lit up the joint and we all started passing it around.

Then, suddenly, both dudes in the same seat as me pulled knives and held them mere inches from my rib cage, one on each side. The dudes in front did the same to Mike. One of them said, "Don't try anything!"

As they approached the Hollywood Freeway, they veered onto the on-ramp and drove onto the freeway, heading north. I asked, "Where are we going?" The only answer—"Be quiet!" My heart was beating fast and I was shaking. I wondered if they could tell how scared I was.

They drove awhile, all the way to Topanga Canyon, then exited and drove up into the canyon. I knew there was nothing up ahead but miles and miles of darkness. I tried to keep absolutely still. At the top of the canyon, they pulled over and stopped near the edge of a sharp drop-off—almost a cliff. It was pitch black, no lights at all except their headlights. They all got out of the car, and one of them told us to get out. Then they made us give them our wallets and strip down, taking off all our clothes down to our skivvies: our jackets (my brand new fringe jacket!), shirts, jeans, and Frye boots (many guys wore Fryes in those days—we both did). They left us with only our skivvies, t-shirts and socks.

Then they lined us up at the edge of the cliff—with our backs to them. I looked at Mike and we both knew they were going to stab us, so I whispered, "Jump!" And we did!

I rolled down the mountainside in the dark and finally hit a tree and stopped—ouch! I must have fallen 30 feet or more. I was still shaky—shivering and dizzy. I thought about rolling down even farther, but I was too scared. I whispered, "Hey!" out into the dark and discovered that Mike was actually close to me as he whispered back, "I'm here." I replied, "Shhh! Let's be quiet and wait till they leave." Finally, after what seemed like an eternity, we heard them get in their car, and we watched as the headlights disappeared into the dark night.

We both climbed back up the hill and started walking down the road. We were still scared shitless. We walked south down the road, toward the ocean, and eventually we saw some lights, which turned out to be the Topanga Canyon Post Office. There was a bar next door. We went in, called the police, and the Malibu Sheriff's Department showed up. They drove us to their station down on Pacific Coast Highway, where I called Mom. She came to get us, bailing me out once again, as she had done so many other times. She liked Mike a lot, unlike Jessie, who she had always warned me about. I had to admit, Mom always made a lot of sense.

She had a long talk with us about hitchhiking, even though she knew we wouldn't listen. Then she drove us back to our apartment in Hollywood, first stopping off and buying us some food.

So my new jacket was gone, along with my other belongings.

From then on, whenever we were on the Strip, Mike would look for those guys. Once, he said he spotted one of them, walking up ahead in the hippy crowd. A bunch of us gave chase, but we couldn't catch up with the guy.

A few days after our near-death experience, I went over to Jenny's parents' house to see if I could get some of my belongings that we had stored in their garage before everything fell apart. When I showed up there, her dad and brother came out and pulled a shotgun on me, threatening to blow my head off. I told them I had only come to get some of my belongings. After cussing me up one side and down the other, they finally backed off, but they would not let me go in the garage to get anything. So I left.

I never did get any of my stuff back, and when Arthur's first birthday came around, I couldn't even spend time with him. Jenny's family all hated me, and I couldn't reason with her aunt to let me even visit. I felt as if there was a black cloud hanging over me.

So I wrote a poem. I was thinking about the Vietnam war—all the violence and the countless innocent lives lost—and about Martin Luther King, Robert Kennedy, President Kennedy (MLK, RFK, JFK) . . . That led me back to thinking about Arthur again, who had only recently begun to walk. I thought about how I, as a hippy pacifist, felt about guns and, idealistically, how I would want my son to be. The result—my first anti-war poem:

11/12/1969

I gave you my name
and you gave me a son
he's starting to walk
I can't wait till he'll run

we'll ride him on ponies
he'll have lots of fun
but don't ever give him
a little toy gun

*he'll go around shooting
you, me, and a friend
but it won't be a toy gun
he'll use in the end*

*he'll find him a real one
in the armed forces
I don't want my son
taking mass murder courses*

*so buy him creative things
not for impression
let him develop
his own self-expression*

*expression is freedom
but don't get me wrong
I may not be free yet
but I'm getting strong*

*I have understanding
of my own hang-ups
I need understanding
so I can be free*

*and then when our son
needs someone to confide in
he always can come
to you, babe . . . or to me*

*I gave you my name
and you gave me a son
he's starting to walk
I can't wait till he'll run*

*we'll ride him on ponies
he'll have lots of fun
but don't ever give him
a little toy gun*

I may have been naive when I wrote "Little Toy Gun," but it had naturally poured out of this 19-year-old hippy poet who was merely thinking of his own son's protection. Years later, following the murder of John Lennon in 1980 by a crazed fan, I would perform this poem with a hand-drum at the candlelight vigil held on the anniversary of John's death, at his star on the Hollywood Walk of Fame in front of Capitol Records. People would gather there at dusk every year, lighting candles and singing his songs. I always received a welcome reception whenever I played and recited my poem.

4

While I was staying at Mike's, I picked up a job to make some money to help him with rent and stuff. It was at the local Ford dealer only a few blocks away, so I was able to walk to work. They hired me as an errand boy, and my job was mainly to keep the bathrooms clean and take the customers' cars to the car wash on Hollywood Boulevard after they had been serviced.

They let me borrow a service car on the weekend sometimes because I didn't have one of my own—exactly like when I had worked at Lanz and borrowed the big blue step-van. I borrowed a car one Friday night and drove it up to the Sunset Strip, where I met two *groovy* hippy chicks, Betty and Sue. Sue and I hit it off right away, and we decided to drop acid. But Betty didn't want to, so we let her drive home when it was time to go.

Sue and I got incredibly high from the acid, so I crashed out in the backseat of the car for a little while. When I woke up, we were halfway to San Francisco! I was shocked and mad, but they said they were kidnapping me to go to a friend's commune in the city. They said it would be great. It was too late to turn around and I figured, yeah, it would be a cool adventure. Afterwards, I could drive back the next day, Sunday, and be home in plenty of time to return the car to work on Monday. So I went along with the plan.

The commune was in one of those several-story Victorian houses so common in San Francisco. We shared a vegetarian dinner with a bunch of other hippies and had a *far out* time listening to music and talking the tribe talk.

The next morning, a bunch of the group was heading out to the love-in at Golden Gate Park. I figured I could go for a little while before I drove home. It was bigger than our Griffith Park love-in in L.A., but otherwise the vibe was pretty much the same—hippies, families, picnics, music, Frisbees and dogs—and, of course, a drum circle. Sue and I grabbed a blanket and headed up a small trail in the park. We found a spot right off the trail, behind some bushes, and we laid the blanket down.

We proceeded to make passionate love right there. Almost as soon as we began, we heard some clomping on the trail and realized it was a cop on a horse. We laid there as quiet as could be. He slowly went past us and luckily did not see us, even though we could see him through the bushes. Whew! We continued our lovemaking, then we made our way back to the love-in, where the rest of our group was still hanging out.

Back at the commune after the love-in, we all passed some joints around. Sue and I climbed up into a loft and made love some more, then fell asleep. When I woke up it was getting dark. I became worried because I knew it was too late to start back to L.A. Reluctantly, I decided we would have to stay the night again. I would call my boss in the morning and tell him what had happened.

Monday morning came, and I was scared to call my boss, but I knew I had to. I called him and simply told him the whole truth. He knew I was a hippy, but he had hired me anyway. He was pissed off, but actually pretty understanding. He merely said to make sure I brought the car back the next morning. I did so, and I thought that surely I would lose my job. But surprisingly, he did not fire me.

4

I still had my hippy friends and we still had our own tribe, with some of the people who had been with Rings of Knight when the band lived in Hollywood. The rhythm guitar player, Ted and his old lady, Maggie, now had a house on Topanga Lane, a little dirt road at the bottom of Topanga Canyon, right where it spilled out into the Pacific Ocean, not far from that Malibu Sheriff's Station. I would often go to Ted and Maggie's and sit by their fireplace, getting high and licking my wounds. Sometimes we would walk the canyon floor down to Topanga Beach with friends, where we'd build a bonfire, drink wine, get high, play guitars and sing. I wrote this next poem there on the beach one day . . .

11/24/1969

sunlight . . .
bring my sunny day
promise what you may
but come here along the way

I need . . .
someone to hold me tight
to kiss me when it's right
and love me through the night

riding in the breeze
. . . so free
goin' just the way
I was meant to be

yet I don't know where to go
to find that soft warm hand
just tryin' to find some life
in this cold wasteland

in the city it's too noisy
I don't think my warmth is there
'cause everyone's just runnin'
in a hurry to go nowhere

so I guess I'll hit the country
just to see what I can see
then maybe when the time is right
my warmth will come to me

*sunlight . . .
bring my sunny day
promise what you may
but come here along the way*

4

In our tribe, there were the three 'Ms' of Topanga Beach, and they helped me forget my troubles with Jenny. There was Maggie, of course—Mama Maggie, we called her. She had a big heart and an empathetic ear. She gave good advice to all the hippies in our tribe, and she seemed wise beyond her years.

Then there was Mara. Now, Mara was this beautiful, short, tanned beach bunny, with long sun-bronzed hair, and all the guys were in love with her. She lived right next door to Maggie and Ted, where she had a small cottage-house with a loft bed.

One evening, after much revelry on the beach, Mara invited me to see her loft. We left the beach and walked the short distance to her cottage. Once inside, we climbed the ladder to her candle-lit hideaway, and sat on her comfortable, fluffy bed. She pulled on a rope, and a thatched roof opened up to reveal the evening sky and the stars above. That night, we made passionate love on her goose-down featherbed under the stars. *Work!*

Mike and I had moved into a one-bedroom apartment on Sunset Drive, right off Sunset Blvd. at the east end of Hollywood. It was a few doors down from where his single apartment had been, and right across the street from a movie studio where they shot porn films. The studio eventually became KCET Television, the local public broadcasting service channel (PBS). Mike was a true friend, my one true friend I had grown up with. We hitched to the Strip every night to hang out, and that is where we met the third 'M,' Melanie. Melanie had come to Hollywood to do a photo shoot for Playboy. She, her friend Linda, and the members of a rock band, October Country, had all driven out to Hollywood from Sioux Falls, South Dakota. They needed a place to crash, and we told them they could crash at our place for a couple of nights.

Well, those couple of nights turned into several months, and our apartment became another hippy commune, with mattresses covering the floor in the living room and the bedroom. Sometimes we would all drive down to Topanga Beach and join in with the rest of the tribe.

One night, sitting around the bonfire listening to music and getting high, Melanie and I decided to drop acid and trip. We bought a bottle of Ripple Pagan Pink wine to drink while we were coming on.

And what a trip it was! We decided to do another kind of trip. We decided to pack up our shit and hitchhike to Las Vegas, then up to Utah, back west to the coast, and then all the way down Pacific Coast Highway (PCH) from San Francisco, back to home. The next day we actually did it. We packed what we could into two backpacks, along with a couple of sleeping bags, and immediately hit the road, sticking out our thumbs with a sign saying—Vegas!

We hitchhiked our way to Las Vegas, and the two of us, both underage, snuck into the side door of a casino—it may have been the Golden Nugget—and played the slot machines right inside the entrance. They had astrology signs on them, and we each took one and played our own sign—she being a Leo, and me, Aquarius.

I'll be damned if we didn't win enough money for a motel room that night and dinner out somewhere. We ran out the door and laughed and laughed. We had gambled, and we had won. It was so *far out!*

The next morning we headed for Salt Lake City. Once outside of Vegas, for some reason it became difficult to get rides. We even had to sleep in our sleeping bags on the side of a freeway on-ramp one night. But we cuddled up together and made love—doing mighty fine! We made it to Salt Lake City, where we camped in Central Park with a whole bunch of other hippies. It was a regular camping area for traveling hippies, so we partied all night with some other like-minded journeyers. We had an incredible experience—getting high and trading travel stories.

After stepping out onto the Great Salt Lake, we stuck our thumbs out again and headed west, back to the coast. As luck would have it, a couple in a VW Microbus, who were going all the way to San Francisco, picked us up.

We had a fun trip with them, making some new friends, to boot! They left us in the city, in Haight Ashbury. We stayed in our sleeping bags for one night in Golden Gate Park, then headed south down PCH towards home.

We stopped in Big Sur for a night, where I knew some people. We had dinner with them in front of a warm, toasty fire, then left the next day, heading back to L.A. It had been *groovy* fun and tremendously entertaining—and Melanie was great to be with.

I don't think I actually ever wrote a poem about her, but I do remember she had incredible tan lines. I remember them to this day—great tan lines!

Some years later, I did write poems about Maggie and Mara, and because they are both so pertinent to my experiences here in 1969, I am going to include them.

3/5/1988

Mama Maggie
lived in the canyon
always kept a log-burnin' glow
in the fireplace

seems it's time
for me to wake up again
brisk morning memories
of a fond friend

many nights singing
on the beach in a circle

*people gathered 'round
who knows where they came from*

*always a place in her heart
for a stray cat
and in her midst
there was always a song*

*keeping the peace and the plenty
. . . her purpose
her rosy red cheeks
always shined when she'd smile*

*which was often, I'll tell you
she was always around
with her long silky hair
she was woman . . . yet child*

*Mama Maggie
lived in the canyon
always kept a log-burnin' glow
in the fireplace*

*seems it's time
for me to wake up again
brisk morning memories
of a fond friend*

*I remember . . .
I took my woman there
to warm her weary body*

*and . . .
I took myself there
to soothe my breaking heart*

*took many a friend there
for strength and compassion
oh, Mama Maggie
we're never far apart*

*for you're always inside me
sometimes rushing through my mind
like the breeze did in the canyon
through the trees often times*

*and you're still up in that canyon
. . . to this day
or so I hear*

*and whenever I think
of the good-old-days
or hear "Twelve Thirty"
I know you're near*

*Mama Maggie
lived in the canyon
always kept a log-burnin' glow
in the fireplace*

*seems it's time
for me to wake up again
brisk morning memories
of a fond friend.*

⚡

9/19/1991

*Mara's mystique
was quite well known
around the bonfire circle*

*where all the hippies
from the canyon
came at night to mingle*

*situated just yards
from the beach
in a shady, wooded glen*

*along the creek of the canyon floor
her enchanted cottage
welcomed me in*

 *she invited me . . .
come up
we'll have some tea*

*burn some jasmine incense
—and candles
just you and me*

*she took me there
when the moon was full
and the fire raged high
on the roaring shore*

*we drank some wine
we were feeling fine
she said . . . come
let me show you my secret door*

*let's make love in your loft
. . . Mara
let's make love in your loft*

*soft and feathery
under the stars
let's make love in your loft*

*in the back was her room
where a ladder led
to the candles and incense
and a goose down bed*

*arranged high on stilts
. . . up we climbed
the excitement grew
as the roof opened wide*

*revealing naked night
. . . starlight
we made love
as the canyon breeze blew*

*under the full moon
all night
where the smell of jasmine
came through*

*let's make love in your loft
. . . Mara
let's make love in your loft*

*soft and feathery
under the stars
let's make love in your loft*

*take me back
to that wooded glen
and the enchanted cottage
that I knew then*

*and you within
with your long brown hair
and your sun-bronzed skin
. . . take me back again*

*take me back to your loft
at the bottom of the canyon
where the ocean
meets the mountains*

*and your downy covers
touch the sky
in your soft feather bed
while I watch the clouds roll by*

*let's make love in your loft
. . . Mara
let's make love in your loft*

*soft and feathery
under the stars
let's make love in your loft*

⚡

I have wonderful memories of Topanga Lane, the beach, and our hippy tribe. They made me feel so much better for a while, after all that had happened to me. But I was still reeling with pain over Jenny and Arthur, and I was still feeling the wounds caused by Katie.

I would try not to think about either betrayal, but often that would lead me to thinking about what Jessie had done. My so-called best friend was a smooth talker who seduced any girl he wanted, including Katie. But he wasn't genuinely interested in keeping them; he merely wanted them for the moment. The girls always seemed to love a bad boy, and Jessie was just the type they were attracted to.

He had been in some trouble, and had been sent to a youth authority (YA) camp (juvie, as we called it). He managed to escape from that, and he came to Hollywood to find me. When he did, he asked me if I could help him hide. Of course I helped him! That's the kind of friend I was—and he knew it. After all we'd gone through growing up together, he knew he could count on me. So I found him a place to stay, a secret hideaway in downtown Hollywood, in the back room of a closed up business that a friend of mine was connected with . . . and that's where Katie had slept with him.

Even though Mom had warned me about Jessie, saying he was not truly a friend to me, that he was merely using me, I would not listen. I guess I was always simply hungry for a real friend.

12/7/1969

*making the rounds
without any sounds
with only the feelings
you have for each one*

*it always has been
and probably will be
but then in the end
will there be one for me*

*all the true feelings
I thought were existing
have gone
and have left desperation*

*the people I need
think they're better . . . indeed
while my love
is my only vocation*

*does anyone care
does anyone know
if you give of yourself
then my love I will show*

*the one that I needed
is gone now I know
too many have left me
. . . a friend*

*this feeling inside me
continues to grow
has someone a hand
they can lend*

*to keep me from
this misery
which grows darker
inside me each day*

*to keep me from
this feeling
that I've just got to
get away*

*she's gone . . . I'm lost
will I ever be strong
she's gone . . . I'm lost
did I do that much wrong*

*they don't need me now
but I'll make it somehow
I'll find out
just what life can be*

*and then later on
when they need a friend
—they'll know
that it always was me*

*they say that they care
and they'll always be there
but will their love ever
be true*

*I think that they care
and they say they're aware
yet . . . somehow
I'm always so blue*

*she's gone . . . I'm lost
will I ever be strong
she's gone . . . I'm lost
did I do that much wrong*

⚡

Sometimes I utterly could not stop lamenting about Katie and Jenny. I had loved Katie so much—my first love. Sometimes it felt as if the betrayal was fresh and raw again. Tears welled up in me and it was all I could do to keep from crying. Then I would think about Jenny and how she had cheated on me too—more than once. My pain was like an aching desperation . . .

12/22/1969

*life is like a river
that's been tearin' thru the ground
sometimes it moves so quickly
you can't know where it's bound*

*and then sometimes
it's very still
it doesn't make a sound
oh, woman when I need you so
you never are around*

*I have so much I need to do
this straight life leaves no time
I'm sick of playing games
'cause now I've barely got a dime*

*I need someone . . .
who'll bide her time by my side
to help me stand up strong
a woman who will stick by me
even if I'm going wrong*

*I've gone so far
I've lost so much
now this warm heart
just needs your touch*

*life is all around you
every day you prove it true
but until you see your life alone
life will remain something new*

*so if you ever think you're lonely
and you need some company
if you want someone who really cares
then come and stand by me*

*I've gone so far
I've lost so much
now this gentle heart
just needs your touch*

⚡

Katie—Jenny—Jessie, they continued to haunt my life—affecting my dreams, my feelings, and of course, my writing. I sometimes would have nightmares about losing everything, and I was often depressed even during the day, making it hard to move on.

12/24/1969

I need someone
whose thoughts are like me
'cause I'm hung up now
yet I am free

I'm out running around
in this cold-hearted town
I'll do good by you
do good by me

I've just got to tell you
how I feel
'cause this life in L.A.'s
not ideal

I just want to be gone
yet I must linger on
someone's got to make life here
seem real

I ran into
a very old friend
and I thought . . .
we're together again

but he hung me up too
so I'm still feeling blue
understanding . . .
a means to my end

I was living a full life
but then
I got stepped on
again and again

it was because I care
is there nobody there
they were using me
that's how it's been

*we've all gone thru so much
yes it's true
but this cruel life
still holds me and you*

*if we're ever to win
we have yet to begin
our ideals . . . in the end
will get thru*

1970, January-April:

Sandy and Lady, My Teens Are Over

One night on the Sunset Strip, I met Sandy. I was having a good time hangin' with some friends, kitty-corner from the Whiskey A-Go-Go in front of the Music Hall record store, where I had recently observed Jimi Hendrix browsing through records.

This cute, medium-sized hippy chick wearing patchwork jeans, Converse tennis shoes and a tight, long-sleeved, tan t-shirt with a beaded fringe vest over it, walked by me with a little black, English Shepherd dog on a leash. Then she turned around and looked at me, smiled and asked if I wore contact lenses. I said, "No, why?" She replied, "Because your eyes are so blue!" And that is how this hippy girl, who would become my second wife, picked me up. Because hippies were so free, hippy girls thought nothing of picking up a boy.

Sandy was about five foot four, with stringy, shoulder length, light brown hair and blue eyes. She and I hung together on the Strip that night, then hitchhiked down to Topanga Lane, to Ted and Maggie's house. We made love on the rug in front of the fireplace in their front room. I had not been with anyone since Jenny, and it felt good to hold someone in my arms. After that, she and I met up at the love-ins every Sunday, in Griffith Park.

Mike had gotten a job as a commercial fisherman and had moved to Northern California. I was staying temporarily with my sister and her husband in Pasadena, and I would hitchhike almost daily to Hollywood, to hang out on the Strip—and now to see Sandy. On New Year's Day, 1970, at the love-in, she told me she was going to have to give away her dog, Lady, because she still lived at home, and her parents would not let her keep Lady there. She didn't have anywhere she could take her to, so we made a decision to try and find an apartment and move in together, to give Lady a home.

Nineteen days later, I turned 20 years old. In what seemed like an instant, my teens were over! And the '60s were over too! The most momentous decade ever in the history of man was no more—that's how it felt to me. I still felt like a teen, but I no longer was. It still felt like the '60s, but it no longer was. Life would go on, for sure; some things would definitely change, while some things would stay the same. I felt a little melancholy, but that was a normal feeling for me—so no big deal. Regardless, I would surely miss my teens—and the '60s.

Speaking of change—yes, I was now 20—only 20—and yet here I was about to move in with another girl. Sandy's parents lived in Inglewood, so we found a little apartment there. It was a cockroach-infested one-bedroom duplex. If you woke up in the middle of the night to go to the bathroom, when you turned on the light the walls would move. Cockroaches were everywhere.

Most of the time, we were broke. I made up a one-pan breakfast dish I called *Flemish*: shredded hash-brown potatoes, eggs and cheese, all mixed up together. Sometimes I'd add mushrooms. We were on a steady diet of that, Kraft Mac-n'-cheese and PBJs. On a good day, we would have tuna fish sandwiches or hot dogs.

Of course, we would hitch up to Hollywood, to the Strip, almost every night. Like most hippies, we did some drugs. We would panhandle money to get some pot. Sometimes it would be Whites/Bennies for me and Reds/Lilly F40s for her, as they were only $1.00 a roll, much cheaper than pot, which was still around 20 bucks an ounce. When we did that, we must've looked funny walking down the street together—me hyped up on uppers and she, with her arm around me, almost nodding out on downers.

I obtained a job at the local Inglewood deli where she used to work. It helped for now. Shortly after I started working, Sandy told me she was pregnant. Although she had been sleeping with other guys on the Strip besides me, she assured me the baby was mine. We both discussed it and decided she would quit smoking and doing drugs while she was pregnant. We both agreed it was a wise decision.

2/14/1970

when you think of me
and how it's meant to be
please know, my love
—it's strong
it's inside you linger on

I hope you take the time
to know
a love like ours
is meant to grow

so many things happening
. . . right now
I know we're gonna make it
. . . somehow

—stranded in the here and now

I love you so
I just need you to know

if you will just stick by me
. . . stick with me . . . believe
you'll have no doubts
you'll never leave

↯

One night after partying in Hollywood, we arrived home to discover that most of our belongings had been ripped off. Everything in our place was thrown about, but not broken, as though the burglars had been searching for valuable items (not in our place!). All my record albums were gone, though, including an original copy of The Beatles' Butcher Cover Album I had found in a used record store.

At least it was a smaller collection, as I had not had the resources to build up another substantial record collection yet.

3/10/1970

*as time still moves along
some more good things are gone
but love's still growing strong
ever lingering on*

*the people are coming
from here and from there
they are coming with smiles
and flowers in their hair*

*I've lost much in a short while
there's so much yet to see
we must live our own lifestyle
we've yet to be free*

*the people are coming
it's you and it's me
we come with our feelings
let everything be*

⚡

3/22/1970

*yes my love . . .
there is someone to talk to
'cause here I am
I've been looking for you*

*I've been looking for her
I've been looking for him
I've been looking for me
I've been looking for them*

*yes my love . . .
there is someone who hears
oh please help me baby
I don't need no tears*

*there is so much
I need to do
the strength I need
it comes from you*

*the time is now
the feeling's so strong
I hope that you know
It's where we belong*

*I know the way to make you do
the things I want to do
and how to make you be
the woman I want you to be*

*it is simply for me to do
all the things you want to do
and to be just the way
you want a man to be*

*yes my love . . .
there's someone who hears
don't leave me now
forget all your fears*

*I've been looking for love
from the stars up above
I've been waiting so long
for this feeling so strong*

⚡

I didn't get to go to *Woodstock*. However, seven months later, in March of 1970, somebody showed up on the Sunset Strip and offered a bunch of us tickets to be the first to see the movie, *Woodstock*—on the day before it was going to premier. The premier was sold out to all the big mucky mucks, but for some reason somebody decided that the hippies should get a chance to see it first, as it portrayed them and honestly belonged to them, after all.

An arrangement was made to show the movie to the hippies in Hollywood—without advertising it, on the day before the actual premier of the film. They sent some representatives up to the Sunset Strip with a bunch of tickets, and then they just handed them out to the hippies on the street. My friends and I received some of the tickets, and I had enough to invite Ted and Maggie, along with a few others in our tribe.

Sandy and I went down to Topanga Lane the next morning. Ted and Maggie said they were in. Another friend, Barry, said, "Let's drop acid right before we go!" I was reluctant at first, but, of course, I was in. When the time came, several of us dropped acid and we all headed out, excited to see the movie—about the concert/festival event of our times.

And was I glad I was 'trippin.' When Richie Havens came on, then Santana, then The Who singing . . . "See me/Feel me/Touch me/Heal me" . . . Wow! I do not even know how to describe how I felt, other than the fact that it continually sent shivers all over my body. It was majorly awesome! My eyes were glued to the screen. It was an experience I will never forget. We were among the privileged few who were able to view *Woodstock* the day before it premiered. I still have the program they gave us when we walked in the door of the theater. That's how much seeing the movie meant to me.

The movie and the festival—both were a celebration of our hippy culture, a big part of which played out in Hollywood on the Sunset Strip, where Sandy & I, and many of our tribe, hung out. We were two young, righteous hippies, hitchin' to the Strip every night. Just two young hippies lookin' for a tab of acid, a roll of reds and a jug of wine—sometimes hiding behind the bushes to drink our wine and start our trip. Two young hippies going to the love-ins on Sundays at Griffith Park, with free food from Green Power—peanut butter and honey sandwiches with Kool-Aid, and a turkey feast on Thanksgiving Day and New Year's Day. Two young hippies with our friends on the Strip, being hassled by the pigs—the Metro Squad of the L.A. County Sheriffs—nightly herding us up and down the street like cattle, because of their anti-loitering law, and the curfew law enforced against hippy teenagers under 18 (as I used to be when I first became a hippy).

⚡

4/3/1970

for those of you people
who've left me
for those
from whose side I have gone

and even for those
whom I have not yet met
hey now . . .
something is coming
the time isn't long

now when the time comes
people will be as one
you know . . .
all of us will be together

yes, when hate is no more
and when love is just love
then we all will be right
with each other

I say love is just love
it is love . . . yes it's love

*you must know people
that this is true*

*we must bring out the love
that's inside of us all
then you'll know
everyone's just like you*

*you are right in your ways
I am right in my ways
everyone is right
in their ways too*

*if you all are expressing
your love
then I'm guessing
that happiness will come to you*

✦

In April, Sandy was five months pregnant. Our child would be born in late August. We started thinking about marriage, but we would not actually do that for another year, since we were reluctant about doing it at all. We both believed that traditional marriage was not necessary for two hippies to stay together and be happy. Many in the Counterculture felt that way and were shackin' up without getting married.

We changed our minds, however, after our son, Shane, was born. When he was eight months old, we decided to get married so we could give him legitimacy by giving him my last name.

4/6/1970

*blue-eyed brown-haired woman
I think I'm gonna marry you
blue-eyed brown-haired woman
I hope you're gonna love me true*

*whatcha gonna do
when I come home each night
—tell me
how you gonna make me feel*

*whatcha gonna do
I hope you make me feel alright
'cause then I'll know
your love for me is real*

*blue-eyed brown-haired woman
I love you yes I do
blue-eyed brown-haired woman
I'm always gonna stick by you*

*if your love is true
you know it's got to be true
now if your love is true
I'm gonna stick by you*

*oh . . . blue-eyed brown-haired woman
please know I love you so
I'll dance with you in my dreams at night
I'll follow wherever you go*

⚡

4/7/1970

*I look at those
who look at me
and even those
who don't*

*I smile when people smile
you see
I smile at some
who won't*

*when I see your eyes
—and stare
I'm looking to know
you really do care*

*so please don't say
stop staring . . . it's wrong
because eyes say so much
yours say . . . love lingers on*

*and woman
when I smile at you
please know
It is no game*

*I smile because
I love you so
you see
I'm not to blame*

so when I smile
and gaze in your eyes
oh woman
you have to realize

I'm not playing a game
this is not a blank stare
I am looking at you
'cause I really do care

⚡

We found out that Sandy's dog, Lady, was an English Shepherd/Setter mix. She was medium size and black, with long, shiny fur, and a small white patch on her chest. By then, we also had two cats we called Tiger and Monkey Face (Monkey for short). Tiger was a slim, tiger looking cat. Monkey was furry and all black, except for a black and white face and a white tip on his tail.

4/8/1970

baby, when you walk with me
Lady, running thru the park
baby, Lady's so carefree
just you and I
when day's gone dark

baby/Lady
I love you two
in each and every thing
you do

if you will only stay by me
you know our love
will always be

baby/Lady
you're so fine
baby/Lady
glad you're mine

pretty . . . pretty Lady
waiting to get fed
lovely . . . lovely baby
let's get ourselves to bed

and now we have Monkey too
and Tiger's here
and me and you
we all will stay together
loving each other forever

⚡

Sandy and I had our first fight—over money, of course. For some reason it sent me right back to thinking about what Jenny had done to me. I felt insecure and instantly went to that place in my head where I felt as if Sandy might leave me too, exactly as so many people in my life I cared about had done. However, it was merely our first little fight, and everything turned out fine.

4/9/1970

so many have
their own private playground
some people think
it is fun

but if you should ever
turn your back on me dear
you'll know that some hurt
has been done

I always have been
understanding
or at least love
I think I have tried

you must think of me now
please don't think just of you
then I know understanding
won't hide

if you don't understand
you must try harder still
if you can't see it now
I know you soon will

if you try hard enough
you can hardly go wrong
you must just feel it out
then we'll keep growing strong

4/12/1970

*smiling people
walk on by
keep on smilin'
tell you why*

*when you smile
your friends are glad
and when you don't
they think you're sad*

*now if you're sad
please tell me why
'cause you know I care
that ain't no lie*

*so smile a smile
that is real
smile a smile
that you feel*

*I say now . . . keep smilin'
alright now . . . smile with me
come on now . . . make it big
a smile that all can see*

*now I say . . . keep smilin'
come on now . . . let it be
because if we don't smile
how can we ever be free*

Sometimes our hippy idealism would get in the way of our little family, causing hurt feelings, even jealousy. Sandy and I both were idealistic. We believed in brotherhood and in our tribe. We would often have friends over, and it would get crowded sometimes, creating some friction between us. But our love bond was strong, and we seemed able to work out whatever problems arose.

4/15/1970

when the feeling's so natural
how can you ignore
yet so many do
they just don't know the score

it's that feeling inside us
the love we all share
you must open up people
and know we all care

you say that my feelings
are wrong
I can't love someone else
and be true to you too

but how can that be
when the feeling's so strong
girl I love you so much
yet I love others too

you don't see how I can
feel this way
so you think I'm just some
foolish youth

but I've tried
and tried hard
yes I've tried it your way
and now someone has showed me
my feelings are truth

someone else heard my thoughts
and agreed
so I must open up
yes indeed

I must express what's inside
love can no longer hide
so please know that your love
I still need

now I'm writing this song
so my love you will know
if you'll just open up
then our love can still grow

*girl . . . I love you so much
you should know this by now
if you still don't know . . . love
I must show you . . . but how*

*it's inside . . . it's inside
it's inside I keep crying
if you can't see the feeling
our love must be dying*

*if you ever are gone
then my love I'll be hurt
yet my love lingers on
so I'll keep scraping dirt*

*to find someone who knows
to find someone who feels it
to find true love that grows
until no one conceals it*

1970, April-June:

The Beatles Break Up, From Inglewood Back to Hollywood

The Beatles were splitting up! Sandy and I were devastated, as were most of our friends. On April 17, 1970, Paul McCartney released his debut solo album, *McCartney*. Upon its release, people were saying that Paul broke up The Beatles, even though, supposedly, John had already left the band in secret eight months earlier. I read somewhere that in September of 1969, following the completion of *Abbey Road*, John had told Paul he wanted a divorce from The Beatles—that he was leaving the band, and they agreed to keep it secret for the time being. I didn't know for sure what was true, but it all added to our despair over the breakup of The Beatles, who we considered the spokesmen for our generation.

I read that Paul's solo album, *McCartney*, was a *one-man band* album, with Paul writing all the songs, playing all the instruments and singing all the vocals (with a few harmony contributions from his wife, Linda). I thought it was an incredible feat for anyone to accomplish, but if anyone could do it, it was certainly Paul! I heard it was recorded mostly in secret at his home studio, during his distress over the split-up of The Beatles, from around December 1969 through March 1970.

In retrospect, it is easy to observe his strong feelings echoed in the songs on the album. Because of recent interviews, there is now more comprehension about what he was going through personally at the time, which makes *McCartney* a more understood and better received album today than it was at its release. It is now easier to imagine Paul alone, expressing his disappointment, knowing The Beatles were no more, but having to keep it to himself. The driving guitar, and the sometimes almost screaming lyrics on the album—so emotional and moving as to be inspirational in their expression—now seem especially poignant.

John Lennon was always my personal hero growing up, but this was a moment in Paul's life where I genuinely related to the emotions and distress he was going through.

When you think about The Beatles breaking up, you naturally think about the last album they did together. Most people think that album was *Let It Be*, because it was their final release in 1970. But actually, *Abbey Road* was the final album the band recorded together. And I have heard that the final song on that album, "The End," is the last song the complete band recorded together. If you listen to it now, with the way it ends, it is a fitting finale for The Beatles phenomenal career.

⁊

That year, there was another amazing one-man-band album, and it stood out strongly as being just as accomplished as McCartney's solo album. Released in December of 1970, it is the self-titled album by U.S. musician, Emitt Rhodes, who was the lead singer and songwriter of the band, The Merry-Go-Round. The album, *Emitt Rhodes*, was recorded entirely by Emitt Rhodes in his home studio in Hawthorne, California (the same city The Beach Boys are from), and all instruments and voices were done by him. I consider it one of the stand out albums of 1970.

I was able to get my old job back at Lanz, Inc., driving the same truck I had driven before, the large blue step-van. What a trip!

When I had been driving for Lanz in '68-'69, I had been picking up finished clothing from the sewing shops in downtown L.A., and those out in the San Fernando Valley; then delivering them to the Lanz warehouse on Venice Blvd., or to their retail store on Wilshire Blvd. Now, I was working out of their fabrics warehouse in Venice Beach, delivering bulk fabrics to the sewing shops, as well as to 1,000 Fabrics, Lanz's retail fabrics store on Fairfax Ave. I was also keeping inventory of all the rolls of fabric at the warehouse in Venice—right on the boardwalk, by the pavilion where the hippies and roller-skaters hung out. I would often spend my lunch hours there, eating my bag lunch and talking to whoever passed by, getting filled in on the local hippy happenings around town.

Sandy and I were able to move back to Hollywood, taking our pets with us. We moved into a little one-bedroom apartment on Leland Way, right around the corner from Sunset Sound Studios, where Janis Joplin would soon be doing recordings for her last album, *Pearl*, which would be acclaimed as her masterpiece.

While we were living in that apartment, the first Gay Pride Parade took place on June 28, 1970, right up the street from us on Hollywood Blvd. It was colorful and celebratory, with Gay people openly showing their rainbow smiles, while dancing and singing, as they paraded through the streets of Hollywood.

And I was back in Hollywood where I belonged—it felt like home again. I was with the woman I loved, and we were looking forward to our future. It felt like a new beginning.

5/6/1970

it's so good to be true
to be loving you
it's so good to be with you
each day

it's so good to be true
to be loving you
'cause your love now
it shows me the way

to find pleasure in work
I don't feel like a jerk
anymore . . . and I say
don't stop showing the way

*just keep loving me true
and I'll keep loving you
and keep walking so tall
then I never will fall*

*walking with you my love
I'm as free as a dove
in this way I can say
our love comes from above*

*so I say . . . yes I will
I'll keep loving you still
till the end you are mine
till the stars do not shine . . . anymore*

*—even then
I'll still love you my friend
for my love . . . there's no end
to the love that I'll send*

*for the love that you give
is what's making me live
I'll keep loving you true
and I'll never be blue . . . anymore*

⚡

6/1/1970

*in this age that we live
many things will be done*

*yet I don't know how much
'cause I am only one*

*I only can observe
whatever comes my way*

*and things I feel
that need some change*

*to try and fix
I must each day*

*in everything I do
and say*

*to make life here more real
my love . . . that's how I feel*

*it's black and white
like day and night*

*the love light
that you send*

*and if it's right
like it was last night*

*I hope this day
will never end*

⚡

6/11/1970

*the love that I give
now I hope it can show
well the more that I give
then the more it will grow*

*each day when I'm leaving
I don't want to go
I just want to stay here
and love you . . . you know*

*the time is at hand
to know where we stand
to bask in our love light
and know what it's for*

*your love is still giving me
all of the answers
to all of my problems
and yes even more*

*it is telling me now
that we'll make it somehow
we'll always be one
—one with all*

*I see tomorrow—somehow
but it doesn't matter now
because we're here
and I know we won't fall*

By this time, Sandy was seven months pregnant. She had not drunk alcohol or done any drugs since we first discovered she was pregnant, and I had not done any psychedelics during that time. Sometimes we were both on edge because of it. On one particular Friday night, we ended up in a fight soon after I came home from work. I had driven the blue step-van home for the weekend, which I was occasionally allowed to do. I was tired, and now angry, so I climbed into it and drove off—with a tab of LSD in my hand that a friend had given me. It seemed like the perfect time to take it, so I did. I drove around all night while *trippin'* up through San Fernando Valley, then west to Topanga Beach, then back to the Valley again, where I watched the sunrise at the corner of Burbank & Victory boulevards, right under a large billboard that read, "Left Turn O.K. For The Dip" (referring to the Philadelphia cheesesteak and French dip takeout place across the street). I wrote this poem at various intervals—all night long, while *fryin'* on the LSD.

6/26/1970

here I am . . .
I'm just fryin'
on this six year song
. . . it's a song to my mother
. . . or somethin' or other

it's not that we're different
how can it be
it's just that we care more now
can't you see

if the feeling is real
then it's one to believe
that we all can perceive what is real
if we feel it's our way
then we'll make it someday

and it's here . . . it's right now
I must show you . . . but how
you must pick up on something
much closer right now

just to see you
just to be with you
if you know this feeling
then it all will work out

*I just want you together
we all must come now
yes where love sticks together
it's here and here's how
it will stand as it stood
but the love's deeper now*

*and I don't even know
if the time is right now
but it's just that I'm feeling
so feeling . . . somehow*

*it's like . . . as if
LSD were made
for conditioning . . .*

*to make us more aware
of what we already know
in the five senses we have
and the power to show*

*it is here . . . it can grow
it can grow . . . it can grow*

*—it can grow
but how can it grow
if we can't show
that with friends we will win
. . . if we'll ever begin*

*if only Jessie were here
right now
but something says it's right
somehow*

*now Ted is here
we'll get it on
because then I know
it will be strong*

*and now . . . I think . . .
I've almost hit it
it's just . . .
we all keep gettin' together*

it's for you . . . Sandy
and me
and our baby
can't you see

it's for you
it's for me
it's for us
it will be

and now kitty cat
can you scratch the doormat
because that's where you came from
and that's where it's at

if you know where it is
c'mon tell me
. . . right now

'cause the feeling is
. . . maybe
we'll make it somehow

and we all will stand strong
'cause we all do belong

it is strong . . . it is strong
and it grows stronger still

if we want it to happen
you know that it will

'cause it's strong
man it's strong
it's been strong for so long

or at least
I've tried to show
in my own way
I care

'cuz it's there
it is there
man it's there
man it's there

it's for you . . . it's for you
it's for you . . . can't you see

*it's for you . . . it's for me
it's for them . . . can't you see*

*that I'm writing right now
will we make it somehow*

*but I'm just wasting time
'cause it don't seem to rhyme*

*I hear the bells . . .
I must go . . .*

*I'm afraid . . . I must go
if they see what I show
they might stop me
    but how
'cause we're makin' it now
. . . and it's 2:24*

*I see it all around me
I know that it is real
'cause I'm speaking now of truth
. . . man
and that's a feeling that can kill*

*it's all here . . . all around me
I know that it is right
I am speaking now of truth
. . . man
and I know that's worth a fight*

*all I got's . . .
my keys and me
just watchin' the sun rise
on Saturday*

*through all of the knowing
man . . . just let me be
'cause I want to still see you
tomorrow*

*yes . . . and now I hear
the birds are callin'
. . . callin' harder still*

*does anyone really know
where it is
I wonder . . .
if anyone will*

*if they'd all come thru here
peaceful
like I could almost draw
the picture*

*it's just Burbank & Victory
on a Saturday morning sunrise*

*just keep truckin' along
and you'll keep goin' strong
but ol' Jessie . . .
he split
'cause it just couldn't fit*

*that the feeling's so strong
if we'll all come along
and it's . . .
"Left Turn O.K. For The Dip"
and we'll all have a wonderful time*

*man I'm truckin' . . . and truckin'
and truckin' so much
I even had to pee
in the back of my truck
and the truck ain't mine now
wish it were . . . somehow*

*and I now have a choice
I can stay here or go
if I go back to her
then I hope love can show*

*and I hope it will grow
and I hope you all know
if I go back to her
. . . man
then all love must grow*

*yes . . . and all love must show
till we're all in the know*

*Saturday morning . . .
get me home to my love
Saturday morning get me home to my love*

*Saturday morning . . .
gettin' me home to ma babe
Saturday morning gettin' me home to ma babe*

*Saturday morning . . .
got me home to my Love
Saturday morning got me home to my love*

*it's not that we're different
how can it be
it's just that we care more now
can't you see . . .*

↯

The next day Sandy and I made up. It was Sunday, and it felt like an easy, breezy day. We went to the love-in and took Lady with us. I was sitting there thinking—idealistically—about us, about work, about the world at large, and about the trip I just took. I was inspired!

6/27/1970

*you say that you have feeling
and your love for us is there*

*but you don't know
what is happening
and really couldn't care*

*remember . . .
anything can happen
then you'll know
you are aware*

*and show your feelings
deep inside
then you'll know
that we all care*

*and we will know
that you care too
then no one
will be feeling blue*

*so open up your love
right now
and then your love
will show me how*

*to open up my love
inside
then . . . never
will I let it hide*

*. . . anymore
I'll know the score*

*the love you show
will make mine grow*

*then all will know
the love we show*

*then all will show
and love can grow
. . . forever*

⚡

6/27/1970

*my day's . . .
a little bit brighter
'cause my love
is lifting me higher*

*my babe . . .
she lights my fire
yes, man
she's my desire*

*I'm just truckin'
on the job
winding down
the freeway*

*know I'm happy
as can be
knowing tomorrow's
a free day*

*free for me
and my sweet love
on our own
to run and play*

*our love will land
in soft cool sand
she'll look at me
that certain way*

*I know she will
she always does
that's why I love her
so*

*I will always
follow her
and we will always
know*

*because it's strong
our love will grow
we'll win the race
we'll hit our stride*

*I hope it lasts
this golden glow
a love as deep
as the ocean is wide*

⚡

6/27/1970

*see the nonviolent soldier
marching off to war*

*all he's got is aching hunger
and you know he's sore*

*—still he keeps a-marchin' on
knowing what that ache is for*

*not for a tank
or a general's rank
not even for a gun*

*it's for hope
and for dreams
and for love
—can't you see
it's got him on the run*

*we all must join him now
we all must help somehow*

*to make that dream-of-dreams
come true*

*a brotherhood
for me and you*

*it's the 'Brotherhood Of Man'
spreading love
wherever we can*

1970, July-October:

The Manson Family, Birth of Shane

Since I was a boy, I have written dream poems. I will wake up in the middle of the night with a poem fully formed in my head, then try to find a pencil and paper to write it down as quickly as I can—before it totally disappears. This is one of those dream poems. I was dreaming about work and driving in my truck somewhere downtown. I looked in my rearview mirror and saw a woman in a car staring at me and smiling. I suddenly awoke with this poem in my head:

7/1/1970

if he's looking
in his mirror
I will ask him
to come back

because the feeling
is so clear
his sweet love
is what I lack

will he come
on back to me
lord I'm lonely
as can be

pounding inside
feeling's so strong
if he's coming
it won't be long

now he's coming
back to me
it's me and him
just him and me

now he's coming
deep in me
I knew our love
was meant to be

↯

Work was always an adventure. Traveling between downtown and the valley every day, sometimes twice a day, was fun for me. The traffic in those days was minimal, so whether I traveled on the Hollywood freeway, or up and down Laurel Canyon, I usually managed to get to my destinations on time, with no problems. Sometimes I would pick up hitchhikers. Sometimes I would spend my lunch hour in the valley. I would generally be having a good time while I was working. I was alone in my truck, doing my job, and it suited me.

Sometimes I would be driving by the courthouse downtown, and I would see the Manson Family girls on the courthouse steps protesting. Their heads were shaved, and some of them had X's tattooed on their foreheads in support of Manson.

Charles Manson and his girls were on trial for the murder of actress Sharon Tate and six other people. Every time I drove by those girls protesting, I remembered my own encounter with Manson's family. It was a year earlier, in '69, when I was still staying with Mike at his place on Sunset Drive.

I was alone one afternoon, hitchin' down Sunset to the Strip, when I was picked up by a bus full of hippies. As the driver pulled away, he asked me where I was going. I said, "To the Strip," and he nodded, "We can drop you there." I climbed into the back, where there were a couple of mattresses, and about eight people were lounging on them—smoking, talking, having an all around good time. I started talking to this cute hippy chick and she told me they were headed for a ranch up in the Topanga Canyon area, where they used to shoot movies. I said, "Cool!"

Right at the moment we arrived at the corner of Fairfax and Sunset, the bus was pulled over by the cops. It turned left on Fairfax, and then pulled over to the curb in front of the Thrifty Drug Store. I had a few joints in my cigarette box that I was saving for later. Exactly like the time Jessie and I had been pulled over on his motorcycle, I put the box down the front of my pants, hoping the cops would not find it there.

An officer approached the bus and told everyone to get out. He told us to line up along the wall, place our hands up on it, and spread our legs. We all did. The cop then proceeded to go down the line, frisking each person. When he approached me, I said, "I was just hitchhiking. I'm not with them." The girl I had been talking with, who was next to me, confirmed that. "Yeah, we just picked him up." The cop looked at me for a long moment and then said, "Get out of here!" I did exactly that. I walked briskly away, across Sunset to the northwest corner, where I turned around and watched the goings on. I decided I'd better not hang around, that I was lucky to get away, so I started walking west on Sunset towards the Strip.

So now it is the end of July, 1970, and I had recently seen the news on TV of the Manson Family Murders. After seeing them on the news, and seeing the girls at the courthouse, I realized they were the ones who had picked me up in their bus. I knew now that I could have ended up at Spahn Ranch with them—because I was into that hippy chick. Who knows what might have happened if we had not been pulled over? Every time I drive past the courthouse, I think about that experience and how lucky I was. I think about that red Marlboro box down my pants. I was lucky I wasn't busted. The first time I was not so lucky.

I always smoked Marlboro Reds in the box. Most of my friends did too. It was our brand. Whenever I saw that 70-foot high Marlboro Man billboard on the Sunset Strip, with his cowboy hat and his horse, I always thought, *Yep! That's our guy!*

⚡

Sandy was now in the final month of her pregnancy. I was excited about our baby coming, hoping it would be a boy. I was also thinking about my first wife, Jenny, and our son, Arthur. Of course, that led me to thinking about Katie, Jessie and the usual ghosts of heartache that haunt my world.

08/1/1970

*he comes out
. . . you go in
I know we all will win*

*but still I am confused
and still I'm being used
by my friends
who're in need of my love*

*it's their greed . . . for the need
of the love we've all lost
. . . pay the cost*

*love is there
for those who care
'cause the need is in me
I wish you'd agree*

*it can grow . . . it can grow
it can grow . . . it can grow*

*it can grow
but how can it grow
if we can't show
that with friends we will win
if we'll ever begin*

*better catch on quick
'cause it won't be 'round long*

⚡

8/4/1970

*you lie in the meadow
of my mind
and that's a place—baby
that only you can find*

116

*in the love light of my mind
the thought of you flows freely
wouldn't it be nice
if my dreams could be reality*

*you could win me in an instant
all the instances I've lost
you have won me—hold me freely
for the chains there is a cost*

*you can treasure or destroy
in the time of instant joy
and in the love light of my mind
—love is truly blind*

*you lie in the meadow
of my mind
and you can't see
but still you think
our love is not inclined*

*but inside this meadow
you will find
a love that's true
and still I say
a love that you can find*

*and now . . .
this love inside
that you don't see
is true for someone else
someone who's true to me*

*but still . . .
I hope someday
that you will find
some harmony and true love
in the meadow of your mind*

⚡

It's a boy! My boy—Shane! But in the midst of my joy, I was thinking about Arthur, how he had been ripped out of my life. I didn't want to feel that way again—ever.

8/21/1970

*you've finally taken my son
from me
now you've got him
on your own*

*I must find a place
you see
a place to hide
just me—alone*

*but why should I hide
or run away
never to play
another day*

*this heartless game
—is it so
who's to blame
do you know*

*I think I do
it's everyone
when you're alone
the hurt's been done*

*since you've gone
who's been forgiving
who's been hurt
and who is believing*

*you know who
is anything true
is everyone blue
. . . or just me*

*where did it go
—love
where can it be
I think I've found one
who is true to me*

*you've finally taken my love
—away
now you're living
on your own*

I hope I see him happy
someday
ever faithful
not alone

⚡

8/21/1970

she was my wife
you are my only life
she done me wrong
you make the feeling so strong

and in the long run
I hope you stay by me
please stick with me forever—girl
and know I'll leave you never

my lovely bluesy woman
sad eyes stare at me
lock your arms in my arms
my heart, you've got the key

now, someday
when Shane has grown and gone
I'll still be there with you
our sweet love will linger on

just you and me—babe
we'll travel everywhere—and then
fulfill our fantasies
we'll be together in the end

⚡

8/22/1970

went thru a cycle
wondering what was true

my thoughts . . . my friends
is anything real
and even my love for you

then the cycle changed
and I went on to something new

to not be so critical
there's no need for tears
just to be here . . . to be loving you

so when this new cycle
has gone thru its round
who knows what will happen
what may be found

I may not be here
my world may be gone
but I hope—no I know
that our love lingers on

one thing I am sure
will always be true
no matter what cycle
I'm going thru

I'll always be faithful
I'll always be true
I'll always be here
to be loving you

. . . the way I love you

⚡

After Shane was born, I had a writing spurt. I wrote almost daily—so many feelings, so much to say. It all poured out over the next few months.

9/1/1970

if your mind
can't hear a sound
and if you don't know
where you're bound

reality
is coming near
just open up your mind
and hear

what's all around
don't make a sound
just listen close
a double dose

*. . . of love
and love can't wait
for hate to put an end
to life with so much strife*

*you must know
that love will show
it's in the voice
of all who care*

*in all the birds
in every tree
and it's inside
of you and me*

↯

I wrote another dream poem. I think this is the only poem I have ever written about flying, although I've had lots of flying dreams. They are some of my favorite dreams because I always feel so free and powerful in them. Flying dreams are incredible!

9/8/1970

*I had a dream last night
I dreamt that I flew*

*I looked to the ground
and there I saw you*

*standing with those
turning upward to stare*

*at me as I flew
with the wind . . . not a care*

*I turned somersaults
in the air as I went*

*never knowing how
my body was sent*

*one thing I do know
the feeling was real*

*I was really flying
do you know how I feel*

flying . . . flying . . . flying
for as long as I please

almost coming all the way down
then going up . . . up . . . up
with ecstatic ease

⚡

Besides trying to get my dream poems written down fast, before they would disappear, the same kind of thing would happen to me at work. I would be driving down the freeway and an idea would suddenly come into my head for a poem. I knew if I did not write it down quickly, it would be gone forever. Usually I would pull over to the side of the road, write it down as fast as I could, and then get back on my way. Of course, on the freeway that could be risky—dangerous.

When small, portable cassette recorders became popular, I bought one to record my poems and ideas on. This made it easier and safer for me to get my ideas down without losing them, especially at work. I would leave it by the side of my bed at night, so I could also use it for my

dream poems. I was able to get them down much better and quicker. Eventually, I gravitated to the mini-cassette recorders when they came out, then the digital voice recorders, which I still use to this day. I always have one close by.

My writing spurt continued. I was writing about many circumstances: feelings about the life Sandy and I were creating; feelings about past heartaches; lots of feelings utterly pouring out . . .

9/8/1970

something happened
I must say
on the 7,000th day

of my life
it's finally split
an end to strife
or most of it

as time goes on
life will tell
of much that's gone
you know darned well

I hope what goes
is greed and war
two things we don't need
anymore

9/10/1970

*be careful of your heart
if you know someone
who can break it*

*but you've got to stick it out
'cause if you don't
you'll never make it*

*now something else
it's not so bad*

*make it right here
not long to be sad*

*if this is a clue
then know it's for you*

*'cause it's here you've begun
and you know there's a sun . . .*

*shines so true
in the blue—blue sky*

*with the clouds
. . . fly so high*

—got some dust in your eye

*then follow me down
to that cool ocean breeze*

*waves that flow with such ease
and that fresh sparkling air*

*you're aware . . . not a care
'cause you're there*

*. . . and it's here
. . . right now
. . . and it's love*

*be careful of your heart
if you know someone
who can break it*

*but you've got to stick it out
'cause if you don't
you'll never make it*

⚡

9/26/1970

*following the changes
through the years
everyone's here
but no one hears*

*and no one listens
      anyway
maybe I'm dumb
but I've still things to say*

*you say it's all right
so I'll try not to worry
when I'm all day at work
know I'll be in a hurry*

*to get back to here
where the feeling's so clear
that the feeling's so strong
'cause it's where I belong*

⚡

9/27/1970

*reminding me of home again
. . . lazy—breezy and warm*

*holding my woman
so tight*

*under the trees shone the light
of the moon*

*loving her
she's loving me*

*in the night
in that sleepy lagoon*

where the sun won't shine through
but dreams do come true

—deep inside of you

⚡

9/27/1970

why don't you listen
why can't you see

a home is for everyone
them, you and me

the moment that's happening
is what counts mainly

now if you can't see it
it must be told plainly

who knows what's tomorrow
the past . . . I don't care

'cause home's where the heart is
and I know I'm there

you see . . . it's the thing
that's happening right now

and yes . . . I know
it's right somehow

to stay here with you
and what we're going through

⚡

Shane is only 6 weeks old and I love holding him. I think about Arthur, and I remember how much I loved holding him too. He is almost 2 years old now. I wish he were here. We'll have to go and visit him soon and let him meet Shane.

10/6/1970

yes . . .
I have a son somewhere
I know where—he's there

125

*he knows I care
and he knows I'll be there
when he needs me*

*and her . . .
she's there too
and still in my heart*

*as long as he knows
that we both love him so
then you know this feeling
of love
it can grow*

*yes . . .
I have my own love
to come home to
and I know her love
is true for me too*

*now . . . she's given me
another son
and you know
we're all one*

*so let's tell everyone
that it's true
'cause you know
everyone's just like you*

*yes . . .
I have a son somewhere
he's living with her
in a good life*

*'cause everyone
is one-as-one
there ain't no need
for strife*

*I know . . . ex-wife
you love him too
just stick by him
he'll stick by you*

and I'll be right here
—you see
so he can always
stay by me

⚡

10/8/1970

why are we here
and why don't we know
just what it is
makes everything grow

what makes life live
you ask, why is it so

for its own sake
my love
for its own sake
you know

life is just life
it is everything
its purpose
a feeling that I can sing

the purpose is
the thing itself
a tangerine tree
the book on a shelf

everything that is here
it's a feeling quite clear
to know what it is
without any fear

that's why life is eternal
because life creates life

I said life . . .
there's no end
to the love that we send
just again and again

. . . again and again

10/12/1970

*I don't really know
if each life has an end
or if we live on
again and again*

*but what I do know
is I'm living right now
and I've got to make it right
—somehow*

*got to make it right
for you and me
got to work day and night
just for love . . . you see*

*but it's not really work
we're just living each moment
—each day
our love showing the way*

*please don't spread gossip
you only have heard
I want to know something
that's real*

*if that something is love
then it isn't absurd
I'll know that it's something
you feel*

*inside there may lurk
the truth of our time
a message that matters
a hill we must climb*

*I don't really know
when your love began
or when you first felt
I was your man*

*but what I do know
is we're loving right now
and we've got to make it right
—somehow*

⚡

10/15/1970

*we are here
we are here
let us make this
quite clear
just be true
to your friends
they're the means
for your ends*

*you're the means
for their ends
so for them
make amends
if you know
that they're true
just have trust
and you do*

⚡

10/16/1970

*how can I tell you
love
what you should know
this feeling inside me
continues to grow*

*I don't mind this feeling
I know it is so
and I hope you see—baby
this love that I know*

*from the heart of me
you are part of me
as I walk by the sea
. . . all alone*

*love has shown me
a path running through
where my thoughts
they are so true*

*and they mingle
within your thoughts
when you begin
to let them flow through
love . . . it's wise for you*

↯

10/22/1970

*collision-proof cars
probably never will be
but what can we do
to stop this curse on life
—you see*

*we've polluted our skies
we've got tears in our eyes
from the friends we have lost
is it worth the cost
to get there more swiftly
—it must be*

*we are moving along
—life
must keep moving strong
ever onward
always forward*

*yes . . .
we've polluted our skies
we've got tears in our eyes*

*many lives have been lost
we are paying the cost
for our living
—the way we live*

1970, October-December:

Jessie Returns, Jimi & Janis

Jessie was back in Hollywood. We let him stay with us for a few days since he had a new job and said he would be looking for a place to rent. Sandy liked him, so it was easy for him to convince me to help again—that and the fact that we had been friends since junior high.

We had quite a history of hanging out: sneaking into the movies, going to the dances, checking out the girls, Bob's Big Boy Burgers, scoring beer and brandy, and cruising around on the Sunset Strip. It is hard to let go when you grow up with someone, even someone who betrays you with your first love.

Right now, I was concentrating on work, Sandy, and Shane—our life together as a new family. Shane was two months old and we were starting to settle down. But Jessie always had a way of worming his way back into my life. I had always been there for him as a real friend, a true friend, as no one else had. On some level, I still hoped he would somehow be there for me too. It would take many more years for me to learn that Jessie would always simply be Jessie, merely using my friendship for him to get what he wanted.

I had asked him for help once, when I truly needed a friend. After Jenny and I broke up, I had asked him if he would go talk to her, try to reason with her, to try to help us get back together. He said he would be glad to go see her. After he did, he reported back to me that it was no use, she did not want to get back together. Later, however, I heard he had slept with her. I never confronted him because I was scared he might say it was true. To this day, I do not know for sure if he did or not. But I suspect it is true. Frankly, it's how Jessie was.

For some reason, thinking about it all inspired my writing, and I wrote five poems about it in a single day:

10/24/1970

do you dig on any . . .
the things that I say
if you don't
I don't think we're together

you must dig on something
to give a little each day
if you don't
then it's like this cold weather

to express to each other
for there's something to gain
from each precious moment
it isn't in vain

do you dig on any . . .
the games people play
what we give to each other

*is what we can say
is the most precious thing
we can claim from this play*

*it's inside
what we know
it's inside
it can grow*

*if we bring it outside
where we know it can show*

⚡

10/24/1970

*always at the wrong time
but that makes it the right time
for someone else*

*well, friends will be friends
and who knows what it is
I think what we feel*

*but tomorrow
is another day
new things I'm gonna do*

*never to be too blue
'cause you know it's the wasteland
and I know what you're going through*

*so please don't be so blind
'cause I need you
I need to get it through*

*that I must talk to you
about what we feel
to make our life more real*

*open up inside
I know you cannot hide—forever
we're all together*

⚡

10/24/1970

*you want to hassle
you don't dig my friends
the sooner they're away
the better*

*all you want is your own
you want the upper hand
and you know . . .
this ain't no love letter*

*'cause you've done me wrong
and I just want it strong*

*now I'm not saying
that I've been so good
but, love
it must be understood*

*we should stay together
you know it's real
loving everyone
that's how I feel*

*or at least we should be
—anyway
our brotherhood
must come someday*

⚡

10/24/1970

*you cannot hold Middle Earth
'cause you do not know what it's worth
to have anything
is it something I can sing*

*do you care
does anyone care
about the way I care
—does it matter*

*'cause if it don't
then baby I won't be here
—to share
what should be there*

*if you're aware
of how I feel
my love
—it's real*

*maybe I shouldn't be here
maybe I don't belong
'cause what it is that matters to me
is if it's strong*

*I don't care who is who—damn it
I hope that I'm not wrong
'cause what it is that matters
is that everyone is strong*

*I mean . . .
like you—and her
and him—and me
dear god, does anyone see*

*if no one knows
then I must split
—I'll know
that I don't fit*

*but I think you all know
and I think you all care
but the thing is . . .
do you want to make me aware*

*that you know it is there
it's a love we can share
—all of us
yes it's true*

*first off . . .
her—and him
and me—and you
'cause I love all of you*

that can't be asking too much

⚡

10/24/1970

*you ask me why not three
of course you know it's true
you know we can go on together
him, me, and you*

*but it's hard—you know—in this world
of possession and jealousy*

*no one wants to let it happen
yes, what about us three*

*will we let it be . . .
just to be loving each other
knowing . . .
that's how it's meant to be*

*back to what is there
it is everywhere
back to what is true
it is me and you*

*back to what is here
it is three
back to what is clear
it can be*

⚡

I kept these poems private, not showing them to anyone. Thinking about Jessie being around stirred up so much shit inside me. I wrote another poem about him the next day . . .

10/25/1970

*no one wants to make me happy
—not really
'cause you don't really know
how I really feel*

*if you only knew
my love is real for all of you
I know it's strange
but I can't change*

*can't you just try
I'll tell you why*

'cause I love you
—it's true

just to have someone
you know that it's good
but you've got to have everyone
it must be understood

they are dreams
they're just dreams
yes they're dreams
it is true

but then . . .
dreaming is real
you know dreams can come true
. . . if they would

↯

Six poems in two days! I was in the middle of an almost two-year writing spurt that would last for the better part of another year—through most of 1971. I think the reason I was writing so much was because, in the midst of my confused feelings about my past, I truly loved our life. Our little family unit was my joy. We did struggle though, financially. Even in the early '70s, it was hard to support three people on a minimum-wage job. Somehow, though, we got by.

10/27/1970

another day . . .
the same old way
picking up my tired body
and gettin' me off to work

but then, you know
I finally get myself woke up
and I realize
it's for you—and for me

and I know I can make it
another day
I know this way
we can be together

*in our own home
never alone
loving each other
on our own terms*

⚡

10/27/1970

*creamy starlight
softened lips
my blue-eyed brown-haired woman*

*and those curves
along your hips
my blue-eyed brown-haired woman*

*know I love you
yes I do
never leave you
yes it's true*

*moving along . . .
this feeling so strong
—for you
my blue-eyed brown-haired woman*

⚡

10/28/1970

*your thoughtful vibrations
move me anywhere
sweet excitations
show me you're aware*

*just what it is
makes our life real*

*a feeling to strive
a feeling alive
I know inside
a living proof
which cannot hide*

*thoughts can be felt
as a strong upward stride
and I think I could melt
from these feelings inside*

*our thoughts are vibrations
and music is a part
sounds of sweet excitations
that move me
like thoughts alive*

⚡

10/28/1970

*think not . . .
that I don't love you
for I do
in your eyes I see
that you've been feeling blue*

*please do not despair
we are alive . . .
everything is there
for those who care*

*now if you feel inside
you care for life
and all . . .
that it was meant to be*

*don't hurt yourself
do not hide
'cause life goes on
you must agree*

*on a clear warm winter's day
blue sky everywhere
it's beautiful in L.A.*

*you know . . .
this is how it is
this is how it's meant to be
so cherish it
remember all these sunny days*

this day is just another joy
it's for you to play with
it's for you to stay with

so enjoy . . .
while it is here
it lifts my heart
it makes my mind quite clear

⚡

10/29/1970

where are you going now
where have you been
what are you saying now
who's gonna win

it's all right here
—right now
if you will just begin
open up inside
you know it ain't no sin

I said open up
open up inside
now open up
you know you cannot hide

not forever
the sooner the better
so please
open up right now

⚡

Ever since I was a boy, my poetry has easily poured out of me. I don't redo or revise those original, flowing poems much. I guess I have a good Muse! She never lets me down.

I am a natural poet, not an educated one. I am a street poet, a hippy poet, a lyrical and musical poet. Moreover, I am a performance poet, using music and hand drums in my readings/performances.

The following poem is an example of how I can be thinking about a moment—right now, then think about the past, then put it all into a positive perspective. And then the words simply pour right out of me.

10/29/1970

thinking of the future
times gone by
thinking 'bout this new year
knowing why

as gulls fly away
out to sea
I hope you think of me
just a thought for me
and how it's meant to be

we are here this year
watching the sunshine break through

it is breaking quite clear
you know . . .
it is love's aging new

it's for you and the world
the waves are breaking high
it's for me and my girl
I'm as high as the sky

⚡

I am often inspired by observing what is around me, and then something will pour forth. I'm glad I usually have pen and paper at hand, or carry a recorder with me.

10/29/1970

watching the old couple
walking by
she is dressed in pink
he is clutching today's paper

will we be like that
when the years have gone by
looking through a kaleidoscope
seeing the patterns we weaved

to know they have been good
—times to be remembered
many changes together
crossroads overcome

*I hope we do in many more
then we'll still be together
when we're 64
doing what the old folks do*

*taking in the day
with time to spare
many good things
still coming our way*

*we'll be there
still together
loving each other
until forever*

⚡

10/30/1970

*reality is coming
—soon
just like the moon
we've stood upon*

*and if you know
a song to sing
it's like this page
I write upon*

*to give you something
we can share
to help you understand
—if you're aware*

*if you relate
to what I've said
then I will know
you really see*

*—my thoughts
because you've read them
for yourself
and you agree*

*you'll know
my love
inside
you're part of me*

⚡

10/30/1970

too many people
too many cars

too many movies
with too many stars

don't need these cars—you see
walking will get you there

people have a hand to lend
knowing that you care

movies are
as movies can be

some relate
to reality

stars are only people
and you know we can go far

as a church must have a steeple
you know, everyone's a star

I said—walking will get you there
just take your time

then we can have clean air
and this song will rhyme

⚡

Listening to rock-n-roll or the blues will often inspire me because music is so important to me. In the words of Jimi Hendrix, "Music is my religion!" Jimi was an inspiration to so many people. His guitar playing was like no other, and when I heard his music—his colorful magic, I knew it would influence all rock-n-roll going forward.

10/30/1970

she's a mean mistreater
but I love her
she's like an ac/dc heater
. . . thinking of her

I love her truly
her love is unruly
when I'm with her
I go crazy
my lovely bluesy woman
I'm a fool
she treats me cruel
and I love her

⚡

I didn't know Jimi Hendrix personally, but I met him once, and I saw him in concert once. I met him when I was browsing through the record racks at Music Hall record store on the Sunset Strip—kitty corner from Whiskey A-Go-Go. As I was flippin' through albums in the record bins, I noticed in the back of the store, there was Jimi, flippin' through records himself. I approached him and offered greetings. I told him that his music was a big influence on me. He was noticeably gracious and said thank you to me, and then we both went back to flippin' through the bins.

I saw him in concert at the *Newport '69 Pop Festival* at Devonshire Downs in Northridge, CA. It was in June of 1969, a short time before Jenny and I split up. I will never forget it! At dusk—almost dark, Jimi's band, The Jimi Hendrix Experience, started their set. As they were playing, the L.A. pigs showed up in their brand-new spotlight helicopters. As far as I knew, this was the first time L.A. police had ever used them. They hovered over the crowd with their spotlight beams shining down on us, blowing up the dust with their loud rotor blades. It positively sucked. The crowd became extremely noisy, yelling at the cops and shaking their arms and fists in the air. It did not, however, stop Jimi from playing or keep us from enjoying his astonishing set.

For years after that, at nighttime, I would often see the LAPD helicopters with their spotlight beams shining down on neighborhoods as they flew over the vast city of L.A. I would always think back to that concert when they first invaded us.

Jimi Hendrix and Janis Joplin both died in the last few months of 1970. Janis had been recording her final album, *Pearl*, at Sunset Sound studios, right around the corner from our apartment. I used to walk by the studios each day on my way home from work. I would trip out on her psychedelic, hand-painted Porsche parked outside. Many years later, I would see the car again when it went on display at the Rock-N-Roll Hall of Fame Museum in Cleveland, Ohio.

Janis was right in the middle of her recording sessions when Jimi died on September 18th. Then, a mere two weeks later—on October 4th, she was gone, too. It seemed so strange. It was hard to believe that two of our greatest rock-n-roll artists in the prime of their careers were gone so quick.

It would seem even stranger when Jim Morrison died nine months later, in July of 1971. Many people would comment about what an odd coincidence it was that three of our greatest rock-n-roll giants had all died within less than one year: Jimi Hendrix on Sept. 18, 1970, Janis Joplin on Oct. 4, 1970, and then Jim Morrison on July 3, 1971. People thought it was unusually strange that all three of their names started with the letter J, all three of them were 27 years old, and all three of them were born within two months of each other in 1943. Coincidental? Who knows. What a tragic loss they were to our generation, but especially to music in general. We can only wonder what heights they might have risen to, had they still been alive to create more of their magic.

10/31/1970 (Halloween)

yes . . .
we all know
and you want to know
if I can show
just where I am

yes . . .
I think I can show you
but where are you
just to hear you once more

at the split
before the new
is there something
to fill this gaping hole
this feeling of emptiness
so hard to hide

I am trying my best
to know where we stand
to do what I can
to lend out my hand

this feeling of giving
what I feel I need
is the greatest feeling
of all

*to try not to stumble
to know I won't fall
with this feeling—together
this feeling for all*

⚡

My feelings for Sandy were easy to put into poetry—sometimes.

11/4/1970

*see you stare
with amazement
as I dare to yearn
for that feeling
the softness of your warmth

lay your chest bare
let me know what is there
can you show it
from inside you
to let me feel it
inside me

if you are beginning
to be aware
then you're beginning
to understand
    to feel
        to know
            to care
to see just where I stand

to know it is here
beside you
feeling the way I do
you'll see that you are a woman
there's so much inside of you

so lay your chest bare
let me know what is there
oh, woman—you are
the softness of your warmth*

⚡

11/6/1970

if it is right at the time you feel it
—which it is
then it's a feeling
you know you can't steal it

it's a feeling must be given
but cannot be given right
unless you feel that it is right
at the time you feel it

but then . . .
who reacts on these
I say—who goes
on these first feelings

it's a feeling must be given
but cannot be given right
unless you give it
at the time you feel it's right

↯

11/6/1970

now let him go

he must stroll through the day

he's looking so pale

locked inside this way

let him run with the wind

get some light in his eye

then you know

he'll be healthy

he never will cry

for lack of sweet sunshine

↯

Being married, raising a child and working full time did not leave time for much else. I was thinking about my own life dreams; wondering if I could ever make a living doing my music, art, poetry, song lyrics . . .

11/6/1970

is there room for one more
will you let me in
is there room for one more
though it's late to begin

please let me in
'cause the feelings
that are in me
they just won't let me be

they say that I belong with you
so won't you please make some room
—please let me in
—let me in right now

⚡

11/6/1970

we have the same thoughts
we have the same feelings
but we think them
and feel them
at different times

we have so much love
deep inside
yet so many don't know it
they just let it hide
with the illusions around them

and I'm happy . . .
I'm happy inside
from these feelings of love
for everyone I meet
and everything I do

yes I'm so happy
—inside
except, I guess
—the dreams
but I feel good

↯

11/21/1970

*I forgive you
for your thoughtlessness
I want you to be true*

*don't drink from the cup
of unfaithfulness
never to be blue*

*knowing love is true
as it should
it's for you*

*return devotion
with devotion
and you will know so much*

*for you
the riches of the world
are there within the touch*

*. . . the one you love
. . . the one who loves you*

↯

11/21/1970

*what do I want from life
just to have a good time
why the hell am I working
just to make a dime
and why the hell do I need you
—all the time*

*you know that what you need
is what you want
and you can have it if you try
if you try, you can get what you need
and all I want is you*

*you can get what you want
I hope it is true
the world is for us
to make sure love shines through*

4

November—almost Thanksgiving. The holidays are coming! Smoking an exceptionally good joint, I started expounding on what life is—or might be.

11/21/1970

the world is nothing
like I thought it would be
the games are so real
they are life

and this world is not now
as I think it should be
knowing . . .
there is so much strife

like a one act play
in show biz
the curtain goes up
you are born

like a one act play
it sure is
the curtain goes down
as you die

with those feelings inside
and the things you can see
like a September ride
and a walk by the sea

like a friend
you and me
and the things we can be

in this life
we are here
yes . . .
we know this quite clear

from this life
we must go
and I hope when we do
we can show

*just what we know
of this . . .
the heaven we are leaving*

*spaced-out . . . somewhere
you are thinking
then something happens
you are blinking*

*trying to remember
as the curtain goes down
and blackens it out
for your conscious state of mind*

. . . and it was beautiful

⚡

11/21/1970

*I see music
as forward motion
it keeps building
and building
in a sense
a way of life
it keeps bringing us
together*

*always has
so much to give*

*I see music
as a feeling
to be found
amongst ourselves
with a little bit of
strife
but so much
good life*

*teaching us
a way to live*

⚡

11/25/1970

*take it easy
little wonder
love is here*

*take it easy
little wonder
it is clear*

*that you can have it
if you want it
'cause you know . . . life
is what you make it*

*take it easy
little wonder
you're so sad*

*take it easy
little wonder
it's not so bad*

*that you can feel it
don't conceal it
'cause you know . . . love
is what you can give*

⚡

12/3/1970

*slow down with those feelings
there's more you can see*

*slow down with your thinking
in the sense you can be*

*more relaxed with yourself
more relaxed—what you do*

*more at ease . . . feeling tranquil
with all around you*

*take it slow
be peaceful*

*but not in the sense
you are lazy*

*you must strive for yourself
and the ones you know are near*

*make it easy on yourself
or it might drive you crazy*

*you can meditate inside yourself
your spirit will be clear*

⚡

12/5/1970

*take me
let down that wall
and take me*

*don't subject me
or reject me
just accept me*

*take me
let it down
take me*

*my hair may look funky
but I'm healthy*

*I'm so full of love
but I'm not wealthy*

*I'm happy right here
the world can be so clear*

—take me as I am

*now take me
let down that wall
and take me*

*don't subject me
or reject me
just accept me*

*take me
let it down
take me*

*my hair may look funky
but I'm healthy
I'm so full of love
but I'm not wealthy*

*the time is growing near
for all I need to hear*

—take me as I am

⚡

I was trying to write more song lyrics, to perhaps get some work with another band. I'd been playing my bongos more often and even my trumpet again, which I hadn't played in several years.

One morning I went down to Santa Monica Beach to watch the sunrise. I was the only one sitting on the sand as the first pink color of sunrise crept up in the east. It had been a full moon the night before, and the moon was still visible, almost setting on the ocean horizon. The colors of the sun came up over the horizon while the pale, full moon went down below it. Incredible! What a song-poem!

12/6/1970

*be my morningstar
I'll be your sunshine
stay the way you are
this day will make you mine*

*the wind that blows you to me
is a thing called love
the teardrops that you drop on me
from up above*

—you are my cloud

*morningstar
shine for me
my life giving rays
will shine inside you*

*morningstar
by the sand and sea
. . . you touch me
. . . I touch you*

*be my morningstar
I'll be your sunshine
stay the way you are
this day will make you mine*

*the warm sun rising
makes the air so blue
the waves are breaking
for just me and you*

—you are my morningstar

*morningstar
shine for me
my deep blue eyes
will shine for you*

*morningstar
by the sand and sea
. . . you touch me
. . . I touch you*

⚡

12/8/1970

*I'm a truck-driving
Song-writing man
I make it
wherever I can*

*I love you all
I hope you see
—inspiration
whatever comes to me*

*I love those with whom I work
I love those with whom I sing
we all must give to each other
whatever love may bring*

*I am teaching you how I write
I am showing you how I feel
I am teaching you how to work with me
—right now*

*I'm a truck-driving
Song-writing man
I make it
wherever I can*

*to make life more real in this land
I am doing whatever I can*

⚡

I wanted to write something that could be a blues song or maybe a sad ballad, and there was so much in my past that could lend itself to those feelings. My past was always with me—Katie and Jenny both—and the music that mattered so much to me—that spoke so much to me.

12/22/1970

*there's no more magic
in the music
since you are gone*

*and the grass
has all gone dead
on my front lawn*

*no one to take care of it
not to care for me
you know I'm crying to be heard*

*no more magic
in the music
not for me*

*love me once more
you'll see
how it can be*

*life's become so tragic
I wonder
where I belong*

*never to know
your love again
it's been so long*

*never to be near again
near enough to you
I know you cannot hear a single word*

*no more magic
in the music
not for me*

*love me once more
you'll see
how it can be*

*there's no more magic
in the music
no more magic for me*

*but if you love me once more
the magic will come back
. . . to me*

⚡

12/22/1970

*is it anything
is it here
why am I writing
is it clear*

*is there anything
left to say
does it matter
anyway*

*the feeling I get
will you let it be*

*just to say
what does it mean
a love unseen*

*is it here
was it ever here
do I belong*

*I know it's strong
inside of me
but is it right*

*—for you
and what we're going through*

*will you read
what I plead—to you*

it's inside of me

⚡

12/22/1970

*oh . . . oh
oh . . . oh no
oh . . . oh
I need you so*

*oh . . . oh
love is true
oh . . . oh yes
for me . . . for you*

*oh . . . my love
from here I'll go
to find a place
somewhere to show*

*you love me so
I love you so
I love you all
I love you so*

*oh . . . my love
I hope you know
I love you so
I love you so*

⚡

Shane was four months old when he experienced his first Christmas, and he was full of wonder about everything. You could see it in his big blue eyes as he stared at the Christmas tree and smiled or giggled as he watched us opening presents for him.

12/25/1970 (Christmas)

*to a baby . . .
a wondrous feeling of moving
not knowing how
or where he is going*

*all along . . .
new worlds
are showing
everything is new*

*but for you and I
a feeling of pain
or a feeling of fear
might be found*

*it's inside
and all around
but cannot hurt us
if we know that love is true*

*just look in those eyes
of a babe
who can show this love
to me . . . to you*

⚡

After the holiday break, I was hitchhiking back to work. I arrived a little early, so I wrote this:

12/27/1970

*Cold-hearted people
always stop and stare
never seem to smile
never seem to care*

*the love you take
is what you lose
so much you lack
you've got the blues*

*the love you give
for you to choose
you don't know how
to pay the dues*

*never to have the blues
. . . anymore*

*Cold-hearted people
always stop and stare
never seem to smile
never seem to care*

*a feeling
that you really need
to laugh
you must learn to cry*

*a feeling
we've all had—indeed
for those who care
will never lie*

*never to have the blues
. . . anymore*

*Cold-hearted people
always stop and stare
never seem to smile
never seem to care*

⚡

There was so much fear out there . . . and in here: fear that I would never get to follow my dreams; fear that they would never let me in; fear that I could never win; fear that the world would just end!

12/31/1970 (New Year's Eve)

*there's a fear
the atom bomb
might be put in motion*

*or that California
will split and fall
into the ocean*

*don't let the big boom
—get you
make you cry*

*don't let that big boom
—get you
break the sky*

*you can fly
inside yourself*

*your love can't wither
on a shelf
inside your mind*

*because I still want to see you
tomorrow*

*don't let the big boom
—get you
or I'll cry*

*don't let that big boom
—get you
say goodbye*

*I want to know
we will be here*

*life is living
all is clear
in this sea called love*

*that it will stay
for what it's worth
—heaven on earth*

1971:

Kids, Love-Ins, and the Earthquake

I turned 21 in the first month of 1971, but I do not remember it being a big deal as far as being of legal age to drink. I think that was because Sandy and I mostly took drugs and smoked pot, with alcohol not being in the picture so much. Besides, we were basically struggling to survive. I was still hitchhiking to work, and Shane was five months old, with all the expenses that involved. With everything going on, who could afford to go out and drink, even if we could find the time? Besides, Sandy would not be 21 for two more months.

She wasn't working, and I was merely making minimum wage on my job. There was no way we could afford child care, so she was a stay-at-home Mom like most young couples in our generation who were parents in the early '70s. We still didn't have a car, so we'd walk down to the Market Basket supermarket on La Brea and Fountain, about six blocks away. We'd buy what we needed, but we had to borrow a shopping cart to get our groceries home. We'd pile Shane in the top of it with all the grocery bags, then trudge the six blocks home.

A few months later, we struggled a little less because by then I had saved up enough money to buy a cheap used car—a baby blue 1960 Rambler station wagon.

Because we had a baby now, we didn't go to the Sunset Strip as much anymore, but we still went to the love-ins in Griffith Park regularly. We hung around mostly with other couples, particularly couples who had kids. I guess that makes sense. People who are married with kids no longer do what single people do.

My good friend Mike was still hanging out with us along with his youngest brother, Sam, and Sam's wife, Donna. My brother, Bob, was often around too. Sam played guitar, and my brother played flute, so we all liked to jam together, with me on bongos and singing.

At one of the love-ins, we ran into Kevin and Jeanine—yes, the same Kevin and Jeanine who had done the wife-swapping experiment with Jenny and me. Now, they had a baby around the same time as Sandy and me. They were at the love-in with their friends Jim and Pam, who I also knew from high school. Jim and Pam were about due for their first baby to be born. They loved the name of our son so much that they named their baby Shawn, to be as close to Shane as possible.

We all started hanging out together, going to each other's houses for dinner and barbecues and giving our babies the chance to play with other babies. We would often meet up at the love-ins on Sundays, throw Frisbees, play with our dogs, have picnics and take the kids to ride on the Griffith Park Merry-Go-Round.

Griffith Park is a massive public recreational area that covers more than 4,200 acres. The Merry-go-round area itself is vast—with hills and a valley area, where hundreds or even thousands of people would congregate for the love-ins on Sundays.

Local bands, and sometimes famous bands, would come to the love-in and play for free, which gave us the opportunity to dance and listen to music. Santana and Jefferson Airplane showed up now and then. They loved to play free for the hippy tribes. The Santana band inspired a generation of Latin drum and percussion players. I loved the sound of their conga players and longed to play like them. I think they may even be the ones who inspired the drum circles that began showing up at love-ins around the country.

In the southeast corner of our love-in, there was a drum circle every Sunday. There were lots of conga players, along with timbales, bongos, African drums, cowbells, flutes, and so forth. All day long—every love-in, the rhythms of our generation were played out into the universe, and I loved being part of it.

Sometimes when a conga player was tired, they would let you borrow their drum for a few minutes and join in. If you were good, they would let you continue to play. I must have been pretty good because they always let me stay in the circle for a while.

I had a natural sense of rhythm. I had played my dad's bongos since I was a kid, but I learned to play congas at the love-ins. I bought a cheap conga drum at a pawnshop so I could join in with my own drum and not have to wait for someone to let me borrow one.

I loved hand-drums, and I would get lost in the rhythms of the drum circle. I loved slapping my hands in the different ways on the tight animal skins to create the high sounds, low sounds, in-between sounds—all in the spontaneous rhythm of the moment. One drummer would usually start a new beat, quietly at first, and then others would join in. Soon, there would be throngs of beautiful slap-beats, all in sync together; well, mostly in sync—as much as our various skill levels allowed. The low, bass sounds would keep the beat going—the basic rhythm, complemented by the middle sounds. Together these created a solid backbone rhythm for the lead players to enter into, with their high, slapping lead riffs, echoing off the synchronized rhythm of the rest. Getting lost in the continuous rhythms of the drum circle was momentous and mesmerizing. Wow! I loved it! I loved how it all felt! I would play for hours at a time.

The drum circle at the Griffith Park love-in is where I cut my chops and indeed learned how to play good hand-drums, which I still do to this day. I even use them to accompany my poetry recitals sometimes.

Drumming was now my go-to for my own enjoyment and release, something of my own in addition to my poetry and art. And speaking of that, I was still in the middle of my prolific writing period, and I was putting pen to paper a lot. Poems about all sorts of subjects were pouring out of me. Even the silliest happenings.

1/8/1971

out in the back garage
the things I have found out
in the back garage

so many things
for us
out in the back garage

*I found an old chair
a comfy old chair
a table and dresser*

*and even in there
I found an old book
on the human anatomy*

*we needed a bigger bed
I found one
we'll give you the old one we have*

*come and play
there are so many things
see what you can find*

*there's enough for you
. . . me
. . . and everyone*

*out in the back garage
the things I have found out
in the back garage*

*so many things
for all of us
out in the back garage*

↯

1/10/1971

*Mama—
I wish I knew a way
that I could pull you
back to Dad*

*Daddy—
you left me long ago
you made me
oh so sad*

*I just found out
that love is true
I found . . .
how true love is*

*it's coming together
it is coming together
I know it is coming
. . . it is*

*I found out how true love
how true love can be
I know you can see
how love is*

*and it's just to look
inside of you
look inside yourself*

⚡

1/11/1971

*the feeling of thinking
an inspirational thought*

*the thrill of seeking
someone to be sought*

*and the comfort of knowing
you love life a lot*

*I'm here with you
right now*

*you know I'm fighting for love
we cannot do it violently*

*force with peace
yes force with peace*

shed your love on me

⚡

A week before my 21st birthday, I wrote my *hippy—flower child—chant to the universe,* and I called it, "Oh Big Sky."

1/12/1971

*oh big sky . . .
are you watching over me
shall I say . . .
what I feel is real today*

*will they listen to me now
will it matter anyhow
what shall I do
. . . for my soul*

*do you think you are a master
do you practice what you preach
so you think your way is faster
tell me . . . what is it you teach*

*do you show us how to love each other
with more feeling every day
are you helping anyone
with more feeling . . . as you say*

*oh inspiration . . .
are you watching over me
shall I say . . .
what I feel is real today*

*will they listen to me now
will it matter anyhow
what shall I do
. . . for my soul*

*if you want to start somewhere
then start by being true
'cause if you ain't true
then we'll find somebody new*

*now maybe you can help us all
with what it is you preach
but please don't say you know it all
there's always more to teach*

oh big sky . . .
are you watching over me
shall I say . . .
what I feel is real today

will they listen to me now
will it matter anyhow
what shall I do
. . . for my soul

⚡

It was easy to express my feelings for Sandy in my poems . . . and my Muse seemed to agree!

1/26/1971

I know that I was different once
I know that I have changed

I know that since I've met you—girl
my life's been rearranged

I know that love is truer now
a love that's changed my life

and since we've come together
there's been such a drop in strife

it ain't no good—it ain't no good
it ain't no good—unless it's understood

and between you and me—girl
it is

love is where you find it
love is to be true to

love is to be giving
giving love to you

I know that I was different once
I know that I have changed

I know that since I've met you—girl
my life's been rearranged

⚡

1/30/1971

*emergencies are coming out
the love inside of you and me
showing how we all can live
together happily*

*loving each other
living on earth
loving each other
living life's worth*

*the life we are living
the love I can see
right now we are giving
how clear can it be*

*emerging love
emerging love
sharing our love
right now*

*our love for our children
the love they can see
a world they can live in
. . . somehow*

⚡

2/1/1971

*yes . . .
things are always changing
but you know . . .
people are still the same*

*lord I know
it's a speedy world
but we're all still playing
life's love game*

*find a woman to love
hold her
squeeze her
kiss her*

*when you know
she's not at home
let her know
you miss her*

*tell her . . .
that you love her so
make her see it's true*

*make her see
she's always with you
everything you do*

*playing life's love game
singing my song
love life is here
where I know we belong*

*here on earth
where it's moving so fast
old mother earth
got to make it last*

*got to make it last
for our children you know
got to make it show
got to make it grow*

*playing life's love game
whatever I do
playing life's love game
playing for you*

⚡

2/2/1971

*look at me
the way I look
hope you see
an open book*

*a book of pages
filled with love
inspiration
from above*

*do you see
the way I look
like a fish
caught on a hook*

*I'm hooked on love
I'm hooked on love
I'm hooked on love*

*if you can see
I won't conceal
then you will know
my love is real*

*inspiration . . .
you can feel the strength
of love*

*the strength of love
the strength of love
it must be coming
from above*

*the way I look
the way I look
I'm hooked on love*

⚡

As my Muse inspires words that pour out of me, so often they are about the world in general—how it is and how I think it should be. What I write often reflects my hippy ideals.

2/5/1971

*the sun shining down
all around
giving life
the life that has come
from the sun*

*it's on the run
we're on the move
then we're slowing down
and learning to groove*

*everything around us
the love we need to share*

*giving to each other
loving what is there*

*higher . . . inward
mind's eye wide
knowing that we care*

*night shine . . . day shine
never hide
knowing love is in there*

*living today
living tonight
living for right now
knowing it's right*

*loving the sun
loving the moon
black and white
working together
might soon*

*make it shine
all the day
all the night
in our minds
'cause it's right*

*'cause we're loving each other
and closing the blinds
on the hatred and killing
of love*

*living for the sun
you know we've just begun
ocean floors are showing
waves are shining
we're all one*

⚡

2/6/1971

*I'm lost on my own world
I'm lost in my home
but these aching bones
just don't want to roam*

*I need some time
but I ain't got no money
I need your sweet love
please don't leave me, honey*

*oh baby . . . I love you
baby it's true
whenever I'm with you
love's still feeling new*

*I'm out here on my own
and I feel so alone
my love is at your fingertips
just dial me like a phone*

*and the number you can dial
is understanding
the information you need
is to care*

*and then when I answer
the things that I'll tell you
—everything
love says is there*

*every feeling we can share
all our thoughts in open air
all the world around to care
for love is here
I hope it's there*

*the number you can dial
is understanding
the information you need
is to care*

*and then when I answer
the things that I'll tell you
—everything
love says is there*

. . . everything love says

⚡

In our small, one bedroom apartment, Sandy and I had a crib for Shane in the bedroom. We slept on a full size mattress on the floor of the living room. One morning, I was shook right out of bed and onto the floor by an earthquake. I had been sound asleep but I was wide-awake now! The whole apartment was moving, and I could not even stand up. All I could think about was Shane! I crawled on all fours into his bedroom, only to find him totally undisturbed—asleep in his crib. I crawled back into the living room and told Sandy he was okay.

We were so glad when the shaking finally stopped. We sat up and assessed the situation, deciding that everything was all right. To our relief, nothing was broken. Some pots and pans, Melmac plates, and silverware had fallen in the kitchen, but otherwise everything looked fine. Somehow, Shane had slept right through it all.

By then, it was a little after 6:00 a.m. We decided I should still go to work, so I got dressed and headed out. Wow—there was a six-inch gap between our front door and the stairs leading up to it! I was extra careful as I went down, step by step.

The city was eerily quiet, and the power was out everywhere I could see. As I headed west on Sunset Blvd. towards Fairfax Avenue, and then south on Fairfax towards the warehouse where I worked, I could see that all the streetlights were out, too. At almost every intersection, cars were going much slower than usual and stopping, almost as though there were stop signs. Windows were broken on Fairfax near Canter's Deli and on that whole block, and I could see damage inside the stores as well.

When I reached our warehouse on Venice Blvd., only my boss was there. He said he was not sure about working yet. I told him that the traffic on Venice and Fairfax looked problematic, and I was thinking of directing traffic until the police arrived there. He said, "Yeah! Go!" So I did. I ended up directing traffic for more than an hour before police finally showed up and took over, thanking me for the help.

I went back to work. My boss had decided to close for the day, so I went home. Back at the apartment, I found out that our water heater had burst and flooded the downstairs apartment. The guy who lived there was okay, though, and everything was cool. Nobody around us was hurt, but what a crazy day! February 9, 1971, would come to be known officially as the San Fernando Earthquake, but we always knew it as the Sylmar Quake.

2/10/1971

if you can't believe
what the papers say
then tell me
what can you believe

so what's to believe
for you cannot perceive
what has happened
unless you were there

*if you were not there
but you wonder what happened
all you can do
is to listen and read*

*but take in all sides
listen well
read complete*

*if you feel
it's the truth of the matter
you need*

*it's so easy to be swayed
and our thoughts become decayed
if we linger on one side
for much too long*

*if the truth was ever made
it was made
by knowing yourself*

*and seeing that one side
can't be doing
all the wrong*

⚡

2/15/1971

*now who is right
and who is wrong
begin the fight
where you belong*

*inside yourself
to understand
to realize
that war breeds war*

*so live in peace
my brothers
live in peace
right now*

*. . . help each other
. . . play with each other
. . . stay with each other*

*live in peace
and understand
that you must . . .
you must share the land*

⚡

The landlord fixed our water heater and the stairs, and we returned to life as usual.

2/15/1971

*love is growing
growing love*

*it's growing stronger
everyday
for the two of us
much closer*

*for the third
who came to play*

*making everything we say
truer every day*

*for you've shown me how to love
with a love that is true*

*and how to be so happy
loving you*

*it's growing more
everyday*

*always growing
let us pray*

*never stop
always growing*

*never ending
day to day*

⚡

2/23/1971

*feeling good
is a feeling that's real
it's a real good feeling you feel*

*feeling bad
is a feeling so sad
but it can't be so bad
when you're looking so good*

*a good feeling—new
a feeling for you
a good thing is coming for you*

*a good feeling—new
a bad feeling—past
a good thing is coming at last*

*if you are gay
it's 'cause you feel that way
and if you are blue
there's something you can do*

*forget the past
don't be the last
to see it won't last
it's understood*

*a good feeling—new
a feeling for you
a good thing is coming for you*

*a good feeling—new
a bad feeling—past
a good thing is coming at last*

⚡

We had another fight . . . I wrote another poem! I realized this was becoming a pattern. Our fights were usually about money, specifically the lack thereof. I worked hard. Sandy took care of the baby. We never had enough to get by. Same shit, different day!

2/23/1971

*tonight she told me
she don't care
if I'm warm or not*

*wish I had one
who would hold me
whether she thinks I'm right—or not*

*Someone
who would love me so
though I haven't got a lot*

*letting me do things
without getting uptight
then I'd know just what we've got*

*the things that I do
are really for her
she doesn't seem to know
the possibilities*

*what I try to provide
to help us get by
to keep us from this state
of feeling so ill at ease*

*tonight she told me
she don't care
if I'm warm or not*

*wish I had one
who would hold me
whether she thinks I'm right—or not*

⚡

Sandy and I were both 21 when we finally gave in to her parents' pressure to get married, which we had decided on our own to do anyway. Sandy, who was handy at sewing, made us some cool hippy outfits to wear. We went down to the city hall in Inglewood and were married outside on the steps by a Justice of the Peace—her parents witnessing. Shane now had my last name and was legitimate for all legal purposes.

3/19/1971

*I dream of comfortable days
and quiet nights
green trees . . . blue skies
no haze and no frights*

*of being by your side
. . . my love
when all other things
have turned sour*

*swinging on our front porch
cuddled together
embracing each minute
loving each hour*

*to sit with the moment
and look at a flower
just watching it grow
. . . don't you know*

*watching the sun shine
and watching it set
watching . . .
the very last glow*

*to sit in the night air
and think of the times
when love was still new
and our songs had their rhymes*

*it's a beautiful thing
to do . . . me and you
and I still love you true
—yes I do*

⚡

3/25/1971

*hey world . . .
you are going to get well
hey there world . . .
it is well you can tell*

*if you love
with sweet love*

*like a dove
with a shove
from above
you will know love is real*

*so tell me . . .
how do you feel*

*hey now . . .
if you look down a well
and wish to come true
it will you can tell*

*if you help everyone
with your love
it's so fun
we can share
some sweet days
in the sun*

*so love me . . .
and I'll love you*

↯

The following two poems are dream poems, taken straight from dreams I had on the same night.

4/12/1971

*the devil of the earth
and the angel of the star
said to one another
would you like to go afar*

*and tell me how you are
and tell me what you see
now tell me . . .
don't you think
that we can let it be*

*yes . . .
the changes that we go thru
and the things that come to pass
ain't it enough
to make a man turn ass*

*now the things
that you may think of
and the things
you may think to do
remember . . .
there are others living here too*

*the spirit of the sun
amidst the body of the ocean
. . . and together
we can sing the song of love*

*the man came to his son
and said . . .
I've got a swinging notion
we can find a place to be
most happily*

*and there is more
to go a-searchin'
there is so much more to see
there are stars beyond this ocean
there are spirits flying free*

*and the devil of the earth
and the angel of the star
shall look at one another
as they are*

↯

4/12/1971

*once I had a voodoo-eyed
long-haired mistress
at first she was a mystery to me
she had an array of sources
for her sorcery*

*she had jungle-flat
long-legged
wingless bats
and hook-nosed
blue-eyed
ring-tail cats*

*but most of all
when the sun came down*

she had love
she made love
she gave love

once I had a voodoo-eyed
long-haired mistress
at first she was a mystery to me
she had an array of sources
for her sorcery

she had love to give
but she gave it away
she gave her love
to another one day

and most of all
when the sun came down

she had love
she made love
she gave love

now . . .
she's no longer a mystery
no . . .
she's no longer a mystery
she's no longer a mystery
no longer a mystery to me

⚡

More of my discourse on *flower children* philosophy and idealism . . .

6/24/1971

mother nature's father's children
of the universe
struggling to live
your different lives
for better or for worse

struggling in the city of smog
fighting your way thru the grime
feeling your head is full of fog
from worrying all the time

*mother nature's father's children
of the universe
which way for to go
now . . . which way for to go*

*love is the answer
yes . . . love is the answer
the love that you give
the love that you show*

*if you give love
if you have love to show
then you'll know
you will be in the know
yes . . . you'll know
you will be in the know*

*mother nature's father's children
of the universe
have you a smog-proof mobile
have you some love I can feel
is that a smile you conceal
this is our world—it is real*

*mother nature's father's children
of the universe
mother nature's father's children
of the universe
mother nature's father's children
of the universe
look at our decaying earth
it couldn't be much worse*

⚡

Another dream poem . . . a dream within a dream.

6/24/1971

*floating . . . falling
in a dream
I saw you standing
on a bridge
I had a shack
'twas high upon the ridge*

*I took you there
we played*

we talked of old times
when our hearts were young
we danced, we sang, we walked
. . . thinking
how our world had begun

then we walked back
down to the bridge
where you found
some hanging beads

you touched them
and they broke
floating . . . falling
down the rocks
onto the ground
. . . revealing where it leads

I went down
to gather them up for you
and as I did
I must have awoke
for I looked back
you were gone
and the bridge broke

⚡

In June of 1971, Joni Mitchell released what many consider her masterpiece album, *Blue*. It spoke to me in a way nothing ever has! I felt as if she were speaking to me personally in her songs—all the songs on the album. I had a major celebrity crush on her, like no one since Ann Margret. I could not get enough of the album, and I even created a drawing inspired by it, which I call, "Joni's Vision." To this day, *Blue* is one of my all-time favorite albums.

In one more month it would be Shane's first birthday. I loved how our simple life was a happy one most of the time, even though we did not have much. At the same time, we dreamed of getting out of the city and living in the country somewhere, where we could enjoy the simplicity of nature's beauty. I started dreaming about our future, and I wrote these two poems:

7/6/1971

I'm a simple-minded guy
I like to talk about
the weather
I'm a very simple man
I'd like to know what you did
yesterday

say you were running thru the grass
the sweet soft downy smell
of heather
the way you seem to be
I want to stay with you
this way

yes I'm a simple-minded guy
hope you are simple-minded too
then you'll give me a simple feeling
making simple love to you

⚡

7/6/1971

trying to work my way out
of the city
work my way back
to the homeland

work my way out
of the city
back to a feeling
so grand

rolling hills
breezy evening chills
river flow
clean air . . . don't you know

working hard
during the day
sitting quietly with you
at night

our children and pets
with free room to play
dreaming of the place
that is right this way

. . . and I'm here
. . . and I'm trying
. . . and I'm working
. . . my way out

⚡

In Pasadena, where I grew up, there was this extraordinary German delicatessen, Stottlemeyers. It had the biggest and best sandwiches you could imagine. Every sandwich on the menu was named after a famous person, with the ingredients being humorously identifiable to that person. For example, there was the John Wayne—roast beef, lettuce, tomato and mayonnaise on white bread; the Sophia Loren—breast of turkey, Swiss cheese, and lettuce on an Italian roll; the Milton Berle—tongue, ham, limburger on an onion roll. My favorite was the Arnie Palmer—turkey, corned beef, Emmenthal Swiss cheese, avocado, and chopped liver on an onion roll. You had to build it only one way—like this: spread the chopped liver on the bottom of the bun, add the corned beef, then turkey, then Swiss cheese. Spread the avocado on the top of the roll, then—Yum!

Stottlemeyers was also a full-service deli, with meats and cheeses, each in their own refrigerated cases; a bread section; a coffee and tea section, and lots of other gourmet items for sale.

In July, I received a call from my sister telling me that she and her husband were opening a Stottlemeyers franchise in Laguna Beach. Because of my previous experience working in a deli, they wanted to offer me the store manager's job. She said that we could stay with them at their new home in Laguna Niguel until we were settled into a place of our own.

Sandy and I discussed it and decided—hell yes! Let's get out of here and start fresh! I was tired of being a truck driver in the garment industry making only minimum wage. It would be a new, better-paying job and a good opportunity for us.

I didn't realize it yet, but my psychedelic drug days were basically done. Once we left Hollywood, the opportunities for taking LSD or psychedelic tripping would not really present themselves. The tribe was no longer in Topanga, and I would be far away from there anyway. Going forward, I would still smoke pot, but alcohol would be taking center stage in my drug use. Yes, the '60s were truly over.

In August we moved away from our beloved Hollywood and disappeared behind the Orange Curtain.

Original Artwork

by C. Steven Blue

1966-1972

1966
"PEACE BETWEEN MAN AND WOMAN"
(designed in 1966 as a tribute to hippy idealism, now a registered trademark)

1967
ink & enamel on artboard

1967
"Spin Art—Purple Dove"
1967 Hollywood Teenage Fair
enamel on artboard

1968
ink on paper

1968
ink on paper

1968
"Love—Peace Between Man & Woman"
collage—tissue paper & mixed media on artboard

1968
"Peace Between Us—Toucan"
ink on paper

1968
"LSD Drawing #1"
pencil on paper

1968
"LSD Drawing #2"
pencil on paper

1968
"Perch In The Corner"
charcoal on paper

1969
charcoal on paper

1969
charcoal on paper

1969
charcoal on paper

1969
pencil on paper

1969
charcoal & ink on paper

1970
"Queen Jane"
ink on paper

1970
ink on paper

1970
"Hiawatha"
ink on paper

1970
"Siddhartha"
ink on paper

1970
"The Prophet"
ink on paper

_1971_
"Checkered Woman"
pencil on paper

1971
"Joni's Vision"
pencil on paper
(inspired by the Joni Mitchell album, Blue)

1972
*"Peace Between Man & Woman—In Flames"
enamel on artboard*

_1972_
"Codac Woman"
enamel on artboard

1972 – 1973:

A New Beginning
Behind the Orange Curtain
and Celeste

I settled in quickly to the manager's job at Stottlemeyers. By the beginning of 1972, I was totally immersed in work and family, putting in long hours at the deli. In March, Sandy became pregnant with our daughter, Celeste, although we would not know we were having a girl until she was born. We had planned it this time, though, and genuinely wanted a girl.

Because I had a station wagon (our baby blue Rambler), my sister had me drive to Newport Beach early each morning before we opened, to pick up supplies from the bakery where we purchased our fresh breads and pastries. One morning as I was driving back, I was in the left lane on Pacific Coast Highway heading south. As I approached a random street corner, a guy up ahead, who was in the right lane, suddenly turned left—directly in front of the car ahead of me. The car in front of me slammed on his brakes, and I plowed right into the back of his car! The cause of the accident quickly made off down the side street. Because I rear-ended another car, the accident was considered my fault.

The front end of my little Rambler was smashed up, but I was able to drive back to my sister's house, where the car sat for several weeks. I did not have the money to fix it.

A few weeks later, again on PCH, I spotted an abandoned Rambler the same year as ours on the side of the road. It was pink instead of blue, and it was a sedan instead of a station wagon, but the front ends were the same. I convinced the Department of Motor Vehicles to release the car to me, as they could not find any evidence of the owner. I took the front end of that car off and put it on the front of mine. Then I sold the rest of the car to a junkyard.

So now we had a baby blue Rambler wagon with a pink front end. Everyone loved to joke about it: blue for boys, pink for girls. Everyone said we would probably have a girl, exactly like we wanted.

Our lives were pretty busy during that time and, sad to say, my poetry pretty much faded into the background. However, I did manage to write a few poems in 1972.

⚡

1/27/1972

*some of the things
you've got to go through
and some of the things
you've got to do*

*I've psyched myself out
quite a bit
but I always knew
when it was time to quit*

*I'm breaking out
it ain't no use
can't stop now
'cause I'm cuttin' loose
from the bureaucratic
hypodermic noose*

*it's a rude awakening
like I've been asleep
and now it's finally
coming back to me*

*strength . . .
motion . . .
motivation . . .
the purpose has always been there*

*now it's time to get through
. . . to it
the logical revolution
. . . let's do it
the ever-changing feelings
. . . go through it*

*all things pass
all things last
all things fade
all things are new
since I've been loving you*

*and now it's rock-n-roll
—sunsets
and comic books in the movies*

⚡

When we were kids, my brother and I had these sleds with wheels on them, called Flexy Flyers. We would find streets with hills on them, which was not hard to do in Pasadena and Altadena. Then, we would each lie down on our stomach on our sled and coast downhill. The Flexy could go very fast—I think we clocked it at over 40mph. It had a steering bar on the front wheels that, if you lifted up on it, it would apply brakes to the front wheels. It didn't work very well though. Mostly we'd crash a lot! We would usually try to ride up a driveway and onto someone's grass, or drive into a patch of ivy—to stop. I woke up one night with this weird dream poem in my head:

2/10/1972

*Flexy and I
flying down . . . down . . . down
passing everyone in sight*

*tired . . . the old man took me
in the car with leather doors
—snap down tight
he swam in the pool
drinking wine
pouring it to his head
yet never a drop was spilled*

*hungriness
ravaged the refrigerator
the father awoke
devouring the rib
and the artichoke*

*. . . wake up
sit here naked
reading and remembering
the poet and the dream*

*. . . fall back asleep
my Flexy and I
flying down . . . down . . . down
passing everyone in sight*

⚡

I had an old stick I'd found on a hike. It was perfect for carving into a good walking stick. While we were staying with my sister, I decided to do precisely that. I found some woodcarving tools at the Sunday swap meet and figured out how to use them. I carved the stick, and it came out so great, everyone told me how good it was.

One day, the stick disappeared from my sister's garage, where I had been polishing it with linseed oil. Everyone said they had no idea what had happened to it. I knew that someone knew, but I never found out. Although I fully intended to carve another one, I never carved anything again.

3/7/1972

*as I walked along the road
on my way . . .
I came across a man
with a beautiful walking stick
he had carved by hand
out of driftwood*

*it just so happened
I also had my own
which I was walking with
at that very moment
I had also done my own
detailed hand carving
to my stick*

*we both loved our walking sticks dearly
but admired each other's
as well
so we decided to exchange sticks
and go along our way
to see what other people thought
about each other's walking stick*

*we would meet up again in Saint Julien
two months later
to discuss our experiences
and exchange our walking sticks
back*

*after two months of very enjoyable
compliments on his stick
I made my way back to Saint Julien
well . . .
my new friend did not show up*

*on the one hand
I was worried
some harm may have befallen him
on the other hand
I assumed my stick
was of more value
and much more beautiful
than his*

↯

I was listening to some music one day—purely trippin' on the beats. Being a drummer myself, I started thinking about my natural sense of rhythm and how I had always seemed to possess it. This poured out of me:

4/19/1972

there still are some things
that are natural
things which you cannot deny
still some things
that can't be man-made
like the sun . . . the trees and the sky

through whispering canyons
along waterfall lines
searching for the wherefore and the why
if you want
you can close your eyes
but don't let the natural pass you by

and rhythm . . .
is something that's natural
rhythm is something that's real
rhythm is something you're born with
rhythm is something you feel

and you don't know how
it comes out of you
you feel it comes from above
I don't know . . .
it's something inside of you
rhythm is something like love

school is a place you can go
to learn about engines and gauges
if you yearn to know light beams
and electronic phases
the real truths in life
and outer spaces

I really can dig mathematics
and the sound of stereophonics
there's so much to learn
if you look
so many things
I could write a book

but rhythm . . .
is something that's natural
rhythm is something that's real
rhythm is something you're born with
rhythm is something you feel

you don't know how
it comes out of you
you feel it comes from above
I don't know . . .
it's something inside of you
rhythm is something like love

there are natural things
that you can find
no matter where you go
there is all the time
and all the places
to learn what there is to know

but in all these things
and all these places
where do you find the glow
in your life
there's so much to do
and so many feelings to show

and . . .
rhythm is something that's natural
rhythm is something that's real
rhythm is something you're born with
rhythm is something you feel

you don't know how
it comes out of you
you feel it comes from above
I don't know . . .
it's something inside of you
rhythm is something like love

. . . it's somethin' like love

↯

Good things so often come to an end. In June of 1972, barely a year after we had moved to Laguna, my sister and her husband split up and sold the deli. I no longer had a job, and we no longer had anywhere to stay. We packed up to leave.

We left without our cat, Monkey Face. He always loved roaming in the hills of Laguna Niguel and often wouldn't come home for days. Then, when we had completely given up on him, he would come struttin' back from another adventure. For a week before we left, we tried to find him. We looked everywhere, and we asked everyone around the neighborhood if they had seen him, but we definitely couldn't find him, and finally it was time to go. Naturally, we figured he knew and was hiding out because he wanted to stay there, where he could roam the hills freely as he'd always done. Heck, he's still up there to this day, for all I know!

Sandy, who was now three months pregnant, went to stay with her parents in Inglewood. I temporarily stayed with my sister in an apartment she rented after leaving her husband. Sandy and I didn't especially want to leave the beach area of Orange County, so I searched for a new job there. I was taking care of business, but I was feeling so alone without Sandy and Shane. I worried every day about her being pregnant and us being apart.

I always have these dreams
that someone slept with my baby
they always want the bad boy
not the good boy

sometimes . . .
when you need real love
it still doesn't matter

wish there was someone
to confide in

lost in the struggle
of the tumble
. . . alone again

just a heartbreak kid
with nowhere to turn
because of what happened
there's no way to return

♪

After weeks of looking, I finally found a job at a place called Gourmet Collective in the Costa Mesa/Newport Beach area. We moved to Costa Mesa in July, into a cozy little duplex at the west end of town, on the hills overlooking Huntington Beach. It had two bedrooms, a fenced yard, and a garage, so it was ideal for kids and our pets, Lady and Tiger.

The new job was different from my last one, as I would not be the store manager. It was a large, two-story gourmet shopping complex, with lots of departments. They hired me as the manager of the gourmet foods department. The store also had a liquor department, a wine cellar, a tobacco shop, and a full-service deli with both hot and cold foods to go. Upstairs there was a beauty salon and next door a restaurant, which was also connected to the wine cellar. The wine cellar could be accessed from either the restaurant or from stairs in the back of the gourmet foods section—my department.

I did the ordering, stocking, and inventory for my section, and I rang up the sales as well. Gourmet foods was right next to the deli, so I often rang up their sales too, as well as wine sales from the wine cellar. One day Raquel Welch bought a $300.00 bottle of wine from me—for her lunch! We also did all the catering for John Wayne's yacht parties on his boat, the Wild Goose, in Newport Beach.

Our lives were looking better with my new job, so we were able to replace the old pink and blue Rambler with a used 1961 Volkswagen Beetle. Surprisingly, the 'bug' didn't have a gas gauge. When you ran out of gas, you would turn a throttle handle protruding from the floorboard of the car, which would activate a reserve gallon in the bottom of the tank. The car would then sputter, sputter, sputter, start up again, and then you'd have enough gas to get you to the next gas station.

My new job had better wages and even included health insurance after the first six months. Unfortunately, that would not come in time for our baby to be born. Welfare, which had been covering us, would still cover the birth, as the job at my sister's deli hadn't paid enough for us to have health insurance—or to ever get our own place, for that matter.

We still had the same hospital in Laguna Beach also, as we didn't want to mess anything up with the birth of our new baby. The hospital was progressive and had natural childbirth classes called the Lamaze method, which we took because that was the only way I would be allowed to be in the delivery room when our baby was born. I had been denied that when both of my sons were born, because fathers were not allowed in delivery rooms in those days. I didn't want that to happen again. I was determined to be in the room to see our baby be born!

As I said earlier, we didn't know whether our baby was going to be a boy or a girl—ultrasound was not widely available yet, especially if you were on Welfare.

When the time came, our baby almost couldn't wait. Sandy's contractions started at home, but by the time we realized we had to go—now, her water broke. We rushed to get in the car with an hour-and-a-half drive to the hospital. We were worried Sandy might have to give birth in our VW bug.

By the time we arrived at the hospital, Sandy was almost crowning. They barely rolled her into the delivery room before Celeste popped out—yes, a girl! They had quickly given me a gown and mask to put on, then rushed me into the delivery room to be with Sandy.

It was astonishing—almost overwhelming, to watch Celeste be born. I was excited, but also a little scared. I coached Sandy and watched as she pushed and pushed, and then suddenly there was our daughter, Celeste. It was too amazing for words! I had never seen or experienced anything like it. The doctor let me take hold of her as she was born, so I was the first one to hold Celeste, who we named after the song, "Celeste," by Donovan. I was so full of joy, almost to the point of tears. A month later, I turned 23. I wrote this on my birthday:

1/20/1973

I'm a happy go lucky guy
I'm happy . . .
I'll tell you why

I've got my woman
to love
and my children
my little doves

they make me feel good
when I come home
so I never
want to roam

I guess . . .
I've used some
I know some
have used me

but now I'm happy
as can be
true to them
they're true to me

⚡

We now had two kids, but my job paid me enough so I could finally get a few items for myself. Better conga drums were my first purchase. The brand I bought was Gon Bops, made in Southern California, and regarded as some of the best congas in the world. Instead of the old pawnshop drum, I now had two good congas—a Quinto and a Tumba. Those two drums would allow me to do all the sounds much easier—highs, middles, and lows. Both drums were mahogany, but had a lustrous golden sheen to them, almost like oak. The trim was shiny chrome and the heads were made of goat skins, which gave off a rich, resonating sound when I played them. The way the sounds rang out of the bottom of the drums was truly musical—mystical, magical to me.

    I also started buying records again at a more frequent pace. My third record collection was finally growing in size. Among my friends, I had always been the biggest rock-and-roll music fanatic, and my album collection was important to me. I had started rebuilding it again when we were in Hollywood, after losing my second collection that time when we were ripped off in Inglewood.

I was always careful with my records. I handled them only at the edges to keep the oil from fingerprints off them, and I usually would not let anyone else touch them if I could help it. I even had thick, plastic covers to go over the complete record and cover of each and every one of my albums.

Sandy and I loved music and played it almost every night. We had a TV, too, but music had always been and still was our main thing.

I also bought a reel-to-reel tape recorder for myself. It was a brand new Sony 2-track, sound-on-sound recorder, which allowed you to do multi-track recording, by ping-ponging back and forth between the 2 tracks. It wasn't dull and scratched up like something from a pawnshop. It was brand new—and shiny—and all mine.

On Saturday nights, after I worked all week at the Gourmet Collective, Sandy and I would hire a babysitter and go to Finnigan's Rainbow to dance, drink, listen to live rock-n-roll and hang out with new friends. Finnigan's was right down the street from where we lived, and it was our favorite place to unwind.

With my new reel-to-reel, I started recording local bands playing live at Finnigan's Rainbow, and then, eventually, at other local places where we loved to dance and party. Soon, I was recording bands all over Orange County, including the two most famous Orange County bands of the time: The Blitz Brothers and Honk.

The Blitz Brothers' drummer, Dick Dodd, had been the lead singer in The Standells—the band with the 1966 hit "Dirty Water." The song is about Boston, and it is traditionally played by Boston sports teams after home victories. The Standells were featured in the movie, *Riot on Sunset Strip*, about the infamous riot I had taken part in back in 1966. Dick Dodd also had been one of the original Mouseketeers on the original *Mickey Mouse Club* on TV. They called him Dickie on the show.

At Dick Dodd's request, I brought my congas to Finnigan's one night when the Blitz Brothers were playing. Dick wanted to learn how to play congas, so he could front the band as the singer, while still playing rhythms. He loved playing my congas, so he bought his own.

When Dick was the front man with his new congas, they needed another drummer for the trap kit. I convinced them to audition my friend, Ben, who was a hard rock drummer. They loved his playing and told him that they would use him when Dick was fronting the band. The band liked me too, so I was given the opportunity to sit in sometimes with my own congas. Often, it would be me on congas, with Dick on the trap kit; and sometimes we would both be playing congas, while Ben played the trap kit. My favorite song to perform with them was The Doobie Brothers song, "Without Love." It was the perfect song for congas. It felt so good to be on stage again, to focus on music again. I recorded some of those nights on my reel-to-reel.

One day in early February, I wrote a new poem based on the music festivals I used to go to in the '60s. I had been thinking a lot about those days recently, especially 1969, when I had gone to so many free concerts and hippy festivals.

I remembered how I had almost gone to Woodstock, but completely missed out. Several of us had gotten tickets, and we were all going together, but at the last minute, our ride flaked on us. We were bummed out! We did not have enough time to try to hitchhike from L.A. to New York, so we sold our tickets. A couple of months later, though, on Nov. 2, 1969, The Moody Blues played at the L.A. Elysian Park love-in. I will never forget it because the night before they had been slated to play a concert at the L.A. Forum with Jefferson Airplane. However, Mike Pinder's Mellotron gear was held up in customs at the airport, and they didn't get it out in time to play. To not totally disappoint the crowd, Jefferson Airplane did the concert anyway.

I had been listening to L.A. rock radio station KRLA that night, so I knew about the screw-up with the Mellotron gear. Then they made an announcement that The Moody Blues would play at the love-in the next day—for free. A little while later, Jefferson Airplane announced that they would come along to play also.

Of course, I went. The Moody Blues were my favorite rock band, well, next to The Beatles. I could hardly believe I was getting to hear them in concert, much less for free at the love-in. *Work!* A local band, Sweetwater, played first, and then some other local groups played as well. Then Jefferson Airplane played, with The Moody Blues coming on at the end, near sunset.

The thing I remembered more distinctly than anything else happened while the The Moody Blues were playing. I looked up in the hills to the west to see people dancing on the hilltops. They were a quarter to half a mile away, but there they were dancing to The Moodies on hilltops. *Out-a-sight!*

Soon after that, I heard that The Rolling Stones were going to throw a free concert in December near San Francisco, in Livermore, California, at the Altamont Speedway. They were going to be joined by Crosby, Stills, Nash & Young; Jefferson Airplane; Grateful Dead; The Flying Burrito Bros. and Santana. Everybody was calling it *Woodstock West*. I absolutely wanted to go, so I talked my friend Tad into going with me. He had a car, so I would not have to hitchhike. We rolled a whole bunch of joints, enough to fill a red Marlboro box (of course) to take with us.

There were 300,000 people at the Altamont Speedway that day. It was huge, the biggest concert I had ever attended up to that point, and it was free!

We had a great time, mostly, but this was not your typical peaceful hippy crowd. Early on, from our vantage point, we could see Hell's Angels on top of a yellow school bus throwing full beer cans at the crowd. Then, during Jefferson Airplane's set, Marty Balin was socked in the head by someone—and knocked out—in the middle of a song! The crowd started going crazy and pushing towards the stage—so many people packed so tightly that it became scary. People were shouting and the band was trying to recover and start playing again.

At that moment, something happened that I'll never forget. Grace Slick started humming into the microphone, low, slow, soft, gentle—and the crowd, magically, quieted. She incredibly took control and calmed everything down to a hush—magic! Everything slowly began to become peaceful again, and then the band resumed playing.

We left early during The Stones' set since it was getting dark, and so were the vibes. Later, we heard about the stabbing on stage during their set. Someone had a gun, apparently to shoot one of The Stones, and he jumped up on stage, but one of the Hell's Angels jumped in and stabbed him to death. This is all chronicled in The Stones' film documentary, *Gimme Shelter*.

It was called the end of the *Woodstock Generation's* 'peace and love' era. I didn't believe it was, but many people did.

So I hadn't made it to *Woodstock*, but I was at *Altamont*. And I saw The Beatles—twice.

Flashin' back on all of that, I wrote a poem, "Folk Festival," about another free festival I attended that year, even before *Woodstock* or *Altamont* took place. It was in Santa Clara, CA in May of 1969.

It actually started as a protest to a huge, three-day paid festival, *The Northern California Folk-Rock Festival*, which was so expensive that most hippies I knew could not afford to go. The music industry was beginning to get savvy to how much money could be made from rock music festivals. They found a way to cash in on the hippy culture by sponsoring huge festivals. They would get all these big-name groups to play, and then they would charge a ridiculous amount of money for the day, or even more for a multi-day pass. They had tried out this scheme at *Woodstock*, but it had not worked out. Many people bought tickets, but it became a free concert when half a million people showed up and busted down the fences.

So, as I said, there was this protest against one of the expensive, weekend long festivals in Santa Clara, in May. I went up there to join the protest. As it turned out, a free concert was held right across the street in a baseball field park, to keep the protestors from getting too out of control. After the protest, I stayed for the free concert and ended up sleeping overnight in the park in my sleeping bag.

Jefferson Airplane was one of the headliners at the paid festival, but they came over to the free one the next morning and played right as the sun was coming up. We all awoke to the awe-inspiring sounds of the Airplane!

As I stated earlier, I wrote a new poem based on the music festivals. It was actually about that festival. Here it is:

2/5/1973

*Santa Clara in '69
was feeling fine
thirty thousand
came to a diamond
to have a good time*

*two days of music
in protest
to how expensive it can be
for a feeling . . .
we had two days of
—for free*

*got to motivate back
to that attitude
and rotate back
to that feeling
the feeling we got
was gratitude
for a feeling
so revealing*

*I'd like to motivate back
and motivate back
. . . rotate back
to that feeling
get on back
to a feeling
so revealing*

*the Airplane was flying
at sunrise
as people wiped sleep
from their eyes
to see the Airplane that shined
with the sunshine
the feeling could hypnotize*

*police stood by
a few blocks away
directing traffic
and showing the way
they weren't there to hassle
. . . I want to say
what a beautiful feeling
on a beautiful day*

*and I'd like to motivate back
to that attitude
rotate back
to that feeling
meditate back
to a feeling
so revealing*

*euthenics was working
that day
everyone was high
in their own way*

*two days of music
for you and me
two days to be
at a place to be free
a revealing feeling
for all to see
two days for free
. . . how peaceful it can be*

*and I'd like to
motivate back to it
motivate back to it
rotate on back
to that feeling
get on back
to that feeling
so revealing*

↯

I was pretty busy: my job, raising kids, recording bands, playing and listening to music. By this time, as if kids were not enough to look after, we had three dogs, four cats, a turtle and a hamster. The kids loved our pets and we did too, but Sandy certainly had her hands full while I was at work. We looked forward to our nights out dancing and drinking on the weekends, especially at the clubs with live bands. Life was busy, life was good, and 1973 flew by.

1974, January-September:

California Jam, Leaving Gourmet Collective

On Saturday, April 6, 1974, we took the kids with us to *California Jam* at Ontario Motor Speedway. Shane was three and a half years old and Celeste was nearing a year and a half. Despite their ages, we knew they would be fine, even at a large-scale hippy festival, since they were used to smaller, local ones, as well as the love-ins.

We went super early in the morning to get a good spot to sit, as the concert announcements said it was general blanket seating on the grass. It was still dark when we showed up, and there were small bonfires scattered along the hillsides above the speedway.

We situated our blanket on the right side of the stage about 100 yards back from it. It was a good spot to see all the action from, but not too close to the people who would be crowded near the front of the stage dancing. We didn't want any chance of the kids getting hurt by people trampling over blankets to get close. It seemed like the perfect spot, as we were also far enough in from the edge of the crowd where everyone was walking, but close enough so we wouldn't have to climb over too many blankets to get out if we needed to take the kids to the outhouse.

It was later estimated that there were between 300-400 thousand people there. When you looked out over the crowd, it was absolutely incredible—like a city of people, carefully climbing over others and careful not to interrupt someone else's space. It was peaceful, and the smell of pot and incense filled the air.

Neither of the kids were interested in the music or what was happening on the stage. Shane, however, was interested in everyone around us. He would actually go up and sit next to people on their blankets, and then interact with them. We had to keep an eye on him to make sure he didn't wander too far. Everyone around us got a kick out of how uninhibited he was. Celeste, on the other hand, slept a lot or merely wanted to eat.

The Eagles played, and they were the band we had come to see. They were one of our absolute favorite bands by then, and it was incredible to see them live! Some of the other bands who played that day were Earth, Wind & Fire; Black Oak Arkansas; Black Sabbath; Deep Purple; and Emerson, Lake & Palmer.

It was an extremely hot day. All day long, the concert promoters were handing out free jugs of water to people in the audience. In a totally welcome gesture, moments before Black Oak Arkansas came on, a helicopter flew over the crowd and dropped thousands of cardboard sun visors with the band's logo on them. Watching thousands of them floating through the air—that was astonishing.

Emerson, Lake & Palmer played last, and it was dark when they came on. During one song, Keith Emerson was playing a full-size grand piano—which started rising up into the air with the stage lights following it! There was Keith, way up in the air and still playing, when suddenly the piano started tilting forward, then began to slowly spin in circles, with Keith still playing all the while. The crowd went crazy!

Both of our kids were crashed out by then. When the concert ended, we had to carry them to the car along with all our blankets and stuff. All in all, it was a lot of fun. It was one of the best festivals I've ever been to—and I've been to a lot!

⚡

Then, in May, Sandy dropped a bombshell. She said she had never had a chance to find herself before we were married. She wanted to go out and do that now, on her own, to find out who she was and what she actually wanted for her own life. She had already made a plan to take the kids and go back to Hollywood.

It was a drop-dead shocker. Déjà vu and disbelief at the same time.

I knew this breakup wasn't entirely her fault. We had not been communicating well for a long while, maybe since Laguna. But my kids?! I could not have my kids ripped from my life once again.

It seemed especially distressing and ironic, since Sandy and I had been working on getting custody of Arthur—to have all three kids together with us. Back when we were still in Hollywood, right after Shane was born, we had visited Arthur frequently. He and his aunt Mimi lived only a few blocks away from us, so it was easy to visit. Sometimes, Aunt Mimi would invite us for dinner. She was the best cook.

Shane was only two years younger than Arthur. Arthur loved to play while Shane watched him with great interest—his blue eyes bulging and a huge smile on his face.

Once we moved to Laguna, it had become harder to visit, since we did not have our own place and could not afford to go to Hollywood very often. However, when we moved to our own place in Costa Mesa, it was easier for all of us to see each other again. Sometimes, we would drive up to Hollywood. Other times, Arthur and Aunt Mimi would take the bus to Costa Mesa and stay with us for a few days.

On one visit, Mimi told us that Arthur's grandparents were trying to take custody of him away from her, but she was fighting it tooth and nail. She suggested that it would be wonderful to have Arthur be with Shane and Celeste—the three of them together with Sandy and me in a real family situation. She said she would be willing to be on our side and actually sign custody over to us. Sandy and I discussed this and decided to try to make it happen. Mimi wrote a letter describing her wishes for us to have custody, and she gave it to us, but then Sandy dropped her bombshell, so now, all of that was going away too.

I was beside myself and didn't know how to handle it, but I did what I usually did when I couldn't handle things—I smoked pot! I also started drinking more. But now, the drinking was more of a crutch, a way to not feel my feelings of heartache, whereas before it had mostly been about partying and letting loose.

I started drinking heavily, and I started hanging out by myself. I was hangin' a lot at a new disco club called Smokey Stover's, in Newport Beach. They had a Sunday night blues/rock jam session, and I would often jam there. Playing music was one of the few things that seemed to bring me any solace. I would often record the jam sessions on my reel-to-reel, which gave me an in with the other musicians there, and made me feel noticed and valued—feelings I certainly was not getting anywhere else.

There was a guitar player named Johnny, who frequently played at the Sunday jam. He claimed to have played with the original Mill's Brothers band, whose recording of the song, "Paper Doll," had been a major hit in the 1940s. Johnny had his own gig with a small combo at a club called The Lip on Balboa Island. He liked my conga playing and asked me if I'd like to join in with his combo playing those gigs. I said sure! So I played with him at The Lip twice a week for a while. I recorded some of those gigs, where we played mostly blues songs like, "Stormy Monday," "Tobacco Road" and "Walkin' Blues." Of course, we'd play "Paper Doll," too.

These distractions helped me to cope a little, but not much. Nothing would change the fact that Sandy was leaving. I did not know what would happen between my kids and me. I was so depressed!

5/13/1974

don't expect the past . . . too fast
to think of missing you
and so many things to do

but what I feel . . .
I already miss you
how fast will you think
of missing me

for the time apart
is a red sunset
but a blue moon

we've got to make a start
to know the true you
to know the true me

so let it be . . . and think
but don't downgrade me too fast
don't make it the past . . . badly

don't make it
the closed situation
but the open that can be

♪

5/28/1974

all the things we've wanted to do
all the plans we've tried to get to
plans for the future
that still hold true
and . . .
I still want to do them with you

babe . . .
I know you've got your heart set
on bein' free
but does that mean
you don't love me

we're married . . . it's we
the way it should be
and I think we can still make it
. . . naturally

on that Tuesday night
when the feeling was right
you showed me what was there
. . . that you still care

it was a sign
a full moon was shining
it seemed to me
that both of us were aware

of something deep . . . not gone
something that lingers on
knowing that love is not just
a moment's fame
and definitely not a game

there's so much
I still want to give
so much I want to do
with you

and now I think
there is a chance
to do something for you
. . . just you

and maybe it's for me too
it's all in what we do
and I think that now
we both can see it through

the time in between
I hope it goes fast
I think we have something
that lasts

you may not know this
but you're always on my mind
. . . wherever I go
. . . whatever I find

but don't be disillusioned
baby cool your mind

'cause I don't want to just
. . . fade away
in the depths of the blind

only leaving us
like so many pin holes in time

and after all
it's a full moon
. . . it's yours
. . . and it's mine

⚡

They say timing is everything, but I don't know about this one . . .

Right in the middle of all of this, Jessie showed up again. He said he needed a place to crash while he saved money from his new welding job so he could get his own place. I was already in so much grief over what was goin' down, and now I was having a full-on déjà vu experience of what had occurred with Jenny. But I needed a friend to talk to, and we had a long history, so I let him stay. I told him explicitly that it could only be for a couple of weeks at the most.

And so . . . guess what happened? Yeah, you guessed it. Jessie slept with Sandy! Where do I even go with that?

I took a drive up Ortega Highway to get away—to be alone and think. I saw some cars parked alongside the highway, so I pulled over to see what was there. I followed a small path down a big hill and came upon this marvelous stream, with little waterfalls and everything. I spent a couple of hours there—silently contemplating my situation.

6/03/1974

*I had to get away
to try and save a good day*

*to find a better way
to say I love you*

*to a place that isn't shown
find a place that isn't known*

*a thought . . .
that words can't really say
is how we lost our way*

*and only to be said for two
it's me and you*

*it's there . . . it's everywhere
but it's inside (please don't hide)*

*for what can love do
but be each . . . me and you*

⚡

6/15/1974

*you ask me—babe
what is the matter
all I can say is
I need to know I'm wanted
I need to know I'm needed
and it's been too long*

*I feel so foolish
a grown man gone wet
—going wet
on a heartstring*

*what is real love
just knowing you're wanted
and you've got my heart—babe*

*you don't have my body
you don't have my soul
but my heart is in control
. . . right now*

sometimes . . .
when your mind is in control
it tells you the way to go

but what is real
in your heart
is what you feel

and I need to know
what is real
in your heart
for me

today is the anniversary
of love lost before
and if you don't know
what it's for
then know—babe
it's for you

♪

A short time before Sandy left, my black cloud briefly parted, as a sliver of a rainbow came my way . . .

I was doing even more stuff alone after finding out about Jessie and Sandy. I was out driving around Newport Bay—just wandering around, simply wanting to get out of the house, away somewhere—anywhere. A beautiful summer day suddenly seemed even more beautiful when I noticed a cute, long-haired girl sitting on the front steps of one of the bayfront rentals in Lido Isle. She was wearing blue-jean short-shorts and I could see her multi-colored panties peeking out underneath them. She saw that I was looking and waved at me, so I stopped and parked. I walked up to where she was sitting and struck up a conversation. Before I knew it, we were inside her place, making hot, passionate love in her living room. We did not even make it into her bedroom!

Robyn was a savior! I had not slept with any woman other than Sandy in five years. I was so devastated that another woman was the last thing on my mind . . . but then this moment wondrously happened.

Back home, I confided in Jessie. But that was a mistake, because he immediately blabbed it to Sandy. Was this a deliberate stab in the back? Regardless, now I'm lookin' like the bad guy. It gave Sandy the perfect excuse to blame me for everything. It didn't matter that she had slept with Jessie. That's one thing I never understood.

I don't know if there ever had been a great communication bond between Sandy and me. There was definitely a physical thing in the beginning, but the ability to talk with faith and trust was always a stretch for us, or so it seemed now, anyway. We hadn't talked in a long time about anything deep. And she also did not believe in my dreams. She said they were only silly, stupid dreams that would never amount to anything.

One night, Robyn came to hang out with me while I was recording The Blitz Brothers at Finnigan's Rainbow. We danced. We drank. We smoked pot. We were so excited about being together, and having so much fun that we couldn't even wait to get back to her house to make love. We did it right in the parking lot—right in the back seat of my VW bug!

From then on, Robyn and I hung out whenever we could. We discussed pretty much everything in each other's lives. She was easy to talk to, and I hadn't opened up to anyone for so long. She was incredible and I liked her a bunch.

Then one day, she told me she was moving back to Northern California. She said that after all the discussions we had been in, and thinking about how heartbroken I was at having my children ripped out of my life once again, she had taken it to heart and started thinking about her own son. She made the decision to go back to her ex in Northern California, to give her son the family environment he needed, and to give her ex another shot.

We were on the same wavelength in so many ways. This was a bummer for me. I did not want to see her go. I was sad about it—very sad, but I knew it was the right thing for her—even though I would be alone again.

Before she left, she presented me with a special gift. She made a special hanging talisman for me, hand-painted on rawhide, and containing all the shells she had gathered from the shore in front of her bayfront rental house. The talisman was a representation of both 'The Star' Tarot card and the symbol for 'Aquarius'—the water bearer, which is my sign. She told me, "This is only to be hung in your music room. You can see it and think of me when you are creating." I thanked her . . . and we said our goodbyes. Goodbyes, goodbyes . . . another goodbye.

6/19/1974

you . . . made for me
—a way out
created a precursor
for my music
to be part of my music room
—only
for you believed in me

you . . . gave to me
—the opportunity
to feel again
oh how I needed
to feel again

you . . . were in my life
but a short time
then became annexed
—north
—for your ex
—for your son
—to be complete

you . . . gave of yourself
your precious treasures
collected far and wide
from the ocean and sky

and you . . . created it
out of love
for me to see
for my music to become a reality
you . . . oh . . . you

the fabric of design
created from your mind
yet given from your heart

—a dream collage
of future thoughts and seasons
the reason of rawhide logic
lovingly arranged

I know this may sound
like a worn out cliché
but . . . do you believe in destiny

I can still smell
your fragrance
from across the room
many-colored bottoms
—drew me
to your sweet perfume

⚡

6/20/1974

*sing a song
of life
sing out
all that strife*

*for the love
in your eyes
makes me realize
how wise it's been
for you now
to make the movement
. . . somehow*

*to show what you know
what else can you do
. . . but grow
to the outward
movement
of the soul*

*a pertinent philosophy
of your innermost feelings
for the sound
of the movement
you've wondered*

*and you know
what you feel
and how I feel
. . . it's been real*

Here are pictures of the front and back of the talisman created for me by
Robyn in 1974,
which I hung near where I made my music:

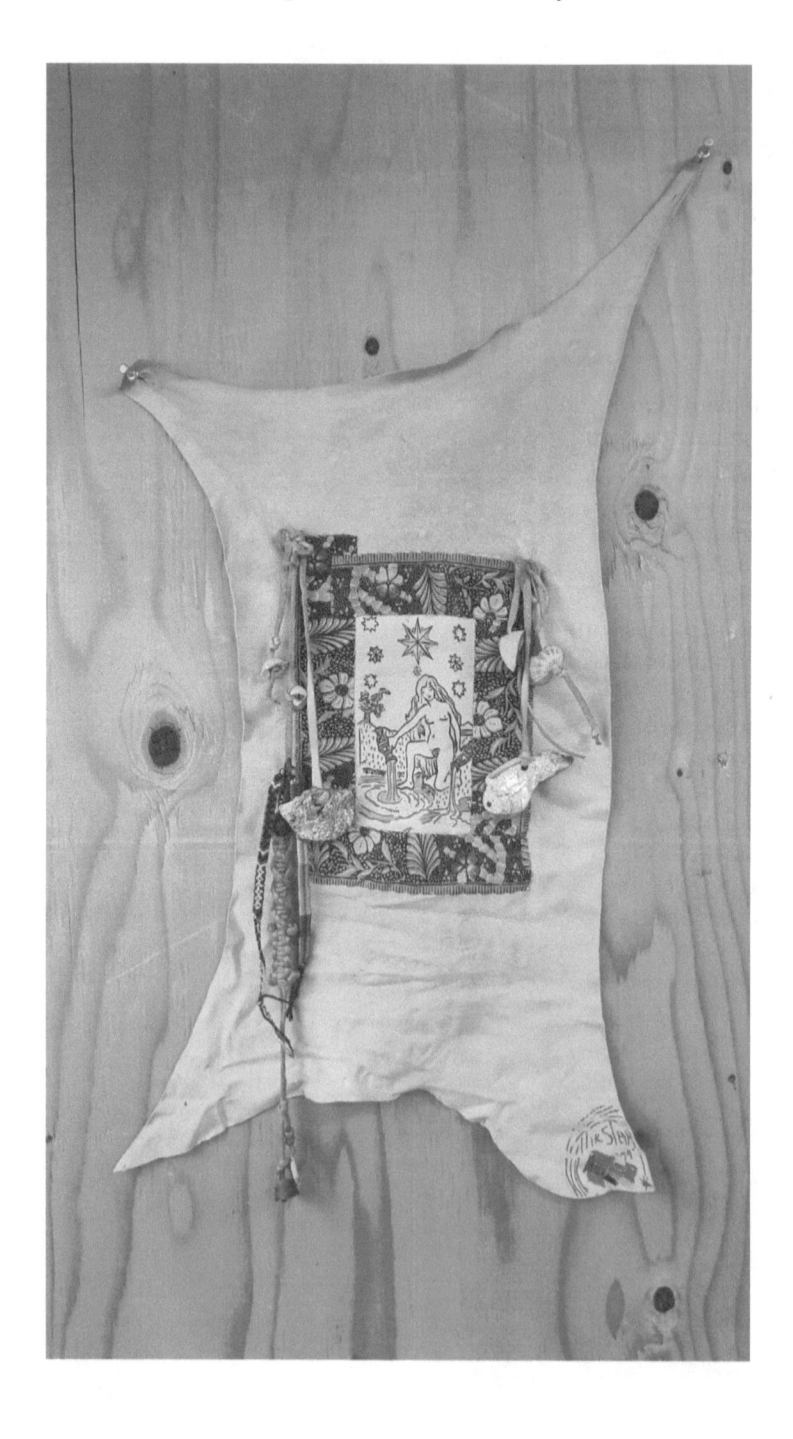

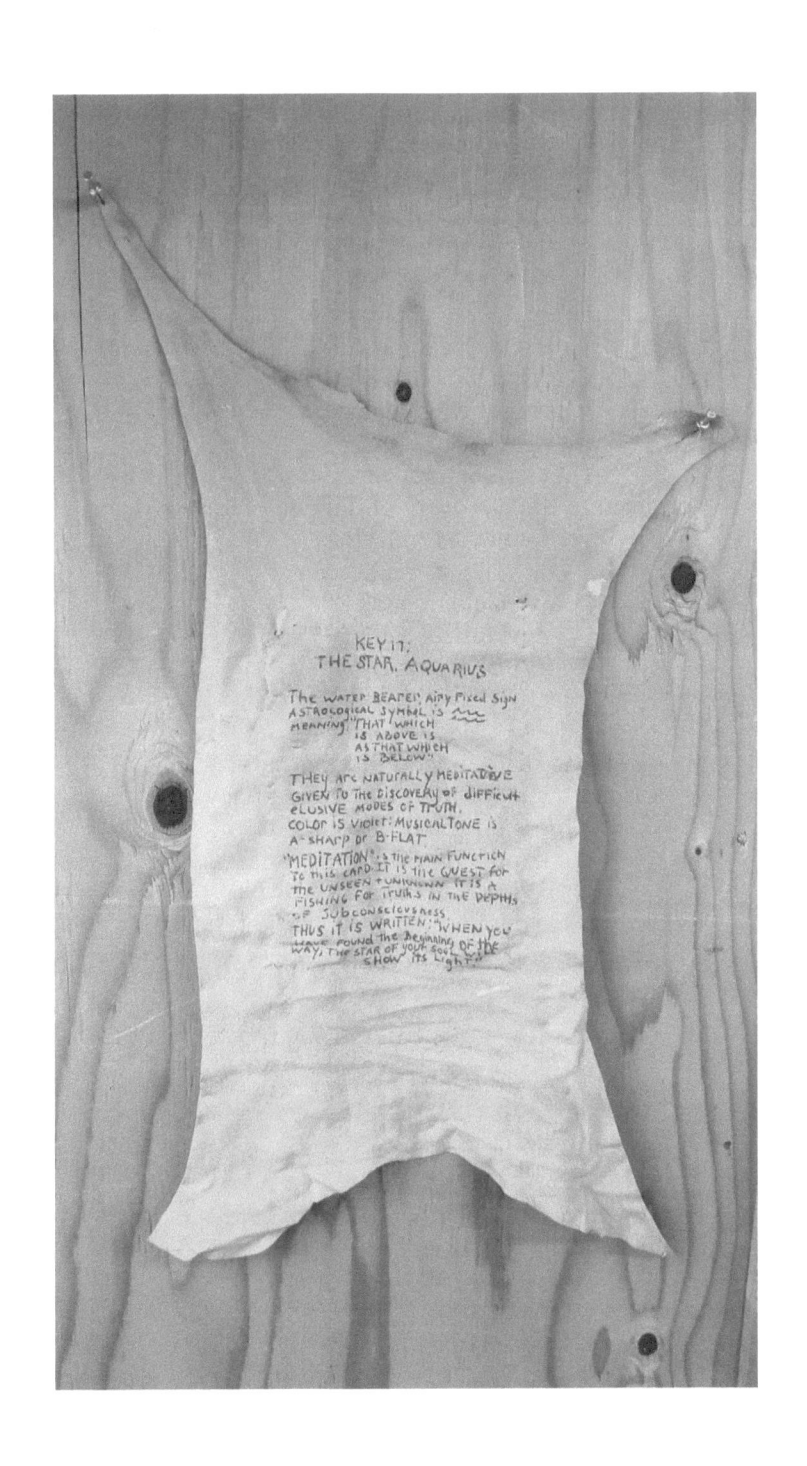

KEY 17:
THE STAR. AQUARIUS

The water bearer, Airy fixed sign
Astrological symbol is
meaning "THAT WHICH
IS ABOVE IS
AS THAT WHICH
IS BELOW"

They are naturally meditative
given to the discovery of difficult
elusive modes of TRUTH.
color is violet: Musical tone is
A sharp or B-FLAT

"MEDITATION" is the main function
to this card. It is the QUEST for
the UNSEEN + UNKNOWN. It is a
FISHING for truths in the depths
of Subconsciousness
THUS IT IS WRITTEN: "WHEN YOU
HAVE FOUND the beginning of the
WAY, THE STAR OF YOUR SOUL will
SHOW ITS Light."

Written on the back side of the talisman is the following:

Key 17:
The Star – Aquarius

The water bearer, airy fixed sign
Astrological symbol is

〰〰

Meaning,
"That which is above is
as that which is below"

They are naturally meditative,
given to the discovery of difficult, elusive
modes of truth.

Color is violet.
Musical tone is
A-Sharp or B-Flat.

'Meditation'
is the main function to this card.
It is the quest for the unseen & unknown.
It is a fishing for truths
in the depths of subconsciousness.
Thus it is written:
"When you have found the beginning of the way,
The star of your soul will show its light."

⚡

At the end of June, Sandy left.

Remember my friend Mike, who I grew up with in Pasadena, who I stayed with in Hollywood after Jenny left me? Whose younger brother, John, was the one who slept with Jenny? Whose youngest brother, Sam, and Sam's wife, Donna, hung out with Sandy and me in Hollywood? Well, when Sandy decided she was going to leave me, she took the kids and moved back to Hollywood, moving in with Donna, who had recently divorced Sam. Donna had talked Sandy into staying with her for a while until she sorted out what she was going to do. How ironic!

Everything having to do with love seemed to have come full circle in my life—in an awfully strange way—involving friends who I grew up with in Pasadena. So let's do a little recap here:

—My best friend, Jessie, slept with my first love, Katie—1966.
—Mike's younger brother, John, slept with my first wife, Jenny—1969.
—Jenny also slept with her first high school boyfriend, Kevin—1969.
—Jessie also probably slept with Jenny—1969.
—Jessie also slept with my second wife, Sandy—1974.
—Mike's youngest brother, Sam, his wife, Donna, talked Sandy into moving in with her—1974.

What a strange set of circumstances! Or, in the words of Robert Hunter, "What a long strange trip it's been!"

Five years I was with Sandy. This was longer than any other romantic relationship in my life.

I made a vow to myself . . . I would never marry again—ever!

⚡

what do you do
when your 2nd wife decides
she needs to go out
and find herself
because she didn't do that
before you were married

sometimes . . .
when you need real love
it still doesn't matter

wish there was someone
to confide in

lost in the struggle
of the tumble
. . . alone again

*just a heartbreak kid
with nowhere to turn
because of what she did
there's no way to return*

⚡

7/11/1974

*mr./mrs.
mist or magic*

*beginning glorious
ending tragic*

*missed her/miss us
mist or magic*

*beginning glorious
ending tragic*

⚡

7/11/1974

*fragmented in the corner
of my mind
sometimes you make me feel
so blind
when your love light
doesn't shine
. . . I wonder*

*this heavy feeling
in my chest
you could put my heart
to rest
. . . if you wanted*

*what else can I do
to make it real
trying to show you
how I feel*

*when I'm feeling blind
you could ease my mind
sharp pin pricks
—striking out
at the holes of time*

*wishing I had the time
and the rhyme
to have you need me
the way I need you*

*bring it to me now
I'm trying to make it
. . . somehow*

planted in the here and now

⚡

Now that Sandy, Shane and Celeste were in Hollywood, I had to drive up there if I wanted to visit them. Of course, Arthur was there too, so I could see him as well when I went to visit. I took advantage of the circumstances to bring Shane and Celeste to Arthur's house so all three kids could be together. His aunt welcomed us and would cook lunch or dinner for all of us when we came.

On my trips, I would stay with Sam, who now lived alone in Laurel Canyon. It was ironic that I was staying with him, while Sandy was living with his ex, Donna. It was the mixed up mess that was my life. Strange as it all seemed, I had come to accept it.

Sometimes I would go out clubbing with Sandy and Donna at Jason's, a nightclub in the Studio City/Toluca Lake area of San Fernando Valley. They loved dancing to the house band, Sweet Jubile. I knew the guitar player, Otha Young, who had been my next-door neighbor when I was still living with Mom. We used to get high together at his place. Otha had briefly played with my friends' band, Joint Effort, back when I was working on the Strip. It was cool to hear him again. He was such an astounding guitar player.

The lead singer in Sweet Jubile was Juice Newton, who would go on to be a superstar in country music. She and Otha were married and he wrote many of her early songs, including her #1 hit song, "The Sweetest Thing I'll Ever Know." She had a voice like an angel and the club was always packed.

One night, after a few drinks, I went up to her and said, "I bet I can guess your astrology sign." She said, "Okay, what is it?" I said, "Aquarius!" And she replied, "Wow! How did you know that?" I told her, "I just had a feeling." I was pretty good at guessing signs in those days and sometimes I simply knew, especially when someone was the same sign as me.

Whenever I could, I went to Hollywood to be close to my family. I tried each time to convince Sandy to get back together with me. She only stayed in Hollywood for a few months, however, and then moved back to Costa Mesa, where she found a small duplex for her and the kids.

I wrote an ode to our love. I couldn't help it. It poured right out of me.

8/2/1974

I'd like to tell someone
what your love means to me
I couldn't make it nowhere
without your love

everything I do
ain't nothin' without you
don't you know how much
I depend on your love

all I ever wanted
was for you to set me free
just to hear you say
that's the way you want me

now I don't know why
I feel this way inside
but it won't change
and I just can't hide it

well I've got to tell somebody
I've got to tell someone
I've got to tell someone
about the love I've found

I've got to tell somebody
I've got to tell someone
I've got to tell the world
about the love I've found

with a little faith
you know that love is free
and you and I . . . girl
have found the key

but when I come around
and you just can't be found
I think about how much
you mean to me

cryin' times are over—babe
now I know we can make it
I know we can . . . we can go on
when love shows thru

well I've got to tell somebody
I've got to tell someone
I've got to tell someone
about the love I've found

I've got to tell somebody
I've got to tell someone
I've got to tell the world
about the love I've found

↯

Meanwhile, something interesting was happening at the Gourmet Collective. Jackie, who worked in the deli department, had become good friends with me. She and her husband, Scott, often hung out with Sandy and me. We would go to the rock clubs together and out to dinner sometimes. They would also come over to our house, and we would all smoke pot and listen to music.

Right after the July 4th holiday, Jackie asked me if I would like to have lunch with her. She knew that Sandy had recently left me, and she was hugely sympathetic. She told me she had something she wanted to discuss with me.

At lunch, Jackie told me she had given notice and was quitting her job. She said that she and Scott were opening up their own deli in Newport Beach. It would be a German style delicatessen similar to the one I had managed in Laguna. Scott's dad had passed away recently and left him some money, so they decided to put it into opening their own business. Jackie said they were looking for a manager for the store and thought I would be perfect for the job. She asked me if I was interested. My life was already in disruption, so what did I have to lose? I told her I needed a little time to think about it, and she said that was fine.

I was only a department manager at Gourmet Collective, but I would be a store manager again if I took the job at the new deli. It would also mean a hike in salary, and that was the clincher. Although my life was in turmoil, I still needed to work, and this sounded like a fresh start—perhaps exactly what I needed. I called Jackie and said, "Count me in."

I gave my notice at Gourmet Collective, telling them about my new offer. I thanked them for the wonderful opportunity they had given me. They said I was welcome back if the new job did not work out. I left at the end of July, deciding to take a few weeks off before the new job began. As it turned out, the store wasn't ready for me to begin until the end of October, so I had the whole summer off from work.

After Sandy left me, some friends and local musicians would frequently come over to my place to jam and work on songs together. They helped me create a demo tape of songs with my lyrics and music we all created together.

One of my friends, Alden, came over more frequently. He was an extraordinary guitar player, and we worked well together. We were able to create what I thought were some great songs, using my lyrics as the jumping-off point. One of the best ones was from my poem, "Rhythm" (4/19/1972), which I had written in Laguna a couple of years before. We also made songs out of "Got To Tell Somebody" (8/2/1974), and "The Number You Can Dial" (2/6/1971) (all three of these poems are found in this book under their dates).

I could record multi-tracks with different musicians, using the sound-on-sound abilities of my Sony two track reel-to-reel. We ended up creating songs from seven of my poems, and we recorded some original songs from other members of the group as well. It was *bitchin'!* I learned a lot about recording from the sessions we did, and I expanded my musical skill set. I was not merely the co-songwriter—I was the lyricist, singer, percussionist, producer and recording engineer—all in one.

It was mind-blowing! I had been given the privilege to create with old friends, as well as new friends—working on my own poems and music. It didn't ease my heartache much, but I was beginning to make my dreams into reality. Who'd have thought? What a trip!

I was still drinking heavily. Some nights I would black out, or actually pass out on the bar, at Smokey Stover's, but someone would always deposit me at home safely. At least I was lucky in that.

I was downtrodden, depressed, and I could not stop thinking about Sandy and my kids. I dreamed of how it could have been, wondered what happened, cried myself to sleep at night, and welled up with anger over having been abandoned—thrown away and left alone again.

It was a little over two months since Sandy had left, but it all still felt so raw. I thought to myself, "Why can't I ever have a woman who is true—who is truly mine; one that I can genuinely talk to and who will always be there for me as I am for her? What is so wrong with me that those I love always desert me?"

9/12/1974

I am waiting
recuperating

for the love of a woman
who will make me forget about
all other women

. . . I am waiting

*yes I'm waiting
recuperating*

*to go with her somewhere
to all the good things there
. . . you know I'm waiting*

*and while I'm waiting
recuperating*

*a-gettin' down on bended knee
you know that's how it's gonna be*

*while I'm waiting
while I'm waiting*

. . . waiting on you

1974, October – 1975:

Soul Mates and the Black Forest Deli

In October of 1974, out of the blue I met Shelly. It was one of those classic scenes right out of a movie . . .

It was a Friday night, and I was hanging out at Smokey Stover's, as usual. Smokey's was the premier disco spot in the Newport Beach area, and on the weekends it was always packed. I was dancing, partying, and doing my usual drinking to unwind. At one point, I gazed across the crowded room—and there—way over on the far north side of the room—there she was! Our eyes met—and our eyes locked. We smiled at each other. It was as though we both knew something—something!

I worked my way through the crowd to where she was. The closer I came to her, the stronger the attraction was. We both saw it—we both felt it—we both knew it! I now stood before her, and I said hello. From that moment on, we were together and inseparable.

We danced all night long until the club closed, doing *the Bump*, grinding our asses together, doing what would one day become known as *dirty dancing*. We had a blast—dancing, drinking, and talking.

We went home together that night to her apartment, where she slipped into this baby blue negligee, then laid down some blankets and pillows on the living room rug, so we wouldn't disturb her little girl, Lily, who was asleep in the only bedroom she had. Shelly lit some candles and turned out all the lights. We proceeded to make wild, passionate love—all night long. Before we knew it, dawn had broken. We could see it through her sheer curtains. We looked at each other, smiled, and kissed deeply again, not wanting to stop.

Shelly was gorgeous! She was about five foot six, but slim, which made her appear taller than she actually was. I loved her long, straight, naturally blonde hair, ivory skin, and infectious smile—but I especially loved her deep blue eyes.

The way she smelled made me delirious—elated. Particularly at the edges of her forehead, right where it met her hairline—like peaches. Especially right after we made hot, passionate love and she still had little beads of sweat there—like warm, ripe, summer peaches. I could not get enough of her sweet smell. And not only there, as there were other parts of her that smelled sensuously sultry and gorgeously delicious. I loved every smell that was a part of her, and I could not get enough!

When Shelly and I fell in love, I was 24 and she was 22. I do believe we were soulmates, and she believed it too. We had been drawn to each other like magnets. From a far away glance across a crowded, noisy room, we had found each other. We couldn't take our eyes off each other, and we had to be together—right then. I know you've seen it in the movies, but this happened to us—for real.

Everything about us was magical. It was like all the classic things you hear about: we knew each other already from another lifetime; we knew what each other was thinking; we would complete each other's sentences; we would think the same thoughts at the same time. It seemed like magical things would happen with us constantly.

Déjà vu moments would often occur, as if some experiences had happened exactly the same way before. Serendipity occurrences happened around us because of our providence. Wherever we went, our happiness seemed to rub off on the other people we came into contact with. It was magical, and we both knew it. We were so on the same wavelength—with almost every subject. It was obvious we were truly meant for each other. It was uncanny.

We were both the same astrology sign—Aquarius. Also, as it turned out, we were both from Arizona. We were born in the same city, Phoenix—even in the same hospital, although two years apart. Yet we had both met for the first time in California, in our mid-twenties, in a disco, our eyes locking, coming to each other, knowing already . . . actually knowing without even speaking. Okay, I know you get it.

Our love was so deep, like no other relationship I had ever been in. Shelly wasn't a love like a steady in high school that I knocked up, and then dropped out of school to do the responsible thing. She wasn't a love like a hippy chick, high on downers, who picked me up on the Sunset Strip one night. And, no, she wasn't even like my first love, Katie, that first love that you never forget. No, this was different—way different. So much deeper, so much more profound on so many levels—in feeling and inspiration—in every way, actually.

10/7/1974

since I have met you
you've blown my mind—straight thru
seems we've found
what we needed to do
when I knew inside
love was waiting to get thru
seems the right way was next to you

so if I catch you in a frown
and whether the vibes are up or down
remember what we've found
'cause it's so nice to have you around

my mind is saying
you're a love weaver—baby
I think we'll make it for the better
and my heart is saying
you're a love weaver—darling
I'd like to stay close to you forever

there comes that time
when you've got to choose
you've just got to know
how to never abuse

*you've sewn up my wounds
you've patched up my blues
and we've both paid a lot of dues*

*when you decided
to confide in me
you set my spirit free
and the feeling that I can see . . .
I think it was meant to be*

*my mind is saying
you're a love weaver—baby
I think we'll make it for the better
and my heart is saying
you're a love weaver—darling
I'd like to stay close to you forever*

*you're a love weaver
you've sewn my wounds
you're a love weaver
you've patched my blues*

*I admire the fact that you're free
but what I am longing for, dear
is just to know you'll always be here
what I feel isn't jealousy
I know I'll never have to fear
and I melt . . . when you are near*

*you don't have to say a word
for there's something that says
more than any thought heard
what flows between us is so revealing
you can tell me . . . with a feeling*

*my mind is saying
you're a love weaver—baby
I think we'll make it for the better
and my heart is saying
you're a love weaver—darling
I'd like to stay close to you forever*

⁂

I took Shelly to my new favorite spot, the river I had found up the Ortega Highway. I told her it was a gorgeous, flowing stream at the bottom of a spacious canyon, with towering rock walls on both sides, and waterfalls nearby. You had to climb down a steep, narrow pathway to get there, but once you reached it, the water was wonderful—not too deep and not too swift, so you could lay in it and let the water wash over you. Shelly and I spent the day there, skinny-dipping and making love in the river. It was just the two of us. No one else was around. We had a small picnic lunch on the riverbank, and we sunbathed on the rocks alongside the river.

10/13/1974

just you and me . . .
riding the mountain curves
goin' down on me
I could hardly drive

climbing down the hill
to the sweet flowing river
. . . so clean
. . . so cool
. . . so inviting

just you and me . . .
stripping down
on the riverside
alone with nature
we've got nothing to hide

just you and me . . .
making love in the riverflow
naked in the sunshine
on this waterfall line

nature's beauty flowing
for just me and you
in the place I discovered
where love can get through

↯

Our lives were filled with bliss over the next six months or so, but also with mixed messages, none of which were Shelly's fault—it was all me. I was beyond conflicted! Sandy and my children were still so enmeshed in my life, and I could not honestly let that go. Part of me wanted to return to it—somehow, while a part of me was happy and contented where I now was. Shelly and I were so in love, and she was an incredible woman. She gave me the kind of love and communication I had never felt before with any woman. Yet so many circumstances still haunted me and, of course, it showed up in my poetry.

10/26/1974

*where do you want to go
what would you like to do
is there anyone you can count on
does anyone get to you*

*don't rely on fair weather friends
who'll smack you right in the face
and if you don't make enough bucks
you'll be put right in your place*

*you think you're very big
say you've worked so hard
to get where you are
well, I'd rather have one person
to understand me
than a brand new Cadillac car*

*a world that's run on money
you know that's where we are
a world that's made of love
could get us very far*

*lady luck will find you
remind you
mesmerize you
—then hit you
with her blinding light*

*she may not have been there
—before
to help you make it thru
but if you just hold on tight—now
she might*

*is a friend really a friend
or is he just trying
to use you too
you've got to know that
. . . eventually
your true friends will shine through*

*don't listen too much to gossip
it usually is not true
and don't be puttin' down others
who might know what you're goin' thru*

*a world that's run on money
you know that's where we are
a world that's made of love
could get us very far*

*lady luck will find you
remind you
mesmerize you
—then hit you
with her blinding light*

*she may not have been there
—before
to help you make it thru
but if you just hold on tight—now
she might*

⚡

I was about to begin my new job and Shelly was excited for me. I walked in the door of the Black Forest Delicatessen on the morning of November 1st, 1974. It was my first day as the store manager at a brand new business.

Black Forest Delicatessen was in a prime location in Newport Beach. It was on the main drag, Newport Blvd., which was the direct route to the local beaches and Balboa Island. It was right next door to Smokey Stover's, which seemed like serendipity to me. It was also directly across the street from Newport Beach City Hall, so I knew it would attract not only beachgoers but local business people as well. It would also attract people with money who lived in the bayfront homes in Lido Isle a few blocks away (where I had met Robyn).

The store was much more than a deli. Yes, we had our gourmet sandwich bar, of course, which drew the lunch crowd. We also had a meat and sausage case, with fine German meats. We received a variety of fresh bread daily and German pastries as well, from The German Home Bakery in Costa Mesa. We made sandwiches with their bread and sold loaves of it to our customers in our bread and pastry case—plain rye, Jewish corn rye with caraway seeds, German pumpernickel, white shepherd's bread, and whole-grain wheat bread. Whole wheels of natural cheeses from all over the world were on display in our cheese case—cut to order. We had a coffee section with a coffee grinder, selling whole-bean coffees from around the world. In addition to all of that, we sold fresh pasta and pasta makers, as well as other fine kitchenware, in a special gourmet kitchen section.

Along the south wall of the store was a long wine cellar with glass doors, all temperature controlled. It covered the length of the wall from the back of the store up to the front, where there was a door that led directly into Smokey Stover's. The top half of the door could be opened leaving the bottom half closed. I thought, *Hmm . . . definite catering possibilities here.* And sure enough, later on I set it up so that during the weekend nights, we could open the window and the Smokey Stover's crowd could order sandwiches and side orders directly from our deli. I was even more connected to the club now.

We also did full-on custom catering, for parties, weddings, etc., both hot and cold food. The hot food, other than our hot sandwiches, came from a local French restaurant that we partnered with for our catering service. We received lots of catering business from the Lido Isle crowd.

Jackie was the store's main proprietor. The other proprietor was her husband, Scott, but he rarely made an appearance. Therefore, Jackie and I ran everything in the store, except during our busy lunch hours and on the weekends, when one other employee, Sarah, helped us out. Sarah also worked for us when we did our catering.

I loved running a retail store again. I had always been a people person, and to me it was always a joy serving my customers and having conversations with them. Over the course of the next year, I would gain many loyal, repeat customers.

We had a booming first holiday season. We sold tons of gift baskets and did a lot of catering as well. We did so well that Jackie let me hire my musician friend, Alden, to help out.

Once the store was running smoothly, Jackie attended to it less and less, eventually letting me handle all the bookkeeping, banking, inventory, and supply ordering.

⚡

Before I knew it, the holiday season was over and it was 1975. Shelly and I went out to dinner for my birthday. We both had to work the next day so we did not spend the night together. I dropped her off at her place, then went home and made a drink. I sat down to drink it and started thinking . . . Here I am, 25 years old, married twice, three kids, and now single again with a brand new career. Wow! Besides all that, I had Shelly in my life, too. With all the heartache I had been through, it seemed incredible, as I hit the middle of my twenties, that all of this had happened to me.

2/11/1975

the go-between
lying unseen between the lines
must show itself

you seem to bring me up
just to let me down
when you know
I want to be around

thinking a lot . . .
about me and you
thinking about what to do

*but now this door that I've come to
I guess . . .
I've just got to walk thru*

*so open up and stay free
and please don't stop caring for me*

*I guess . . .
free is what I've got to be
but you're still very much
a part of me*

*it's a hard decision to make
when you don't know which road to take
you know . . .
I wouldn't want to hurt you*

*I don't know what to do
'cause when I found out
what you're going through*

*you know it hurt me
hurt me all the way through*

*I want to be happy
I've got to be sure
but some things
I just can't endure*

*when someone is narrow
too selfish . . . or lies
they seem to be the ones
who despise*

*and what they just don't realize
is that truthfulness
is where freedom flies*

*I'm free to be me
you're free to be you
but two-gether . . .
what we could do*

*so be open-minded
let it flow thru
'cause the truth is
what I'm giving you*

*I love you so much
I don't know what to do
I just hope'd . . .
you'd see me thru*

*the go-between
lying unseen between the lines
must show itself*

⚡

2/28/1975

*if you find yourself thinkin'
about what I might be doin'
baby . . . please give me a call
and if you don't know
what kind of plans to make
it don't take no time at all*

*so find out if I'm there
'cause you know I'm gonna care
about what's goin' on
'bout what you're gonna do*

*baby . . . if you want me
just call me
said—babe
even if you don't want to ball me
just recall how lonely it can be*

*if you think I was mistaken
in the love that I was makin'
baby . . . please let me know
'cause since I've been a-losin'
you know it's so confusin'
and I don't know which way
to go*

*so let me know
just how you feel
'cause you know
you shouldn't conceal
what's goin' on
what are you gonna do*

*baby . . . if you want me
just call me
said—babe
even if you don't want to ball me
just recall how lonely it can be*

*was I mistaken
in the love I was makin'
please let me know
or baby . . .
let me go*

⚡

3/24/1975

*you say everything
in the right way
and at the right time
and it's all right in my mind
but it's the wrong time for lovin' you*

*I'm sorry for what I've done
. . . to you
I know sometimes I was wrong
now all I've got is a song to sing
so let me sing it to you*

*you've got to live and learn
and when your whole world takes a turn
don't let it hold you
remember what I told you
—I'll be there*

*what does love bring
but hurt and sorrow
a feeling for today
a hope for tomorrow*

*isn't it strange
how people change
it's enlightening to see
what you end up to be*

*you've got to live and learn
and when your whole world takes a turn
don't let it hold you
remember what I told you
—I'll be there*

. . . I'll be there

⚡

And once again, the roller coaster ride that is my life continues . . .

In June of 1975, after only seven months in operation, the Black Forest Delicatessen was going to be sold. Jackie informed me that she and Scott were selling it and moving back east. She said the business was too much for them to handle, and they wanted to get out. I had the feeling there was way more she was not telling me—that she would never tell me.

This was a successful business. I loved running it and had many loyal customers, and I did not want to have to leave it. So I asked Jackie if there might be a way I could buy it. She said if I could come up with a down payment and some seed money, she and Scott would consider selling it to me.

I talked with everyone I knew about the opportunity, and I finally came up with two friends who were willing to enter into a financial partnership with me as long as I would continue managing the business. They would be financial partners in name only, investing money but not having any hands-on involvement. This was exactly what I wanted. I was incredibly excited. Jackie and Scott both approved, and we all moved forward.

In July, the liquor license was transferred to my partners and me. Then Jackie convinced me to put our seed money into the store account so we could start re-stocking the shelves and deli cases, so we did that. Scott was back east setting up their living situation, so there was a slight delay in them actually signing the store over to us, but I trusted that everything would be fine. That was a big mistake, one of the biggest business mistakes I would ever make.

Trusting people had always been my downfall, and this was a huge tumble. The day after I deposited our check, I arrived at the store in the morning to do my usual setup. My key would no longer fit in the front door of the store. I went around to the back door—no luck. I was locked out. I went to the bank and found out that I was locked out of the bank account as well. I was raging inside! I did not know what to do.

After a couple of days trying to find Jackie, calling her, going by her house, I discovered that Jackie and Scott had disappeared. I never heard from them again. They had stolen our money and locked us out. My partners were convinced I was in on it, and I certainly had trouble convincing them otherwise. I don't think I ever actually convinced them.

Suddenly it dawned on me—I was the bookkeeper. I kept all the store records, so I knew that the payables and receivables ledger had the record of our money being deposited. If I could get the ledger, I could prove our deposit and, along with the transfer of the liquor license, it would be the proof needed, to show that the store belonged to us.

I devised a plan. In the alley behind the store, there was a small window up high, next to the back door. If I could climb in that window, I could get to the ledger. I figured I could do it late at night when no one was around.

That night, I went next door to Smokey Stover's and had some drinks to get my courage up. After the club closed at 2:00 a.m., I sat in my car for around an hour, waiting for the neighborhood to quiet down, and then I made my move. Climbing up on some milk cartons, I managed to get the window open and slid my body through it, closing the window behind me. I realized I was a bit drunk. Still, I was as quiet as I could be, moving through the darkened store to grab the ledger. I had it in my hand and was about to head out the back door when there was a loud knock on it and someone shouted, "Open up—police!" I opened the door, and there was a police officer with his gun drawn.

The officer took me out into the alley where a police car with flashing lights was waiting. Evidently, someone had seen me crawl in the window and called the police. I tried to tell them what I was doing, but they said I was breaking and entering. I tried to convince them that I was the owner, but they said I was not in their records as being the owner at this address. I tried to convince them to at least hang on to the ledger so that I could prove myself in court, but they said they could not do that. They could not remove any property from the premises.

I was arrested and spent the night in jail for breaking and entering. Once again, Mom came to my rescue and bailed me out. The case was eventually dropped, as Jackie and Scott never filed charges against me. I found out that they told the police it was merely a misunderstanding.

Without that ledger, I could never prove I was the owner. I talked to a lawyer, who informed me that the liquor license transfer was not enough to prove ownership of the store. Without the store having been signed over to my partners and me, I had no real provable case. Everything was lost. I had no recourse.

About a month later, the store was open again. I went in to see what was up and there was a Middle Eastern man there. He said he had bought the store from Jackie and Scott. He was turning it into a Middle Eastern deli. I asked him if he could give me any information on Jackie and Scott, but he declined to do so. When I became a little insistent, he asked me to leave.

So that was it! My one chance to have a business of my own, to build on, to thrive—gone—robbed from me by my own friends!

The rough times in my life would usually inspire words to pour out of me into poetry. This time, however, I was too depressed. I did not write anything for a year . . .

1976 – 1977:

Breakdown,
The Road There & The Road Back

Shelly was my saving grace. Her love restored me—reassured me, and before I knew it 1975 was over and here we were in 1976. I was 26 years old. My 20s were now more than half over. Wow!

I went to see my kids and Sandy as often as I could, still trying (for some reason) to make things work out between Sandy and me—even though I also loved Shelly. I knew in my heart it was because I wanted to raise my kids. I wanted to be their main influence.

Shelly knew I was conflicted. She couldn't handle me still fawning over Sandy and dwelling on what had happened in the past, and who could blame her? We fought about it, and she broke up with me a couple of times over it, but we'd always come back together.

I was still torn up and confused over everything with Sandy and my kids. I longed for the days of family—my family. It seemed as if that was the recurring issue in my life. I missed my kids so much and I wanted to be the main influence in their lives—which I could not be now. How do you even express to someone what it is like to have your children ripped out of your life? It was too much to bear!

Watching them grow was one of the biggest joys of my life—their first words, walking for the first time, singing them to sleep, teaching them how to eat. I was heartbroken over all the other first things in their lives that I would not get to experience or influence.

Then there was Shelly. She was my solace. I loved her so, but it had happened so fast. I felt like maybe the timing wasn't right, because I had not had enough time to grieve, process my feelings, or get any kind of closure. But what did I know? I had no idea why life unfolded the way it did. Sandy, the kids and Shelly—wow! It was all so confusing.

Now, after over four years in the gourmet foods industry, I was ripped off, unemployed and depressed. I didn't have a new job yet. I had no enthusiasm for even trying to find a job.

I was having a nervous breakdown and I didn't know what to do. I couldn't eat, I couldn't sleep, and I couldn't cope. I was in so much pain, and I didn't know which way to turn. I had no idea what would become of me.

♫

I always have these dreams
that everything will be okay
but someone slept with my baby

they always want the bad boy
not the good boy

sometimes . . .
when you need real love
it still doesn't matter

*wish there was someone
to confide in*

*lost in the struggle
of the tumble
. . . alone again*

*just a heartbreak kid
with nowhere to turn
because of what she did
there's no way to return*

↯

As if I didn't have enough to deal with, right at the time when my life was in turmoil, my dad suddenly appeared. I hadn't seen him in three years.

That time, back in 1973, Sandy and I were still together, struggling to get by, raising two kids on only my income. We could have used some help from him, but instead he showed up one day—out of the blue, looking for money for himself. I hadn't seen him in years. I thought he was just visiting us to see his grandkids, but I should have known better. He actually was there because he wanted me to help him buy a car. He told me the one he was driving was on its last legs. The audacity! He had basically never been there for me, not even paying any child support when I was with Mom, so I guess it should not have been surprising. He was still a flaky, mean, selfish drunk. I explained to him that there was no way we could help him, and he left in a huff.

This time, however, he showed up to offer me a job traveling on the road with a sales company, selling housewares. He told me it was an easy job. I would be traveling, seeing the country, living in hotels and eating out all the time. Dad had always wanted me to be a salesman like he was. I would find out later that he got a percentage of all the sales I made—so it was still about him. But for me—right then, it sounded like a fortuitous opportunity. I would be getting far away from all my problems and heartaches. That sounded like a good solution to my troubles, so I said yes.

I told Shelly my plans and she was not happy. We had gotten back together after a recent blowup and she thought everything was going to be fine. But I wasn't able to express to her my feelings about my kids. I didn't know how to express that to anyone, even her. She thought I was getting past my feelings for Sandy and concentrating on her and our life together.

We both knew, however, that I needed to do something about my depression, and I could tell by the expression on her face that she sensed it would be good for me to get away. I know now that she had a lot more sense about things than I did at the time. So I said my goodbyes to everyone and hit the road for what would end up being the better part of two years.

↯

I was feeling a freedom I had never known. Having been married at such a young age, having a child at 18, then marrying again with two more kids by the time I was 22—there was so much I hadn't experienced—even though the hippy life was supposed to be all about being free. I was ready to make up for lost time.

Dad had not told me the truth. Direct sales was hard work. But I was also having a blast! I lost myself in the work, and I found myself again on the road. I rediscovered myself—by myself—who I genuinely was when it was only me I had to worry about.

Yes, I had had a nervous breakdown. And yes, I was now feeling free. On the road, being alone actually felt righteous. Even so, I knew deep down that running away would not fix things. I had run away before when nothing felt like home. I was feeling that way again—knowing that familiar emptiness inside.

There was a hole inside me that I did not know how to fill, due to my family disintegration and relationship failures. I had lost Katie, Jenny, and Sandy. And, yes, even Jessie, my best friend, was lost along with the others I had loved. His betrayals still haunted me. For the rest of my life, it would be difficult for me to have men as close friends.

There is a saying, *No matter where you go—there you are!* You cannot run away from your troubles. Wherever you go, you take them with you. Well, I was not aware of that yet, and I would not be until many years later, when I would become clean and sober (in my 30s). Then, I would work on my abandonment issues in therapy and regain a sense of self-confidence. I would find that alcohol, drugs, and even relationships, could not fill that hole inside me. Only working on myself, accepting myself, and finding a new foundation in recovery, would help me find peace. But that was years away yet. In 1976, I was still trying to fill that hole inside me with alcohol, drugs, and women. After all, it was still the free-love era, and uninhibited sexual freedom was where it was at. Women were on the pill, so it was easy to be with someone and not worry too much. For now, I could console myself with one-night stands, brief affairs, and living the fun life my new job afforded me.

I had never had much—always struggled for everything, but now I had money to spend. Several of my crew members were partiers like me, and there was always a good time to be had—with good food and good drink. Bars, restaurants, nightclubs, live music and dancing—we did it all. And we did it all around the country! Over the course of the next two years, I would travel through 30 states—extensively—plus Canada.

↯

7/18/1976

now that you've left me
I don't mess with games no more
I just look for warmth
when she opens her door

whether it be for one night
. . . or just the sight
I know when it's right

if I were in my time
and my space . . . baby
you'd understand

if I were in my time
and my space . . . baby
you'd take my hand

↯

I met a young gal in Iowa. She wanted to come home with me to L.A. but I said no. No way! I met a beautiful woman in Wisconsin, in a bowling alley. I wrote a poem for her:

8/4/1976

don't cry any tears over me
for we met like the wind and the tree

I floated here . . .
to your steady ground
not knowing
where I was bound

with your fair grey eyes
and skin softly browned

just think
about what we have found

we met like the wind and the tree
so don't cry any tears over me

I came to you
and you came to me
and it seems
it was meant to be

but as I leave you
and you go from me
think of our love
that was free

*think how good . . . love
we feel*

*think of our love . . .
so ideal*

*and maybe on another bright day
this warm breeze will blow back your way*

*for we met like the wind and the tree
so don't cry any tears over me*

⚡

8/20/1976

*white water rock . . .
what I want to say
designs along the highway
remind me of the day*

*when I was a kid
carefree and loose
sucking on a joint
drinkin' organic juice*

*I had a lot to care
no need for despair
the love that was in the air
was something we all could share*

*then you came along
you stole my heart
but in time . . .
you tore it apart*

*now I sit here far away
remembering the day*

*when love was young
and love was free
yes . . . that's the way
it used to be*

*love was like a dream
that had come true
remember . . . love
that was me and you*

white water rock . . .
what I want to say
sitting by the stream
remembering the day

⚡

I was especially busy on the road. The freedom of the open air consoled me as I traveled. It felt as if the open highway gave me something to look forward to—the next town and the next adventure. The more I drove, the farther I went, the better I felt. My optimism returned, but I had not written anything for months. Then on my birthday in 1977, watching the sunset, I thought of Shelly:

1/20/1977

as the sun slowly breaks
below the clouds on the sea
on the western seaboard
you're bound to be

it was coming to me
on a wave of inspiration
thoughts of you
like the waves on the sea

the thought of the sun
rising on the horizon
how it always shines
when I see you in me

the man with the shadow box
casting the sea
thank you my muse
for putting these words in me

the blues in the sunset
like the blues in your eyes
the sun fading softly
thru clouds in the skies

remember I love you
remember it's true
you'll always be with me
whatever I do

I wish you were here
to share this with me
so many things
we could see

⚡

6/15/1977

drivin' down
the avenue of tears
these are the livin'
and lovin' years

the tryin' years . . .
the cryin' years . . .
yes these are the times
of hopes and fears

crowded with clouds
and misty shrouds
workin' my way
thru the haze

bidin' my time . . .
'till I break on thru
gatherin' up the days

⚡

I was traveling with a sales crew of around 30 people, each of whom had their own vehicle. I was driving a '74 Ford Econoline van, which I had bought with my earnings. It was slightly used, but a great vehicle for carrying our products. We would all meet up at a big warehouse in a new city, where the company had already established a temporary base and flown products in. Someone from the company would fill up our vehicles with what we were going to sell: bakeware, silverware, pots and pans, and steak knives. Then they would hand us an inventory sheet of how much product we were carrying. We would spread out all over the city, or even to surrounding cities, to sell our goods to businesses and individual people, right out of our vehicles.

On a night I will never forget, our group was stationed in Lincoln, Nebraska. Several of us were staying in a two-story hotel on U.S. Hwy 80, a few miles west of the city. I was in a second-story, south-facing room. It was a Friday night and I was watching *The Midnight Special*, which at the time was one of my favorite rock-n-roll variety shows on TV. The show featured live performances by some of the most famous bands of the day.

Suddenly, in the middle of the show, a flashing PSA notice came on the TV: *Tornado warning! Take cover! Tornado Warning! Take cover!*

I had never seen an announcement like that before, and I didn't know what to do! I looked around the room to see where I might take cover, and it seemed as if there was absolutely nowhere to go. I couldn't fit under the bed. The space under the table the TV was on was way too small. I thought about the small closet, which I would have to stand up in—that was no good. Then I thought about leaving the room and looking outside the hotel for somewhere to hide. I quickly changed my mind, as that did not seem like a good idea either.

I went and looked out the south window—and sure enough, out in the distance to the south, I could see a huge tornado coming right towards me! As I watched, I saw lightning bolts shoot out of it and hit the ground, creating spinning lightning balls that rolled across the ground. I had never even heard of anything like that. I thought it was incredible, but it also scared the shit out of me! At the same time, I was hypnotized by it—but I still didn't know what to do.

As I continued to watch, the tornado came closer. Then it miraculously veered off to the west and away from the hotel. It finally disappeared in the distance and I sighed, relieved that I was safe and not killed in a tornado.

I found out later that looking out the window was the most dangerous thing I could have done, as a tornado coming close enough would have blown the glass out of the window and right onto me. I thought, duh! Boy was I dumb!

Throughout the approach of the tornado, all I had been able to think about were my children, especially my daughter, Celeste, who was now four and a half years old (I loved to call her Tara—her middle name). On the day after the tornado, I wrote this poem:

7/10/1977

Tara-firma . . .
On the ground
Lightning striking
All around
Striking . . .
In the night
Showing his might

Tara-firma . . .
Coming home
I feel so alone

For a song . . .
That's where I belong
What am I doing here?
It's not so clear

*In fact it's cloudy
All around
Lightning's striking
On the ground
It strikes so clear
And I wish you were near*

```
L
  I
    G
      H
        T
    N
      I
        N
          G
              .
                .
                  .
```

*Piercing the night
Striking . . .
When it's right
Like a thousand stars
So bright
It strikes
With brilliant light
Fierce and bold
It seems so cold
Leaving you with chills
Imagine
Riding a lightning bolt
Like a thousand carnival thrills*

*It hasn't been my week
But I'm thinking
About what I seek
To be freely going
Where I was meant to be
Just trying to find the real me*

*I know where it is
But I don't have the time
Working so hard
Just for a dime*

*But it's just like a song
    Or a dance
        Or a show*

*If you feel you are there
Then you know you can go*

*Looking out . . .
Through tornado skies
Lightning flashing
In my eyes*

*Show me the way
To get there
. . . It's true
Show me the way
And I'll show you*

L
  I
    G
      H
    T
  N
    I
      N
        G
        .

      .

*Piercing the night
Striking . . .
When it's right*

*Like a thousand stars
So bright
It strikes
With brilliant light*

*Fierce and bold
It seems so cold
Leaving you with chills
Imagine
Riding a lightning bolt
Like a thousand carnival thrills*

*Like an omen in the sky
You fly by
In my mind I can see
Where I long to be*

It's close . . . you see
Not far away
Just trying to find
A better day

Tara-firma . . .
Coming home
I feel so alone
And there's–
        L
          I
            G
              H
            T
          N
           I
             N
              G
              .
             .
           .

⚡

    Our crew manager, Ken, and I would go out drinking together sometimes when we were in the same town. We both loved to party and we both loved to dance. We went out to dinner one night while we were stationed in Birmingham, Alabama, and then went to a nightclub afterwards to hear some live music. When the club closed at 2:00 AM, our waiter asked if we would like go-cups for our drinks. I asked him, "What do you mean? We can't take alcohol out onto the street with us." Then Ken said to me, "Yes, you can. It's completely legal here." I was like—*yeah! bitchin'!*
    So we took our drinks and headed out. Ken said, "Let's look for an after-hours club." I asked him what he meant and he said there were private after-hour clubs in Birmingham where you could still drink after-hours if you were a member. If you paid a cover charge, they would make you a member for the night and you could keep partying. I was all for that, so we headed to a place he knew of.
    We went in, sat at the bar, and ordered drinks. I looked around and saw that we were the only white people in the place. I looked at Ken and said, "Aren't you worried, with all that cash in your pocket?" (Ken collected the company cash each day from the sales crews and had several thousand dollars in his pocket.) He said, "Nah! Don't worry. I'm fine."
    Suddenly, this cute Black girl came up to me and said, "Hey, aren't you Steve from American Bandstand and Shebang?" I was blown away that she recognized me, especially since it had been, like, 10 years since I had been on the shows. I laughed and said, "Yeah! That's me!" She said, "Well, you

gotta dance with me!" She wasn't simply asking. It was a direct statement of fact! So we slid out onto the dance floor and started dancing together.

Pretty soon, other girls were playing their favorite songs on the jukebox and wanting to dance with me. I found it significant that they accepted us so easily in their club. I knew that if one of them had been the only Black person in an all-white club, it would have been different. They would not have been made to feel as comfortable as I was feeling. So I spent the rest of the night on the dance floor doing some serious soul shaking with several incredible and gorgeous Black babes.

Meanwhile, Ken had made friends with the bartender, who turned out to be the owner of the joint. When it came time to leave, the owner said, "It's awfully late. I'm escorting you to your car." He showed a pistol under his jacket and said, "Follow me." I guess Ken had told him about having a lot of cash, so we had a safe escort back to our car. So, Birmingham! Yeah! We partied!

⚡

I was sitting in my van on the shore of a lake one evening—don't remember where, drinking a beer and smoking a joint, while listening to Lynyrd Skynyrd's "Free Bird" on the radio. That started me thinking about Shelly, since we had often listened to that song when we first started dating. I was missing her, thinking about how close we were, and wondering if there still might be something in our future.

8/17/1977

new moon phase
and rock-n-roll sunset
"Free Bird" flying
silhouettes shining

reflection on the lake
shining over me
reflecting in my mind
where only I can see

sitting on the sunset
stoned like Klaatu
drinking a beer
with nothin' else to do

the moon in the mirror
is shining through
for just me and you
and "Free Bird" too

*it's a new moon
setting on the west
the ducks on the lake
heading home for their rest*

*and I'm in one of the places
that I like best
resting here
from the never-ending quest*

⚡

I drove through Yellowstone and straight into Montana, where I made friends with a hippy chick in Great Falls. We kept in touch and met up again later on down the road, when I was working in San Francisco and she came there to see a friend.

8/20/1977

*deep blue eyes
with flown back hair
feels so good*

*wish she would
come along
feel so strong*

*love is sweet
love is cold
but thinking about you
I feel so bold*

*yesterday
           came back
                    too soon*

*thinking of you
and the new moon*

*love so free
what it could be
dreaming about you and me*

*the first time that I saw you
looking straight at me
I longed to be inside
your fiery love*

and it feels like the first time
when love was brand new
a love . . .
you just can't get enough of

deep blue eyes
with flown back hair
feels so good

wish she would
come along
feel so strong

woke up . . .
wish you were next to me
that's the way it should be
but you're gone . . .
time to move on

dreaming of you
hope you think of me
until the next time
we can be

deep blue eyes
with flown back hair
feels so good

wish she would
come along
feel so strong

ϟ

Leaving Montana, I drove due north—straight into Canada, and stopped off in Calgary, where I got caught up in the biggest blizzard they had experienced in 20 years. Great timing!

I was staying in this little motel when the biggest part of the blizzard hit, so I ended up being stuck there for two weeks. It was so cold you couldn't go outside for more than fifteen minutes without your lungs freezing.

There was a little cafe across the street. Every morning, I would bundle up as warm as I could and run as fast as I could in the snow across the road and into the cafe before I froze to death. I would eat breakfast and grab more coffee, then run back at warp speed.

Sometimes my mustache would actually freeze in the time it took to run between the café and the motel, and I would have to defrost it after I flew through the door and into my room. I would do the same routine for dinner unless I could get something delivered, which was precarious at best.

There was no way I could start my van to get out of there because my engine was frozen. I had wondered why I saw extension-cord plugs sticking out of the front end of cars there. Now I knew! Canadians would plug in their cars in winter so the engines would not freeze up. I was not sure where they put the plug, whether it was a battery heater or oil pan heater, but it allowed them to start up their cars with no problem in wintertime.

When the storm finally subsided, I went out to start up my van and my battery exploded. It actually friggin' exploded! I called a tow truck and had it towed to the nearest repair shop. They told me this was common for cars that did not have some kind of heating element. They said the water in the battery had frozen and expanded, and it would have taken awhile to thaw. It mostly happened to foreigners who were unaware.

Calgary was beautiful. It was a large, modern looking city with a river running through it. Being a city boy, I was happy to be there. So much of Canada is vast open land, so the city felt welcoming. About 50 miles west of Calgary were the spectacular Canadian Rockies, expanding north and south as far as the eye could see.

Calgary has a space needle like Seattle's, which is called the Calgary Tower. I decided to go up in it. Standing inside, at the very top, it is over 500' high. The view was *out-a-sight!* I could see the entire city and the Bow River running through it.

The immensity of Canadian land expanding beyond the city to the north, east, and south was magnificent to see. To the west, the majestic Canadian Rockies were covered in snow. I was awestruck! The grandness of it was mind blowing, and it engulfed me.

I pondered it for a while. I took some photos with my Nikon Nikkormat FT 35mm camera that I had recently bought at a pawnshop. The photos came out great but could not do justice to what I had seen with my own eyes.

I spent some time selling in Canada and did great because Canadians had never seen our products before. Steak knives and bakeware were the most popular. I was often able to sell to businesses in bulk, for employee promotions for the Christmas holidays. I was making lots of money and socking some away.

There was an interesting thing I found out about Alberta that was different from home in a cool way. If you entered a restaurant, you could not simply sit at the bar and drink alcohol. You had to sit at a table and have the drinks brought to you. Therefore, when you entered a restaurant, you would not be sat at a table of your own. They would simply sit you anywhere there was space, at shared tables with other people. It was different from what I was used to, but it was an interesting way to meet people.

I met this cute little Canadian girl in Calgary, and we had some *groovy* times together. She was young, had only recently started working, and did not have much money, so I took her out to nice restaurants and places she had never been before. You know the story about the traveling salesman. Yeah, well, that was me, I guess.

9/29/1977

Shahnah
      like the wind
           that rules the sky

soft and tender
      or roaring
           as you fly

Shahnah
      old soul
           leading spirits high

nothing can top the sparkle in your eye

for a woman
      you're so young
           you taste so sweet

softly spoken
      supple lips
           your kisses can't be beat

mature you are
      diamond star
           clear spirit of the sun

so young
      and yet so old
           a new life you've just begun

Shahnah
      like the wind
           that rules the sky

soft and tender
      or roaring
           as you fly

Shahnah
      old soul
           leading spirits high

nothing can top the sparkle in your eye

love me
      take me
            love me
. . . feel me love

take me
      love me
            hold me
. . . feel me love

Shahnah
      like the wind
            that rules the sky

—nothing can top that sparkle in your eye

⚡

I left Calgary and traveled north to Edmonton. It was another magnificent city with a huge river running right through it. I loved Canada! It was so vast and beautiful, with rolling plains that went on forever.

After spending several days in Edmonton, I left the province of Alberta and drove east into Saskatchewan. Now I was traveling more in rural areas, which I thought looked like the U.S. must have looked in the 1920s—wooden buildings in small roadside towns. Almost like the old west.

I ended up in Regina, a smaller city with a lake right in the middle, Wascana Lake. It was my last stop before heading back into the states and driving home.

What a *far out* adventure my months in Canada had been. It was a gorgeous country—majestic, wide open and welcoming. People all over the two provinces I traveled had treated me with kindness and respect. I would miss it, but it was time to go.

Before leaving, I reminisced a bit about some of the wonderful Canadian women I had met, danced with, partied with, and even had brief relationships with.

11/27/1977

we've both been through
the pains of love
and being alone
but there's so much
we could have done
before I'd gone

you like your independence
well baby . . .
I like mine too

*but you're my kind of woman
there's so much inside of you*

*you are the love
that could have been
but wouldn't take the chance
just couldn't stand the risk
of a four-day romance*

*love is when it happens
it's something you can't plan
so take it where you find it
have it while you can*

*in the times
when you are lonely
think what we could have had*

*believe me . . .
if we'd been together
it wouldn't hurt so bad*

*for thinking of love
that doesn't go sour
you'll remember
in your lonely hour*

*and what a nice thought
that could be
it could have been
you and me*

*you are the love
that could have been
but wouldn't take the chance
just couldn't stand the risk
of a four-day romance*

*love is when it happens
it's something you can't plan
so take it where you find it
have it while you can*

*four-day romance
four-day romance
just couldn't take the chance
on a four-day romance*

12/6/1977

*I am thinking of you right now
are you thinking of me
I am thinking of the warmth
where we could be*

*this feeling's pouring out of me
our love . . . it feels so good
this inspiration
doesn't happen enough
I wish it would*

*don't you see now
don't you see how
you've got to take the chance
        get up and dance*

*the dance of me and you
till the morning dew
the dance of me and you
. . . love anew*

*you are going your way
and I'm going mine
but we've got some time
. . . you know
time right now to grow*

*you say you fall so easy
that you get hurt
but you've got to take the chance
you make my feelings so alert*

*don't you see now
don't you see how
you've got to take the chance
        get up and dance*

*the dance of me and you
till the morning dew
the dance of me and you
. . . love anew*

My travels with the sales company were finished for now, and it was time to go home. I would get back right in time for Christmas. I thought about Shelly, how nice it was going to be to spend the holidays together. I thought about my kids . . . and everything else that would be waiting for me. The thoughts were good; they were hopeful; they were peaceful.

I headed south out of Canada, then west over to Washington. I decided to take my time and travel all the way down Pacific Coast Highway, the road that had defined so much of my life. I took PCH through Washington, Oregon and then California, all the way down to Orange County, where I stopped and spent some time with Shane and Celeste. Shane was now seven years old and Celeste was five. Seeing them made a wonderful grand finale to my two years on the road.

And I knew a major life decision lay ahead . . .

1978 – 1979, March:

Back From the Road, Return to Hollywood, and Stage Production

When I returned from the road, Shelly welcomed me back with open arms, and I stayed with her while I sorted out what my next move would be.

Her apartment was small for the three of us, so we decided to leave Costa Mesa and move into a cute little house in La Palma, a quaint little suburb between Buena Park and Cerritos. It was a newer, ranch style home with two bedrooms and a fireplace. Her daughter, Lily, would have her own bedroom, and she would be able to go to a public school that was close by.

I had a major life decision to make about what direction to take long-term. I was not getting any younger and I wanted to do something where I had some kind of real future, with the possibility of making good money as I had been making on the road in direct sales.

I had been living high-on-the-hog, staying in nice hotels and eating in fine restaurants, but it was super expensive to live on the road. I became thriftier in the second year and managed to sock some money away for when I came home, to hold me over for a while. That money would not last forever, so I had to decide what shape my future was going to take.

I was not going to be a traveling salesman anymore, as I wanted to be home with Shelly and close to my kids. I did not want to go back into retail in the gourmet foods industry either. Managers did not make enough in retail—barely enough to get by. You could not make real money unless you were a store owner, and I did not see myself trying that again without my own money to invest.

I knew what it was like to make decent money now, and I did not want to go backwards. However, there were few options for a guy who had dropped out of high school and not gone to college.

My new stepfather, Charlie Brown (yes, that was his real name), who Mom had married shortly before I went on the road, had offered me a job where he worked—in I.A.T.S.E. Local 33, a stagehands union in the entertainment industry, doing stage production work for television and live theatre in Hollywood. I thought about it during my time on the road, but now upon my return, I gave it more serious consideration.

I arranged to have another talk with Charlie about it. He told me that it was a good-paying job, with benefits, like healthcare and retirement. He said it was hard work, though, and long hours, but with time-and-a-half pay for overtime, and good money to be made if you worked hard and excelled.

I thought about everything for a while, but it was basically a no-brainer, so I took my stepdad up on the offer. Besides, that way I could be back living in Hollywood again.

We arranged to talk again so that he could explain more to me about the entertainment unions. He told me that I.A.T.S.E. stands for International Alliance of Theatrical and Stage Employees. There are many unions under this banner, all across the U.S. and Canada. Local 33 is the Los Angeles chapter that represents all live theatre union venues, as well as some television jurisdiction (which is shared with the various film Locals).

Local 33 works on the three network television studio lots in town: ABC, NBC, and CBS. They also work for other local TV stations, such as KTLA, KHJ, and KTTV. At these studios, they shoot mostly daytime television, such as game shows, soap operas, and talk shows, as well as some sitcoms, variety shows, and nighttime talk shows. They also do the news shows (both network and local news).

The film Locals, such as Local 44 and Local 328, work on any shows that are shot at the film studio lots, such as Universal, Sony, Warner Bros., Paramount, etc. The film studios shoot movies—of course, but they also do the big, prime time TV shows that are shown at night.

The film Locals have a different Local chapter for each department they work in, whereas Local 33 works in four different departments in its jurisdiction. For the most part, the film Locals do not do any live theatre, and Local 33 does not do any film.

Charlie then explained to me how the seniority group system works in Local 33. As soon as I started work, I would be a 'Group 5,' and I would be on probation for 18 months. During that time, whenever the union called to send me out on a job, I would have to go. It did not matter if it was day, night, or even the middle of the night. If I did not go whenever they called, I would be out! They owned my ass for 18 months—period!

After the probationary period, I would become a 'Group 4' and could apply for my union membership card. At least another year or two would pass before they would bring me up in front of the membership for a vote, and a 'member in good standing' would have to vouch for me. If I passed the vote, I would officially become a member and get my union card. After that, it would still take many years to get into the highest seniority group, 'Group 1,' which is where the best jobs could be had.

Once I started working, I would have a 'call-in' time. The union has a 'callboard,' where you phone in each day to get your job. The 'callboard' has a list of each day's job offers, for both television and legit. This 'call-in' time goes according to seniority. Group 1s' call-in time each day is at 1:00 pm—Group 2s at 2—3s at 3—4s at 4—5s at 5. This way, the Group 1s get the first pick of all the jobs on the list, and the rest of the groups fall in line. The Group 5s, however, cannot pick their own jobs, as they are on probation. The 'call steward' who answers the phone will tell you where to go. If you do not get a job when you call in, you are at the mercy of the 'call steward' calling you any time, day or night, to give you a job. And as I said, you have to go! Once you become a Group 4, then you can pick and choose from the list of jobs that are left when you call in.

Over the years, I would learn that the Group 5s and Group 4s did all the grunt work and heavy lifting, but on-the-job training was how you learned the skills of the four different departments Local 33 represents on stage: Lighting, Sound, Props, and Grips ('Riggers' and 'Flymen' are also part of the Grips department).

—The Lighting Dept. handles everything having to do with lighting/electricity on stage.

—The Sound Dept. handles everything having to do with audio on stage.

—The Props Dept. handles all the things inside the sets that are not tied down—pictures, tables, chairs, rugs, flowers, food and utensils, etc.

—The Grips Dept. (grips are carpenters who work on stage) handles the construction of walls, sets, scenic drops, and scrims on stage.

—The riggers handle anything that has to be rigged from the crossbeams high above—in the ceiling (grid) of the stages—such as motors, chains, pipes, hanging ropes, etc.

—The flymen work the 'Flyrail System.' The flyrail is a system of ropes and pulleys, balanced by lead weights, located on one of the side walls of the stage. The flymen pull the ropes on the flyrail to fly the stage's pipes up and down. Mainly grips and electricians use the pipes. The electricians use the pipes to hang the lamps and power cables used to create the lighting for the show. The grips use the pipes to hang scenic drops, curtains, and other pieces of scenery used on the show.

Besides the four onstage departments, Local 33 also works in construction shops. There are both television and legit theatre shops. They are mainly Carpenter Shops and Electric Shops, where the sets and lighting equipment are constructed and maintained for the different stages.

I would eventually end up excelling in the Lighting department, both on stage and in the shops, but I don't want to get ahead of myself.

Charlie then told me that I would have to wait diligently by my phone from 9:00 a.m. to 9:00 p.m. every day, for the first call to come from the union. I would need to be ready to go to work right then, or I would lose my opportunity. They might call this week, or it might be next month, but no matter when, I had to be by the phone to accept the call and go. If I did not answer the phone when they called, my opportunity would be lost. Once I received my first call, my probation period would start, and then they might call anytime, day or night. I would have to go to work on whatever job they sent me to—every time they called.

As I was paying for Shelly to go through nursing school, I decided to get an L.A. Times paper route to help bring in more money while I waited for the union's call. Because the paper route was early in the morning, it would allow me to get home in time to be by the phone—9 to 9.

1/12/1978

just sittin' here
watchin' time go by
waitin' for the call

so much to do
to get out of here
. . . this time
you know I won't fall

yes . . . bad luck has come
and bad luck has gone
and bad luck has come again

but this time
when I get out of here
you know I'm gonna win

*waitin' for my job
waitin' to move
it's time to cut loose*

*'cause it's the lovin' I've seen
the lovin' I've known
and it's growin'*

*a new day is comin'
it's been on the rise so long
and it's showin'*

*just sittin' here
watchin' time go by
remembering me and you*

*the plans we made
the dreams we had
. . . this time
they're gonna come true*

*yes . . . good luck has come
and good luck has gone
and good luck has come again*

*but this time
when I get next to you
I know we're gonna win*

*rememberin' you
rememberin' my youth
it's time to cut loose*

*'cause it's the lovin' I've seen
the lovin' I've known
and it's growin'*

*a new day is comin'
it's been on the rise so long
and it's showin'*

*waitin' for my job
waitin' to move
watchin' time go by*

*rememberin' you
rememberin' my youth
it's time to cut loose*

⚡

We were discussing my poetry one evening, and Shelly asked me if I could write a poem about any subject. I said, "Sure! I can write about anything! Just give me a subject, any subject." So she said, "Okay, write a poem about that fire in the fireplace!"

1/16/1978

morning-glory nightingales
dancing in the fire
shining . . . sparkling . . . in my mind
like burning embers of desire

glowing . . . spinning . . . brilliant glare
popping . . . crackling . . . here and there
flashing flames and tips that flare
dancing in the air

the fire is burning low
the night's been going slow
I love to see it flow like this
I hate to see it go

morning-glory nightingales
dancing in the fire
shining . . . sparkling . . . in my mind
like burning embers of desire

morning-glory nightingales
what's been found
awareness has set sail
turn 'round

⚡

I was having my morning coffee one day, while waiting for the union's call. I was remembering the times on the road and how much fun they had been. I got to thinking about the time our crew had been based in Denver, Colorado for a couple of months. There was this extremely cute chick on our crew named Linette. She was a stone fox—sexy and petite, only four foot nine and skinny, with pure blonde hair in a pixie haircut! She was from Australia and had come to the U.S. with her sister, Terry, who was also on the sales crew.

Linette and I decided to go on a sales jaunt together and headed south, ending up in Colorado Springs, where we had a great time selling, both of us actually doing well. We had a lot of fun together and had a brief, wonderful affair. When we arrived back in Denver, she loaded up and took off with her sister and another crew member to go up north into Wyoming to sell in Cheyenne. They wanted to go to one of the many fireworks distribution warehouses while they were there and buy a bunch of fireworks for the 4th of July.

Meanwhile, I decided to travel up to Boulder, Colorado by myself and do some selling there. I had heard what a great college town it was, and I thought I could have a lot of fun bar hopping while I was there.

I found this wonderful little cabin rental on a river a few miles north of town, at the entry to the Rocky Mountains. I called Shelly and she said how much she missed me. I told her I would fly her out to Denver and she could spend a few days in this cabin with me. She loved the idea and convinced her brother to watch her daughter while she came to be with me. We had a great time and I realized how much I truly did miss her. But later, after she left, Linette found out that I had been with Shelly, and that was the end of our wonderful, brief fling.

2/8/1978

you came here
from another land
a young woman
striking out on your own

everything here
was so new to you
but my . . .
how you have grown

now you know the way
of love in the U.S.A.

some will take you
love you today
then leave you alone
tomorrow

but if I had you
in my arms
you'd never know
that sorrow

oh Linette . . .
what can I do
oh Linette . . .
you make me so blue

and oh . . .
if I could get to you
oh Linette . . .
I'd see you through
and you'd never be blue
—anymore

you told me you came here
to get away
from a love that you
weren't sure of
to try and find yourself
and maybe find a new love

once we talked
till the sun came up
we seemed to come together
right away
we took a trip along the Rockies
we got closer every day

then you went travelin'
on your own
looking for a star
now I don't see you
. . . anymore
don't even know where you are

oh Linette . . .
what can I do
oh Linette . . .
you make me so blue

and oh . . .
if I could get to you
oh Linette . . .
I'd see you through
and you'd never be blue
—anymore

⚡

My experience being away from home and my success at selling had given me self-confidence again. Once again I felt optimistic. Moreover, I was with Shelly again—and glad of that. I could see our future together as being bright and beautiful. I could see ahead to our successful careers, her as a nurse, and me as a stagehand.

She wanted to get married, but I had told her at the beginning of our relationship, when I was still reeling from losing Sandy and my kids, about my vow that I would never marry again. I loved Shelly, but I obviously could not bring myself to make that commitment again. My mind was set on it. I knew, of course, that Shelly would have trouble with that. She definitely wanted to be married, but I always avoided the subject as much as possible—even though deep in my heart I knew she was the one. Shelly was my soulmate!

As I said, I had been helping Shelly by paying for her to go through nursing school. When she came home from school one day, she told me she no longer wanted that. She said she had met a producer who was going to help her be a model. He kept telling her she would be a great model. Soon after that, she told me she was going to leave and move in with him, because that way she could be up in L.A., where he could help her modeling career more. She added that it did not actually matter, because I was never going to marry her anyway.

3/12/1978

sometimes baby . . .
you hold me down
I think about the things I could do
but then . . . I love you

sometimes you say
I suffocate you
and when you get mad
you always threaten to leave

well this time baby
. . . so long
I've been hangin' on too long
I know it's wrong

and this time . . .
when I get myself together
it will be better

that's the way it's gotta be
so baby . . .
I'll see you soon

oh baby . . .
when you left
the last thing you did
was cry

*I didn't know you would
with our love
      or could*

*baby, when you left
the last thing you did
was cry*

*I didn't know you would
with our love
      or could*

*you say that you're leavin'
this time it's for real
you say it's a sign of the times
you just can't stay*

*well this time baby
I hope you know
I can't take it anymore
gonna walk out that door*

*I gotta find my own way
—on my own
but I hope you know
I still love you so*

*oh baby . . .
when you left
the last thing you did
was cry*

*I didn't know you would
with our love
      or could*

*baby, when you left
the last thing you did
was cry*

*I didn't know you would
with our love
      or could*

↯

*what do you do
when somebody steals
your soulmate
and she says she's leaving
because you wouldn't
marry her*

*they always want the bad boy
not the good boy*

*sometimes . . .
when you need real love
it still doesn't matter*

*wish there was someone
to confide in*

*lost in the struggle
of the tumble
. . . alone again*

*just a heartbreak kid
with nowhere to turn
because of what she did
there's no way to return*

♪

I finally picked up my first call for a job with the union. On my application for the union, I had listed sound/audio as my stage experience. I figured my experience performing on stage, as well as recording bands, would help qualify me for the union stage production work. That could be the reason that my first call was a Sound call, striking a concert at the Pantages Theatre for the rock band, The Tubes. It went smoothly enough and my on-the-job training had begun. The advice Charlie had given me was, "Shut up. Do your job. Listen and learn." It was advice that would come in mighty handy as I watched people who were 'know it alls' make a lot of mistakes. I listened. I learned. It served me well.

    I traveled back and forth to L.A. for a couple of months doing various jobs, day and night. It was crazy traveling at least an hour each way, especially when I was tired after a long job. Finally, I stored my stuff and left La Palma to stay with some friends who lived near downtown L.A., while I looked for a place of my own.

4/14/1978

*a temporary place to stay
to just get me through
. . . today*

*out there somewhere
is someone
who knows where I'm comin' from*

*and when I find out
that's when you'll know
'cause you'll be hearin' this song*

*it's warm . . .
and I can't sleep
I've been thinkin' about you*

*summer's comin'
it won't be long
you know I feel so strong*

*sometimes . . .
when the time is right
you know I feel so alive*

*it's early morning
the moon is out
and it's so quiet outside*

*it's been so long
the time is due
things come and gone
like me and you*

*but changes come
and changes go
and still there is
so much to know*

*'cause each change brings
so much that's new
and if I had a song to sing
you know I'd sing it to you*

♭

I found a nice little two-bedroom duplex on Glendale Blvd. in Silverlake, set back in from the street, with apricot trees in the front yard. It would be a perfect place for my kids when they came to visit. I found out later that it had actually been the ranch-hands' bunkhouse for the famous silent western movie star, Tom Mix, back in the 1920s. It was also directly across the street from a cool German Restaurant, The Red Lion Tavern, where I would often eat dinner and drink German beer on tap.

4/28/1978

gazing at the crystal mirror
what do I see
memories and longing in my eyes

all my life . . .
reflecting back at me
is there to realize

what is true
what I've been through
it's all there to see

but you cannot touch a reflection
like you can't hold the wind
that blows through the tree

all I can do
is to look and see
the things that shine back at me

like the memories of feeling free
    of walks by the sea
        of you and me

leaning on the sky
gazing in the mirror
seeing you there
seeing me here

leaning on the sky
gazing in the mirror
now the things I see
are crystal clear

↳

5/2/1978

*the plans we made
the things we gave
to each other
the dues we paid
worked like a slave*

*and I'm still working hard
yes it's true
but now it's not
for me and you*

*it's all memories
I don't believe it
it's all memories
I can't conceive it
it's taking so long
to accept it
I can't believe that it's true
. . . only memories of you*

*we grew so much together
for so many years
it wasn't always good times
. . . going on*

*although I was gone for so long
the feeling was still strong
as time . . .
as time lingered on*

*but now I know what's done is done
can't think in terms of two
of me and you—no more
I know the score
I know what I'm living for*

*take me back
to that place we were before
take me back . . . baby
give me some more*

*it's all memories
I don't believe it
it's all memories
I can't conceive it*

*it's taking so long
to accept it
I can't believe that it's true
. . . only memories of you*

*if time could tell how you feel
and you know it does
if love was really real
if you had felt the way I do
then our love might still be true*

*and now I'm sitting here
thinking of you
and all the things we used to do*

*of the full moon when it was young
making love in the morning sun
and all those little things
we went through
when we were one*

*take me back
to that place we were before
take me back . . . baby
give me some more*

*it's all memories
I don't believe it
it's all memories
I can't conceive it
it's taking so long
to accept it
I can't believe that it's true
. . . only memories of you*

*now I take time
on my own
and stay to myself
as much as I can*

*. . . trying to get by
. . . trying to make a stand
. . . trying to get where I'm going
. . . trying to break on through
. . . and these memories . . . of you*

I settled into my job, excited about the prospects of this new career in show business. In the beginning, I worked mostly in television, setting up and striking sets, or in lighting—on game shows, soap operas, and the local network news.

There was a bunch of us Group 5s who all came into the union at the same time. We would usually end up on the same jobs/calls, so we grew to know each other. One of them was Julian Chambers, whose brothers were the famous L.A. band, The Chambers Brothers. We worked on many calls together and became friends. One day, he gave me a special, limited edition CD, mostly given to only family members and close friends. It was the Chambers Brothers first album, *The Time Has Come*—one of my favorite albums. It always reminded me of that turbulent year, 1968, when we lost MLK and JFK.

One of the shows Julian and I worked on together was *Hollywood Squares*, which was shot at NBC studios in Burbank. We would mostly do the setup and teardown of the show—called 'load-ins' and 'load-outs.' The load-in would take a whole day. So would the load-out—after a couple of days of taping shows. The main set of *Hollywood Squares* was so tall, it barely fit under the top of the huge elephant doors of the NBC stage it taped in. It was maybe 20 feet high and 30-40 feet long. It was on wheels, but it was so huge and heavy that it took at least 10 stagehands to push it down NBC's giant hallway and into the stage.

Because my stepdad was one of the union's best electricians, I got a lot of Electric calls. I quickly learned that the electricians were usually the first ones on stage and the last to leave. Many considered it the hardest work of all the departments—constantly hauling large coils of power cable, and climbing ladders to hang stage lamps, some weighing 20 pounds or more. It was heavy work that most stagehands didn't want to do. Most wanted to work in Props or Sound—the easiest physical work. Group 5s hardly ever got Sound calls. They were the premium jobs, mostly sought after by those with the highest seniority. After my first Sound call on my very first day, I didn't get any more Sound calls for a very long time. I decided that learning the Electric department would be good for me, as I'd always find work—the work so many did not want to do.

I longed to work in live theatre (known as legit theatre in the biz). Having done my own performing live on stage, I knew the energy and thrill of playing in front of a live audience. Working backstage on events performed in front of live audiences was where I felt I belonged. There is something about a live show, not pre-taped as television is. Whether it is a rock-n-roll concert, a Broadway show, opera or ballet, a live show is a new experience every night—created by the energy between the cast and the audience. It's electric!—no pun intended. Later on in my career, when I acquired more seniority, you would find me working in legit theatre whenever I could. For now, though, I was simply happy to be working.

When the union did send me on a call in legit, it was almost always loading/unloading trucks and/or doing the load-ins/load-outs, for a theatre show or rock-n-roll concert. Group 5s would get called to do the show's load-in, then go home, while the higher seniority groups worked on the show itself—the 'show call.' Once a show was done, they'd call many of us back to do the load-out. So, load-ins/load-outs—load-ins/load-outs! That's about all the legit I got to see for a while.

Then, one day in May, I called in at my call-in time and got right in—almost immediately. The call steward told me to go to the Shrine Auditorium the next morning at 8:00 am—in the Electric department. When I got there, I found out that we were loading in The Royal Ballet from England. They would be there for several weeks premiering a brand new ballet, called *Mayerling*.

At the end of the day, the Head Electrician of the Shrine told me that I would be staying on for the run of the show as a deck electrician. He said to report back the next morning at 8:00 am.

I was excited beyond belief! My first legit show! I would be there for the run of the show—almost three weeks. I would find out later, the reason they needed more electricians was because there was a huge turnover on stage for the different ballets they would perform. Each one required different sets and lighting, so electricians would have to strike and set different things each day.

It was exciting. I was thrilled to be part of a working crew on a world famous ballet. In the course of my career, I would come to know that ballet performers are the hardest working people in show business. Their lives are completely immersed in, and totally devoted to, the work that they are doing. They totally live and breathe it.

During the show times of the ballet, I would stand in the wings waiting for any lighting cues. I would watch the ballerinas as they came up to the wing, rubbed their ballet shoes—soles and toes—in the rosin box (which made a crystal, crunching sound), then flew out onto the stage like butterflies in flight—effortlessly it seemed! But it wasn't effortless; it only appeared that way to the audience. Watching the ballerinas rehearse during the day, I realized just how hard their work was. They were amazingly dedicated people, and I instantly fell in love with ballet.

Each day, between our set ups, many of us would go to lunch over at the restaurants around the USC campus—which was close by. I was among several stagehands who hung out with some of the chorus line dancers during our lunch breaks. I ended up going on a few dates with one of the dancers. Her name was Denise, a very cute ballerina, who was a little shy, with an infectious smile. She reminded me of Linette, the Australian girl from the traveling sales crew. Like Linette, she was petite with a pixie haircut. But Denise also had a marvelous British accent.

I still had my Nikon camera from my time on the road, and I took some pictures of the dancers I knew, when they were on stage in full costume during dress rehearsals. I gave copies of the pictures to them when I got them developed. I even had an opportunity to take some photos of Denise away from the stage, in her various costumes. She even did some dancing poses for me. I still have those and cherish them.

The three-week run came to an end and the Royal Ballet moved on. My first legit show was finished, but it was one I would never forget. Denise and I kept in touch for a while, but then she stopped writing.

In early June, I got a call to go to Stage 74 at Sunset-Gower studios. It was an Electric call working for ABC, who had recently leased several stages there to produce shows. When I got there, I found out I would be working on the rigging of the new stage for the ABC soap opera, *General Hospital*, which was moving there from Cahuenga Studios.

I walked through the giant elephant doors of Stage 74, which were cracked open. It was a totally bare stage—a huge soundstage of four walls, with nothing but soundproofing insulation on them. On one of the far walls was a long, steep, wooden staircase leading up to the grid, which was also made out of wood. It was amazing to me, as it was something I had not yet seen. All the grids I'd seen in legit theatre and on the TV lots were made out of steel.

While talking to some of the other stagehands who were milling around, I found out that the Sunset-Gower Lot was actually the old Columbia Studios. The stages had been built in the 1920s, and many famous films had been shot there, such as, *It Happened One Night, Mr. Smith Goes to Washington, Funny Girl,* and the "Three Stooges" comedy shorts. From what I could gather, the stage we were on was over 20,000 square feet—humongous.

Bob, the head electrician, was a close friend of my stepdad. I guess that's why I got the call. Before the crew started working, he asked me if I would like to volunteer to be a rigger for the electrical dept. If I did, he would keep me for the entire rig of the show, which was scheduled to be about five months long. I told him I would love to be there for the whole thing, so, yes, I would volunteer.

I had not done any rigging before, but I knew it meant I would be going out on the crossbeams of that wooden grid, where there was the possibility of falling. That was pretty scary, and I wondered what I was getting myself into.

The grid was over 40' above the stage floor, and the crossbeams were about 3'-4' apart, with nothing but open air in between them. Because of the danger, riggers were paid an upgrade of $4.00 more per hour—hazard pay, they called it. That sounded good, but I was still scared about doing it. A guy named Brian was the other rigger that I would be working with, and he was an experienced rigger. That gave me a little reassurance, as he would be training me.

In case you don't know what a 'grid' is, it is an open ceiling area below the actual roof of a soundstage. The crossbeams on the grid are where you hang things that drop down to the staging area below. It usually has a 'catwalk' along the outside perimeter that you can walk around on to gain access to the different areas of the stage below. You can hang things right off the catwalk. Anyone on the crew can do that, but the riggers have to climb over the catwalk railing and onto the crossbeams themselves. They have to walk out on a beam to access any area other than the catwalk.

Bob instructed Brian and me that we would have to walk the beams to the points where we would hang all the lighting power cables that were going to be used on the show. This was in the days before personal safety harnesses and safety cables were used in grids for riggers to hook onto so they wouldn't fall.

I had never done anything like this before. Lucky for me, I was a normal, agile, 28-year-old, with good balance. This was not for the faint of heart! We hoped that those old wooden beams from the '20s were solid, and they indeed proved to be.

For the beginning of the rig, the carpenter dept. had riggers and grips on man lifts, who dropped chains and hung pipes on them, all over the staging area. All the pipes were dead hung from the grid and were about 20' off the floor, just the perfect height for the Electric Dept. to use for hanging and cabling all the stage lamps that would be used for lighting the show. The grips would also use the pipes for hanging curtains (called 'blacks').

Once the pipes were rigged, the electricians came in to hang the power cables for powering the stage lamps. This is where Brian and I came in. Over the course of several weeks, we hung 800, 20amp lamp cables for the show. We walked out on a crossbeam to each position where we were going to hang a lamp cable. Then we sat down on the beam and waited for the Electric crew to bring the coil of cable up in a man lift from below. Each coil was 200' long. With one of us sitting on each side of the coil, we would lift it up onto the beam, and then balance it there while we let in enough of the cable for the female end to reach the dead hung pipes below, where the stage lamps would be hung and plugged into the cables. Then we would tie the remainder of the coil off with tie lines that we had (by the dozens) hanging from our belts. After that, we would stand up, step over the coil, and move on to the next position to hang another cable.

Once all 800 cables were hung, members of the crew went up to the catwalk, while Brian and I went back out to each cable, untied it, and pulled the male end across the beam to the catwalk, where someone from the crew would grab it. Then we would feed the cable while the crew dragged it along the catwalk to a position where there was a giant hole in the wall. They would drop each cable through the hole, down into the lighting booth below, which was called the 'boardroom.'

All the cables were numbered on both ends. In the boardroom, someone would plug each male cable end into an appropriately numbered dimmer in a huge dimmer rack. The dimmer racks were then plugged into a lighting board, where all the stage lamps could be programmed for use in the show. On the lighting board, each light/lamp could be turned on independently, dimmed to whatever level the Lighting Director desired, then added to a cue for the show. During the show, the lighting board operator would bring up the various cues at the LD's request.

Sometimes during our break times, Brian and I would climb a steel ladder on one side of the grid, where there was a hatch that opened onto the roof of the building. We'd go out there and stand at one edge of the roof, light up a joint, and stare out at the hustle and bustle of the Hollywood landscape below us—and the Pacific Ocean to the west.

I was taking some pictures with my camera, mostly from up in the grid, looking down through the pipes that had been rigged, to the stage floor below. Then a birddog found out!

The unit managers were the onstage ABC coordinators, who coordinated everything between the union and management that had to be worked out having do with the show. The union members called them 'birddogs.' Stan was our birddog on the *General Hospital* stage. One day he saw me taking a picture and he approached me. "You can't do that!" he said. "Public picture taking is not allowed on any stage productions at ABC." I told him that I had been taking pictures since the beginning of the rig, thinking it would be interesting to see how a bare stage was rigged for a show. I added that I did not know it wasn't okay to take them, and I showed him a few of the ones I had already printed. He really liked them. He said that because I had already taken them, he would like to show them to some people on the main lot, to see if it was okay for me to keep them.

He came back the next day and told me that management would like me to do a photo shoot of the complete rig for ABC, all the way up to the first day of shooting the show. He said that once the actors and production company were on stage, I could no longer take any shots. He said that ABC would pay me for developing the pictures I would take—and a little extra.

So I took photos, from the bare stage all the way up to the first day of shooting. I took hundreds of shots, from all angles of the stage—up and down. I printed them and gave the whole batch to ABC. They ended up paying me $500 for the job, on top of the printing costs. Therefore, not only did I get the experience of rigging the show, I also got to photograph it—and get paid. Wow! It was like a second job on top of the main job.

Rigging *General Hospital* was a great learning experience for me. Bob was so pleased with my work that he tried to get me a 'staff' position at ABC, which meant that ABC wanted to hire me as a permanent staff stagehand, working exclusively at ABC. However, the union would not let me do it, as I was still a Group 5, and still on probation, but I got five weeks of work out of it, and I made a lot of new friends. I would go on staff at ABC some years later, when I had more seniority. I would become a lighting board programmer/operator, running the very first computer lighting boards in the industry. I would also be a Head Electrician, running my own crews on various shows.

✭

Even though I was working long hours, somehow I still found time to write poetry. Here is a story poem I wrote early on in my new career, but not related to work at all.

9/1/1978

memories of 1967

*you know you come
from down below
from the poor side of town*

*you walk along with your crutch
while she's dancing free style*

*you think about
how the bad luck has been
as you pass her by
while she gives you
such a free smile*

*but you could help her
with your common sense
keep her from being raped
by this world of difference*

*a world of difference
is where we are
a world of love
is where we could be
if we could travel
as far as we can see*

*things have come far
in such a short time
but people still live
in such different worlds
although they are
so close together*

*she is rich
and you are poor
she's used to money
you're used to being sore
as you think about all
the reasons why*

*but you could help her
with your common sense
keep her from being raped
by this world of indifference*

a world of indifference
is where we are
a world of love
is where we could be
if we could travel
as far as we can see

⚡

Not long after the General Hospital rig, I got a call to go to the Hyperion Reclamation Center, in Playa Del Rey, as a grip. It turned out to be just a fancy name for the Los Angeles Sewage Plant. I thought it was kinda weird to be going there for a stage call. As it turned out, we would be striking a movie set from the movie, The Killer Bees. I wondered why we were striking a movie set, as we were not a movie Local; but I had to do the job, so I did not question it.

As it turned out, the set was actually underground—down in a sewer tunnel! We went down there and it was smelly—pukey smelling. Not only that, but there were thousands of dead bees on the ground—all around the set. I must say, this was the strangest/worst call I had gotten from the Local so far. We struck the set as fast as we could and got the hell out of the sewer! We loaded the set walls onto a truck, and that was that. At the end of my career as a stagehand—almost 30 years later—I would still regard it as the worst call I ever had.

The second worst would be setting up Pink Floyd's *Division Bell* tour at The Rose Bowl in Pasadena, in April of 1994.

I was on the Sound crew, and it was a hot day—over 85 degrees—and outside. Most people in our union thought that Sound calls were the cushiest calls in the Local. This definitely was not one of those.

Several of us were given the task of hauling loudspeakers to the very top of the stadium, which was up 77 rows. To make matters worse, the speakers were big and heavy, so heavy it took two people to haul each one up the aisle to the top. Not only that, they could not be carried up the rows with one person in front and one person in back of the speaker—they were too bulky, and way too heavy for that to work. They had to be carried side by side—one person on each side of the speaker, holding its built-in carrying handle.

Unfortunately, two people could not fit in the aisle between the rows at the same time, as the aisles were too narrow for that. So we had to take turns—one person in the aisle holding one side handle of the speaker, and the other person climbing over the seats while holding the other handle—as we slowly made our way up the aisle to the top. Then we'd switch off, giving the seat climber a break to be in the aisle, while the one from the aisle took his turn climbing over the seats. Back and forth—over and over. It was grueling. We did this for 10 hours, with a one-hour lunch break.

Just imagine trying to carry those loudspeakers up 77 rows to the very top of The Rose Bowl—in over 85-degree heat! It was one of the most physically challenging days I ever experienced in the union.

The only saving grace for me was that I had bought a ticket to see the show the following night, as Pink Floyd was one of my absolute favorite bands, and they were incredible live. I could not wait to see them, and they did not disappoint. I was in a seat just above the field, so I had a great view.

Just as it got dark, a gigantic flower bud rose up out of the ground, right in the middle of the stadium. It rose up into the air, and then opened up fully—blooming like a real flower. As it did, it revealed fantastic lighting effects and laser beams. It was one of the best produced and best sounding concerts I had ever seen—besides *The Wall*.

I saw Pink Floyd perform *The Wall* live at the L.A. Sports Arena in early 1980. I went to the concert with my friend, Rick, who was the night manager at the Chateau Marmont Hotel. Rick and I did a lot of adventures together—and a lot of drugs. But going to see *The Wall* was probably our biggest adventure ever.

If you've seen the film version of *The Wall*, then you have some idea how remarkable it was. But there is no way the film could ever compare to seeing Pink Floyd perform it live—and for the very first time.

During the first half of the show, Pink Floyd played from behind the wall area, as the stage crew constructed the wall right in front of the band, using large cardboard bricks (2 1/2' by 5'). The bricks were painted white on the side that faced the audience, with the logo of a British brick company printed on the back of each. By the time intermission came, the band was completely hidden behind the full height and length of the completed wall, which stretched all the way across the arena—stark white.

After intermission, the band was set up to play in front of the wall, while spectacular lighting effects and animation were projected on the face of the wall itself. Physical reveals appeared in the wall at times during the show, sometimes with the band sitting up high in an opening of the wall while playing. Then, for the next song they would appear playing on the stage floor again, in front of the wall. At one point, an airplane came flying across the arena from front to back, and then it crashed into the top of the wall. In addition, there were giant puppets that rose up from the floor, inflating into three-dimensional animated characters, while rising up 20 feet high or more—some with lit up, telescopic eyes that shined down upon the crowd.

At the end of the concert, the wall crumbled down, smack dab on top of Pink Floyd—while they were still playing. The rectangular cardboard bricks had been carefully choreographed so no harm would come to the band members, but the effect was complete. To watch the wall topple down on them was an amazing sight! At the end of the show the lights came up, and I ran down to the stage, grabbed one of the large bricks from the wall and, in the midst of the crowd, dragged it out the door with me and took it home. I still have it.

↯

Back to the present time—early 1979. Since I was back living in the Hollywood area, I called up my friend Sam and asked if he would like to get together to catch up—and jam. He was glad to hear from me and suggested I come over to his place. He was still living in Laurel Canyon, where he had been since his split with Donna. I went over and we hung out, got high, played some music and had a good time. He told me he was getting out of L.A., as he could not stand it there anymore. He was heading to the country.

2/16/1979

I went by my friend's house
to say high . . .
what's the score
he said he don't think
he's gonna work no more

said he'd rather be poor
the way things is
'cause everything's just showbiz

he'd rather be outside
gonna pack up his truck
take it for a ride
take his last buck

go up to the mountains
till he gets broke
take some smoke
here . . . have a toke

he's gonna pack it up
ain't gonna work no more
he's gonna pack it up
'cause he knows the score

he's gonna pack it up
don't care if he's poor
he's gonna pack it up

then he'll trade his truck
for a couple of mules
forget all the gaul-danged rules

as long as he can
keep on eatin'
he won't have to come down
and be competin'
in the city

*it ain't no pity how he feels
watching all the people
in their automobiles*

*he's just happy
to be free
bein' what he's meant to be
work till 1980
fix up that truck
finish with his taxes
I wish him good luck*

*he's gonna pack it up
ain't gonna work no more
he's gonna pack it up
'cause he knows the score*

*he's gonna pack it up
don't care if he's poor
he's gonna pack it up*

⚡

Jamming with Sam started me flashing back again, to those exciting days of 1967-1969, when I was involved with my first band and hanging with our hippy tribe on Topanga Beach—with raging bonfires and music. As I was thinking about those days, a poem poured out of me, a tribute to that first band I worked with.

3/9/1979

*Rings of Knight
was a rock & roll band
they had the best sound
in the land*

*playing rock & roll
. . . all right
playing rock & roll
. . . all night*

*the people danced like now
it's true
the people danced
like me and you*

*but they were dancing
to rock & roll
rock & roll
with a lot of soul*

*Rings of Knight
was a rock & roll band
they had the best sound
in the land*

*playing rock & roll
. . . all right
playing rock & roll
. . . all night*

*they had that funky guitar
chicken-pickin' too
keyboards like The Beatles
drums that burst right through*

*and if you knew them like I knew
you'd want to hear them too
Rings of Knight . . . "Floatin' On A Cloud"
rock & roll . . . calling out loud*

*Rings of Knight
was a rock & roll band
they had the best sound
in the land*

*playing rock & roll
. . . all right
playing rock & roll
. . . all night*

*the army got some
changes came
and they never sounded the same
but still . . . the feeling was there
it was everywhere*

*Rings of Knight
was a rock & roll band
they had the best sound
in the land*

playing rock & roll
. . . all right
playing rock & roll
. . . all night

⚡

Speaking of music and bands, the guy living upstairs from me in the duplex, whose name was also Steve, was in a heavy metal band—The Claw. He was a bass player and we would jam sometimes. Bass and congas go great together—a solid rhythm section.

One day I heard some cool keyboard music coming from Steve's apartment, so I went upstairs to check it out. It turned out Steve was jamming with Doug Ingle, the keyboard player from Iron Butterfly. What a mind blower! I stood at the side of the room listening to them jam. It was incredible. They took a break and we all started talking. Then Steve said to me, "Hey! Why don't you go get your congas?" I said, "Yeah!" I ran down stairs and dragged them up to Steve's place, where the three of us jammed for several hours. We had a blast. It was awe-inspiring.

Steve and Doug were full of enthusiasm as they told me they were playing a gig together in a few days. It was at a soul club in South Central L.A. They asked me if I wanted to come and sit in with them. I said, "Hell yes—for sure—*far out!*"

The club in South Central was a super cool live music and bar scene. It kind of reminded me of that after-hours club in Birmingham, Alabama. I was absolutely into it. I drank, I danced—we played, we rocked. We clicked just like we had when we were jammin' at Steve's. The audience liked us, and they showed us their appreciation with exuberant applause and shouts.

I was thrilled that I had actually been given the opportunity to sit in with Doug Ingle, the man who wrote "In-A-Gadda-Da-Vida," one of the classic rock songs of all time, with arguably the best organ solo—ever, in the history of rock and roll.

1979, April-December:
Back With Shelly

Six months after Shelly left me, I received a phone call from her. Things had gone sour with the producer.

Both of us were living in L.A. now, so after talking a while we decided to meet. It was great to see her, and I realized how much I missed her. She told me she missed how it used to be with us, that she remembered how good we always seemed to be together. I told her I felt the same way and that I had never stopped loving her. We decided to try dating again and see how it went.

She told me she had started a job at KTTV, a local L.A. television station where I also did work calls sometimes. Once I knew that, I would look for her whenever I was working there. We would go to lunch and hang out when we could.

As we started to date, I wrote some more poems; some about us, some thinking about things past and present, dreams—of course, and anything else on my mind that would simply pour out.

4/12/1979

I'm down . . . I'm down
got to get back up again

I'm at the crossroads now
will I choose the right direction

my fear is that I'll have to
pay for the sin

of dying without knowing
what I believe in

hey man . . . hey come on
where you been . . . where's it gone

hey man . . . what you gonna do
look out now . . . it's comin' through

hey man . . . we gotta know
where do all the taxes go

hey man . . . when the west wind blow
you gonna be covered with snow

⚡

4/27/1979

your genius moods
are like unto a rock
—stone free

I wish I could be free to love you
free to go
free to be where you are

. . . expression
. . . tranquility
you are what you should be

—accepting
what you can see
realizing your own reality

once I went . . .
from this groove up here
back about a year

to what we were going through
back then
we just couldn't win

we were trying to make it
but we were trying too hard
to see

the undermining intimidation
of real feelings
trying to be free

in the light of day
it got in our way
. . . the trying

I'm done with crying about this
—for now
'cause we'll make it out somehow

we'll be what we're meant to be
growing . . . learning
—but freely

*I'll see you
in the true light of day
you'll see me the same way*

⚡

4/27/1979

*I'm searching . . .
looked over there
looked everywhere
but what am I looking for
just to grow some more

yes . . .
learning is a process
—life-long
don't even think
you've grown enough

a student of life
carrying your crosses
you know sometimes it's rough

but you are made
of tough stock
like a trigger in a cock
         position
your superstition is gone
knowledge lingers on

and where you are
dancing on a star
is where we all should be
—free
to learn what we will

wisdom is a skill
knowledge is a key
—both to get us
where we will see

be what we want to be
learning and growing
not just floating
like kelp in the sea*

*creative expression
yearning to come thru
it always brings me
back to you*

*what can I believe in
I feel like old days new
I think of all the trouble
I went thru
—just to love you*

*I lost my head
you ate my bread
now I'm down
lickin' my sores*

*I lost my head
you ate my bread
now I feel like
eating yours*

*I feel like a wretched
beggar boy
begging food
from you*

*even though
I'm in my own home
I feel like I'm stuck
with your glue*

*I can't break away
from what's holding me
but now I've got to
. . . got to
. . . got to be me*

*expression
freedom
at once I can see
a light flashing
blazing thru eternity*

*feel your . . .
feel your own pain
—look
—look again*

*it's all happened before
you know what the pain is for
so try again*

*forget her
and live your life
the way it should be
it's yours to win*

↯

5/6/1979

*oh Shelly Ann . . .
do you ever feel you can't express
what you want to say
because it's such a strong feeling
and words just get in the way*

*oh Shelly Ann . . .
the way we feel things together
at the same time
it doesn't happen with others that way
we really do rhyme*

*I love you . . . baby
we're alike in so many ways
and I think that . . . maybe
we'll be close for all our days*

*at least I hope so
—anyway
what more can I say
but I love you*

*oh Shelly Ann . . .
I'm not sure what you want to be
am I really part of you
or do you still want to be free*

*oh Shelly Ann . . .
hear my heart . . . can't you see
that no matter what you do
you'll still be part of me*

*I love you . . . baby
we're alike in so many ways
and I think that . . . maybe
we'll be close for all our days*

*at least I hope so
—anyway
what more can I say
but I love you*

*oh Shelly Ann . . .
why do I anticipate you
walking through that door
and why do you leave me
always wanting for more*

*oh Shelly Ann . . .
why does my heart jump
at the thought of you
and why could I never
really say we're through*

*because I love you
we're alike in so many ways
and I think that . . . maybe
we'll be close for all our days*

*at least I hope so
—anyway
what more can I say
but I love you*

⚡

When I first moved to Hollywood with Mom in 1966, we lived on Formosa Ave., two blocks west of La Brea Ave. and two blocks south of Sunset Blvd. On Sunset, another two blocks west of Formosa, there was a Pioneer Chicken. It became my favorite fried chicken in the world, and they even had baskets of gizzards and livers. Yum! I ate there a lot when I was a teenager.

There was another Pioneer Chicken on the corner of Sunset and Fountain, right where they came together in the far eastern edge of Hollywood. Now, in 1979, I was working one block from there at a place called Triangle Lighting, part of a larger theatrical business named Triangle Scenery, so I was able to eat my favorite fried chicken a lot. There was also a *roach coach* truck that came to our building during the morning coffee break, at lunch, and during the afternoon break. I loved their breakfast burritos and breakfast sandwiches. I would always get them with chocolate milk.

Triangle Scenery was housed in a big, four-story triangular shaped building, located where Fountain Ave., Bates Ave. and Effie St. all came together to form a triangle shaped block of land. Originally built in 1916, it had housed the Mack Sennett Studios in the silent film era.

Triangle Scenery housed a complete legit theatre ensemble of staging departments. We built all the sets, lighting, scenery, drops, and wardrobe for the L.A. Civic Light Opera, and we also built and rented equipment for other legit theatre traveling shows. Even the scenic designers worked there, creating the blueprints for everything we would build.

In legit theatre, the most common 20amp plug for stage lights at that time was called the 'Bates' plug, so named because it was created where I worked when it had previously been named Bates Lighting, before being changed to Triangle Lighting.

Triangle Lighting was located in the basement of the building. I first worked there as a basic bench electrician, fixing lighting equipment and learning everything about putting the lighting elements together for touring legit shows. After about six months, I was upgraded to the foreman position running the lighting crew. The carpenter shop was above us on the ground floor, as was the scenic art department, which painted all the scenery and scenic drops for the shows.

On the far side of the scenic art department there were these massive wooden frames, around 50' wide by about 20' tall. There were long holes in the floor and ceiling, which allowed the huge frames to travel up and down like an elevator, so the scenic artists could paint these massive, colorful scenes for the shows, which were called *scenic drops*. They would lower the frame to paint on the top of the drops, then raise it up to paint in the middle, then raise it even more to paint on the bottom.

In our department below, I would be working on some lighting equipment when suddenly one of these massive frames would come down and I could see the bottom portions of these beautifully painted scenes. When they were raised back up, which was most of the time, we would have to be careful not to fall into the 50' long holes where the frames would move up and down.

I loved running the lighting crew, building the shows and learning everything about putting on legit shows. Besides building and repairing lighting equipment, I had the opportunity to learn how to run the solid state lighting boards, which controlled all the lighting on a show. Later on in my career, I would learn one of the first actual computer lighting boards at ABC television. I ran the first one from Strand Century Lighting Company—the Light Palette #001! I would then be in high demand as a lighting board programmer/operator for much of the rest of my career, which would even include being the Lighting Director for The L.A. Lakers at The Staples Center in 2000-2001, working with Shaquille O'Neal & Kobe Bryant during their first championship season since 1988.

4

6/2/1979

hey baby . . .
I've got to talk to you
come on over here
let me make something clear

the past is gone
though the memories are dear
and if you wanted me
I'd be right here

but go where life is leading you
that's what you were meant to do
and that's what is attracting you
to the land beyond this life so blue

you've got to be a doer
    and do it
do what's right for you
    and get to it

a change is due you now
and what you've been through
—somehow
has brought you to it

you know you have come far
to the time to be what you are
it's what you've been waiting to do
and now it's here for you

you've paid a lot of dues
you know it's true
and now it's time to strike out
for something new

got to be a doer
    don't do it
don't sit around
    and just chew it

—but do it
get involved
find out what's going on
and you'll want to do it

*let someone know you cared
though sometimes you were scared
on how to show it*

*but you know that it is true
that what you are going through
is what you've got to do
baby—you . . . know . . . it*

*got to be a doer
    if you do it
don't be the one
    who blew it*

*don't just talk
like those who think they knew it
show them that you've really
been through it
—and do it*

*live the life
you've been wanting to live
give forth the things
you've been wanting to give*

*do the things
you've been wanting to do
—go
find out what belongs to you*

*got to be a doer
and go through it
got to be someone
who wants to do it*

*to go with you somewhere
share everything that's there
—and you knew it*

*catch it
    this time
        if you can
don't let those moments fly away
the feelings that relate to you
the things you have to say*

yes—catch it
   this time
      if you can
don't let it slip away
into grains of sand
on the beach of another day

got to be a doer
   and do it
do what's right for you
   and get to it

a change is due you now
and what you've been through
—somehow
has brought you to it

⚡

Although Shelly and I were both working a lot, we were dating a lot, too. It was the summer of 1979, and summer was always the best time of year in Hollywood. There were always concerts to attend, and, of course, it was the best time for going on picnics and taking walks in the park.

    One day we drove up to Fern Dell Park at the top of Western and Los Feliz. We took a picnic lunch, which we ate under a shady tree on a blanket. Then we walked on the stream-lined paths in the park—hand in hand, enjoying the warm, summer day, the beauty of the park and each other. Later I wrote this:

7/9/1979

going through changes
the same as before
but not quite the same ones
as we grow more

sometimes it takes longer
to get where you are going
though you realized where it was
all along

strolling down pathways
through the park
you by my side
in the dusk before dark

*seeking the road
of our longing
living the dream
of belonging*

*brown and red bird
in the palm
colours on the flowers*

*crimson burgundy
in front of tall green bamboo
—shoots
to white clouds in the blue*

. . . just for you

*sun through the trees
with leaves that tease
rustling in the summer breeze
somewhere to be at ease
with only nature to please*

*can you please me
or just tease me
will I know*

*I want to grow with you
but I really mean grow
I want to go with you
I want it to show*

*do you know how I feel
is our love really real
I've got to be me
can't you see*

*brown and red bird
in the palm
colours on the flowers*

*crimson burgundy
in front of tall green bamboo
—shoots
to white clouds in the blue*

. . . just for you

. . . just for you

Things were looking good again. I had a proper job making decent money, precisely like I had wanted, and I was excelling; making a name and reputation for myself in the union as being smart, hard-working and dependable.

Shelly and I were getting deeply involved again. We decided to have a serious talk about the possibility of moving in together again, to see how it could be. I thought I could have a real relationship with Shelly, and I told her I had room for her and Lily where I now lived. We decided to go for it and see what would happen. So now, our future was in front of us again. What would happen? We would have to wait and see . . .

10/30/1979

thinking about moving in together
. . . again
oh the feeling
how long it's been

it's almost like starting
all over again
I wonder if this time
we can win

the way you make me feel
. . . sometimes
like no other woman could

the things we learn
from each other
can really do us some good

if we can just hold on this time
if we can just hold on this time

hold on . . .
with your dreams baby
shine on . . .
with your life

climb on . . .
to my star honey
let go . . .
of your strife

*hang on . . .
to our love darling
and it will always
shine through*

*and we'll see it all
. . . together*

*and we'll grow
in
  what
    we
      do*

*I remember when we lived together
. . . before
each time our love grew
more and more*

*but when we lived
on different sides of the door
we wouldn't see each other
for six months or more*

*sometimes . . .
we'd both get so sore
and stubborn as we could*

*but we learned things
from each other
that really did us some good*

*if we can just hold on this time
if we can just hold on this time*

*hold on . . .
with your dreams baby
shine on . . .
with your life*

*climb on . . .
to my star honey
let go . . .
of your strife*

hang on . . .
to our love darling
and it will always
shine through

and we'll see it all
. . . together

and we'll grow
in
  what
    we
      do

. . . if we can just hold on this time

. . . if we can just hold on this time

Okay, so now my teens are over and so are my 20s. I'm about to turn 30, so I guess I have to go and be a grown up now — :(

See ya . . .

The End

. . . . . hmmm

Okay, I guess that ending was a little bit abrupt...lol. I honestly like it though, don't you?

But . . . for those of you who need or desire a little more conclusion to the story, a little more resolution if you will, here is an alternate ending that ties up some of the loose ends . . .

Then, just like that, it was my 30th birthday. My teens and 20s were over. I hated turning 30! It was hard enough that I was no longer in my teens, but no longer in my 20s either? This was indeed hard for me to take, and it made me take a long hard look at myself.

There is a saying from my generation, "Never trust anyone over 30!" But that's where I was headed now, so I had to ask myself, *What does this mean for me?*

Do I have to act like an adult now? I mean, I have always been the responsible one anyway, and I have always tried to do the right thing. Even though I messed up a lot during my wild, roller-coaster youth, I was always the one taking care of everyone else and making sure they were okay, often while sacrificing my own dreams. I had to make some serious choices at a particularly young age. I had no one to guide me. I totally went by my own instincts. I believe I did do the right things, throughout. I dropped out of high school and went into the workforce, even though what I wanted— badly—was to continue my studies to be an artist and musician. I looked out for those I loved. That was who I always was. That is who I still am.

After returning from the road, I took my stepdad's offer and went into stage production. Was this the right thing? It did seem like the natural thing to do for me, especially after how I had grown up dancing, working in clubs, and playing music—plus it gave me a real career!

Then, suddenly I realized it was not only that my teens and 20s were over, but that an entire era was coming to a close. The free love era of the '60s and '70s, both lustful and loving, was coming to an end. AIDS was on the horizon, and we would never again experience this kind of sexual freedom.

It was not merely sexual freedom that was ending, though. I would miss the hippy idealism, the spirituality, the simplicity, the mutual understanding of Peace, Love and the Brotherhood of Man. We hippies lived in the here and now and made the most of every moment. We were striving to help each other up, to keep each other safe. We treated others as we wanted to be treated—like the Golden Rule says.

Compassion and empathy ran deep in us. These were ideals that we could take with us into the future. We could pass our hippy values on to our children and even, as the Moody Blues said, "To Our Children's Children's Children."

So much had changed in the world and in my own life. I had a steady job now, in a career that I was happy in. It gave me the opportunity to visit my children more and have them visit me too. I was more involved in their lives, watching them grow, even able to help them financially more.

Shelly had a steady job also, and our relationship was on solid ground, perhaps for the first time. I know she still wanted to be married, but I was not quite ready yet. We didn't talk about that, though. Things were good between us, her daughter was in a good school, and we set about being a family as much as we could.

I still had a hippy heart. I still had my hippy idealism. I still felt youthful, hopeful, optimistic! Yes, it was sad to be turning 30, but I was happy with the way things were.

Where would I go from here? Well, I would simply have to wait. We'll see what the future brings . . .

Epilogue

Well, I made it through the '60s and '70s. I'm about to head into the '80s, the decade we will call *The Me Generation*—media-induced commercialism and consumerism, creating a thirst for instant gratification and a massive return to materialism over environmentalism.

As for what happens to me in the 1980s—my life will surely change, but in many ways it will stay the same. I will still have to work on other peoples' dreams to make a living, but I will find the strength and self-confidence needed to renew my enthusiasm for my own discarded dreams.

And what about love? In my 30s, love's betrayal will find its way to my door yet again, causing my disintegration into full-blown alcoholism, cocaine use, then crack addiction, which will threaten my job, my future—my very life! But I will be one of the lucky ones. In 1987, I will get clean and sober and come out the other side. Recovery will save my life and give me the ability to help others as I have been helped, not merely to survive, but to have the ability to live a fulfilling and meaningful life, with a strong foundation in my recovery. A new life and new love will await me. I will rediscover the artistic talents that have been with me since childhood.

At the time of this writing, I am retired and have been clean and sober for more than 35 years—part of another story yet to be told.

You can find some of my recovery story in my already published book of narrative verse, *S.O.S. ~ Songs of Sobriety ~ A Personal Journey of Recovery*. It is a poetic memoir that chronicles the first 10 years of my recovery process, written—like this book, in chronological order. It has been an inspiration to my readers who are in the recovery process, as well as to other readers seeking comfort in their own lives, or seeking to help someone they know who is struggling in the recovery process. That recovery process is what led me to the ability to finally write this book you hold in your hands.

1955
Route 66—on the road to Arizona to visit Nini

1955
My brother and me in Arizona

1965

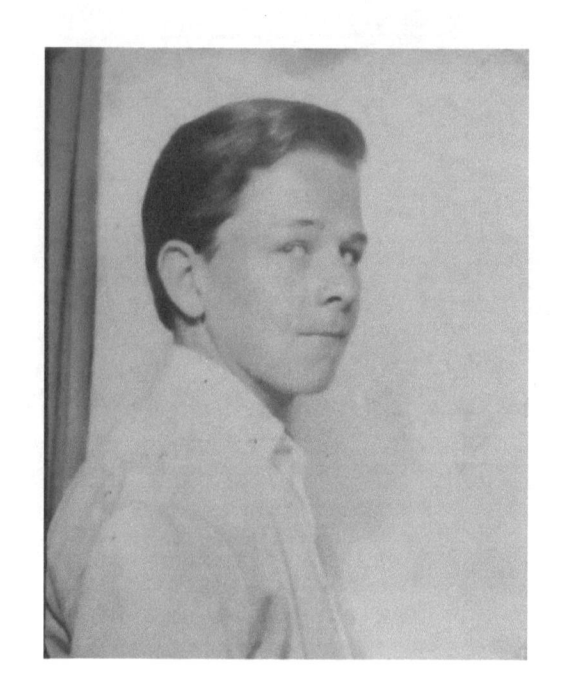

1966

1967

1967

1969

1970
me holding Shane

1971
in the handmade wedding outfit Sandy made
—smoking a roach

1972
behind the Orange curtain

1976
on the Pacific Ocean
(following my nervous breakdown)

1976
on the road

1977
on the road
(my 1ˢᵗ selfie)

Part 2:

Bat's Ass Blues

narrative verse
on the nature of perception:

introspection, fantasy and dreams, political,
social and spiritual/religious commentary

Selected from over 50 years of poetic inspiration,
this section was composed during the pandemic of 2020-2021

• • •

I am but a humble street poet
I hope you like my ramblings
I put them down here
to entertain you

Set #1:

self-perception and temporal contemplation

the bright-eyed man
walked wearily in the sand
deep in thought
he pondered the dreamers
and the schemers

as he gazed into the night sky
a shooting star
blazed its final request
and the bright-eyed man
beseeched the moonlight

how do I live my dreams
when all this reality
demands my time
to which the full moon
winked and replied

is this reality
or does it merely drift
on the mist of dreams
and imagination

* * *

my stuff is rough
it's bare bones
I hate to answer
telephones
I want to look you
in the eyes
when we speak

but it ain't no use
in this fast-paced world
to ride a horse
or court a girl
if you take your time
to get there
she's just moved on

and what becomes
of the alley cat
on the night
of the hard driving rain

when the lightning speaks loud
and everyone crowds
in the shelter
of warm window panes

I live my life
in a pot-bellied stove
I'm an oak tree
with ages to tell
I'm the earthquake commander
a green salamander
a salesman
with nothing to sell

but did you see me
on the night of the new
when everything changed
in an instant
the air was so clean
and the grass was so green
that a new age
did not seem so distant

in the quiet
an angel calls
—awakened
by the engine stalls
of the inner city
pondering its sleep

the dream is a draftsman
a hill-dwelling craftsman
a step in a puddle
on the road to forever
and life is a boat
in a great castle moat
we all circle
yet must row together

now is then
and yesterday's tomorrow
but how can we live it
like we mean it
when we're running so fast
that the race cannot last
and the space in between
lies unseen

or is that to lay
in a meadow and ponder
the meaning of
the wild blue yonder
the stars at night
or a daffodil
the momentum is great
as it rolls down the hill
of imagination
gone to seed

—I'm a wildweed!

why do I feel
so safe in the rain
and long to sit
behind waterfalls
I gaze at blue crystal
I tell tattered tales
and listen . . .
when eternity calls

maybe this just goes
on and on
or maybe the hunger
can't fathom the dawn
it's the spark in the dark
behind your eyes
when you sleep just the moment
and then it is gone
—and you weep

sheltering skies
pour forth from your eyes
and germinate the seed
of my fast growing need

—I'm a wildweed!

* * *

in the far reaching furrows
on the frontier of the future
beyond the fear-founded feelings
of failure
lies this moment

precariously perched in the present
—am I
and I tumble in thoughts
of the true path of passion
seems the fashion these days

and I find I'm amazed
by the simplest things
that a fresh moment brings

can I linger here long

may the seconds tick slowly
as I slip through the shadows
of serendipity sessions

for the plans that are painted
from the palette of presence
are most promising
    and pure
        and profound
and it's nice to be around

do I sense these sensations
for the same round of reason
that I'm writing these rhymes
to arouse you

are moments just fleeting by
—tricklings of time
I may come to
    I'm here now
        I pass them
            they're through

remember them fondly
they spark something new
the next measure of moments
that surrounds you

* * *

it always cracks me up
how a tree grows out
from the side of a rock
on the long road hill
of a mountain pass
as another speed demon
zips on by
in his lowered
little Honda

* * *

two voices drift softly
on the winter breeze
the heater crinkles
in this weather as it awakens me
from the dream of writing you
a poem
you soft, moist-kissing redhead
theatre goer of another past dream

you read me the ratings
of previous lovers
—the entry is mine
as I attempt to write you
the poem
of a young girl, sound effects and all
zooming down the hill
in a yellow boxcar racer

* * *

insignificant . . .
amid the towering concrete and glass
       structures
and mid-town shuffling pedestrians
       I live
          virtually unnoticed

my sturdy stem
struggling up through the crack
of a weather-weakened crease
of the seemingly never-ending squares
of this man-made walkway

my delicate yellow petals
hungrily reaching for the sun
       undisturbed

except by the passing gusts
of swirling city dust
on their way to settling
in dark corners
of trash can cluttered alleys

oh no—watch out—thwack!
a passing foot—kicks
  me into
   oblivion

* * *

tall ships
sail out on the water
into that long and lonely seascape
of never-ending horizons

so it seems
when you're on your own alone
so far from your home
in the highlands

the never-ending battle
the waves of emotion
they travel on your mind
as ships do on the ocean

to bring you to another shore
of intimate understanding
as you're peering through the porthole
for the first sight of the landing

the sounds of the sea
come back to me
on the quiet side
of my being

the love that's lost
beckoning me
back to the land
of believing

the fog is lifting
in the mist of mind's eye
the light is shining
from the shore above the sky

and I'm just sitting here
wondering why
I never went to sea
the waves break all around me

* * *

an aged tree . . .
struggles to grow free
from itself
its outer branches turned inward
twisting, turning
pushing in and up
then outward again
as it struggles
through life
throughout the years

—a countless calendar
for all intents and purposes
an ode of our inhumanity to nature
if it could speak

the prima-ballerina . . . retires

structured steel . . .
struggling to be free
of itself
countless cables of iron
twisting across, downward
around each other
then upward again
giant steel beams
pinnacle upwards
as if struggling for life

—a welded calendar
dedication of humanity
to science and entertainment
is what it seeks

the prima-ballerina . . . is born

poetry . . .
you are the ballerina
the song of your dance
takes wings in my heart

—it soars
it flies inside me
but you are the swan

poetry . . .
like a flowing verse
is your rhythm

your movements
melt together
like snowflakes
in the sun

twirl me into a trance
take all of me
into your dance

no feather . . . no down
your passion is poetry
—you are
the ballerina

* * *

I want my words
to be as beautiful
as a songbird sings
grace of a blue heron
soaring in the sky
harmonic inspiration
of guitar strings

I want my words
to reach you . . .
down to your inner soul
the love that clings
onto your heart
the feelings
you can't control

* * *

stature and cultured sand
colored pictures in glass
craftsman capitol
at the peak of persistence
eight ohs and ouches
hold you down

swimming to Ortega
on palm tree rafters
the cliff water singing
takes you home

star mania's gone at last
a sulky reminder
of the old days
spinning fast
on the merry-go-round
with sunglass shadows
under lacy eyes

penetrating presumptions
on a Sunday saturation
crash test dummies on the road
puckered lips and painted hearts
pretending to have weeks of fun
on a 40

you sit on your front porch
contemplating the world
and wondering why
but you're traveling
at the speed of light
right where you are

you flip your hair
and sip a cappuccino
a paper smile
and a single pearl
capture you
as across the room you gaze

why is a creature
of your beauty and grace
sitting alone
on a Sunday afternoon
a late arrival
and one of your stature
could not go unnoticed
in L.A. for long

homeless heroine
pushing a go-cart
the music is in your mind

reminds me of hipper times
freer rhymes
before mall entertainment
and patriotic peace-keeping missions

oh, ride me
on a window sill
and keep the colors coming
take bronco girls
in riding pants
and send them off
to boot camp

and the city
mirrors my peculiar
but penetrating presumptions
of the preposterous

a lost culture stands
in stained-glass wonder
multi-colored fragments
images pieced together
to form a crystal clear
picture window

through which can be seen
a life of warmth, compassion
faith and vitality

that vanished
on the rainbow mist
of a Sunday saturation

* * *

I'm searching for an answer
to the fading crack of dawn
the warmth of daylight waning
while the night goes on and on

do people just get stranger
or is something really wrong
with my depth perception

interject me with some feeling
signify it with some proof
you can understand the magic
that inspired me in my youth

and is so hard to come by now
seems no one has the time
to strike the message truly
fit the rhythm to the rhyme

the image is nearly frozen
the cast is almost bronze
the coolness of the chosen ones
whose hipness goes on and on

in never-ending sit-coms
on the ever-prevailing tube
until it infiltrates your psyche
like a perpetual engine lube

yeah— I'm still glad you are here
but you're a dim light in a dark room
It's hard to feel you when you are near
in all this gathering gloom

could it be you signify
the truth that has been lost
could it be we're poorer
all the coins that have been tossed

maybe we are all worse off
but just don't seem to notice
maybe we should just shut down
and blame it on the potus

I'm searching for an answer
to the fading crack of dawn
the warmth of daylight waning
while the night goes on and on

do people just get stranger
or is something really wrong
with my depth perception

* * *

down shifting . . .
why is everybody stopping
it's 11:30 at night
this lane will get me there
—quicker
a truck would say
if it could speak

as it slices its way
in front of me
like a freshly sharpened knife

is that a dog pound
in the back of your pickup
or are you just overly protected
I want to shout to the man
with the wolf hounds in his truck

as I punch . . . punch
the FM buttons
as if wishing
the right rhythms
with my index finger jabs

searching for a song
to sooth this momentary anxiety
of another unexpected
stop and go—off hour
freeway traffic jam

and for a jam session
I'd rather hear rhythm and blues
than nutra-sweet synthesizers
       gutsy
       straight forward
       to the point
       unpretentious
and you know where to stomp your feet

give me a dance-able
clap-able
three part harmony
with a low down bass beat
anytime . . .
(except maybe when I first wake up in the morning)

just in the . . . "Nick Of Time"
you come on the radio
as the traffic starts
moving again
and I press through the gears
while I hum along
to your bluesy guitar

passing the barking dogs
I look over
to the pickup's driver
who peers out from under
his crinkled straw cowboy hat

I wonder what soothes him
in moments like this
I want to shout
hey . . .
how about some Howlin' Wolf
but I pass

* * *

red light - blue light
swerving down
five lanes of busy freeway
smooth control
the traffic flow
for safety down the way

a man stands
by the roadside
his head bowed
to the ground
arms behind him
hand-cuffed tight
it's loneliness he's found

just another night
in the city
the many things I see
a thousand lonely people
pass me by

another night
on the freeway
it always seems to be
so many lonely people
wonder why

hurry people
on your way
don't take the time
to know
that even in the city
flowers grow

don't take the time
to see
the sunset by the sea
the skyline
or the moon
that shines above me

lonely girl
stands on a bridge
like she's gonna jump
into the air

people gather
while the next exit down
a helicopter circles
with a spotlight glare

lonely man
lonely girl
I'll say a prayer for you
I pray—somehow
you'll see the sun
shine through

tomorrow
    oh tomorrow
        no more sorrow
to see the sun shine
beg, steal or borrow

red light - blue light
swerving down
five lanes of busy freeway
smooth control
the traffic flow
for safety down the way

four youths lined up
on the shoulder
they've been out on the town
tonight

but they painted it
just a little too red
now four young faces
are full of fright

just another night
in the city
the many things I see
a thousand lonely people
pass me by

another night
on the freeway
it always seems to be
so many lonely people
wonder why

hurry people
on your way
don't take the time
to know
that even in the city
flowers grow

don't take the time
to see
the sunset by the sea
the skyline
or the moon
that shines above me

all the lonely people
I see
I'll say a prayer for you
I pray—somehow
you'll see the sun
shine through

tomorrow
    oh tomorrow
        no more sorrow
to see the sun shine
beg, steal or borrow

* * *

sand dollar
burgundy
ruby tears
create a sea
tainted scent
washes over me
reminds me of
the rowdy years

wind and waves
and spirit clusters
ink the earth-bound rust
—that lusters
love's first revelry
tossed aside
in the night

pray once more
that bare skin
bothers
cover up
the last clear
hollows
friend and foe
defend the midnight
from the mourning call

send 'round your parrots
    ravens
    blue wings
stir your pain
with sack-worn seeds
don't forget
to burn the candles
—bright
on Hallow's Eve

see the clear-lit
cast of curtains
part the time
that now is certain
steal the wheel
that stands
at beckoned call

turn it quick
before the tide shift
hungers for
the morning's fog lift
nothing's left
to keep the night
in check

did you catch
the screaming cattails
drenched in flames
behind the wind gales
broke the spell
just 'fore the break of day
and just in time
night
    slipped
        away

periwinkle pitchfork / shredded on the moon / can you find December / in the saddest part of June / it's a broken danger / morning crafter mend / can it be forever / in the caterpillar pen / written on the frowning / spoken on the brow / can it ever bring specific / meaning to the now / it's a crude demeanor / a progress to discover / you know you've never seen her / when she's running to recover / apoplectic heart song / in the USA / if you got the words wrong / fly to Mandalay / damn it all / sing it loud / come on man / let's go / if you got your ticket / then let's hurry to the show / tap to speak or Google it / grandeur on the grange / if you can still hop a horse / it's home on the range / gather in groups / like lettuce / crunch in your mouth / like ice / scattered like leaves / in the bellowing wind / damn / we've now gone to it twice / will it ever / be the same / if we don't race to the end / can you ignore it / can you explore it / isn't it just round the bend / why did it ever / demand us / why did it ever / play loud / why did it ever / infect us / and cover us in the dark shroud / come I implore you / down to the sea / watch the sun set / like it always could be / dance in the moonlight / dance in the sun / hold me forever / 'cause it's just begun

Set #2:

paid my dues
for the retrospective blues

life is like a river
that's been tearin' thru the ground
sometimes it moves so quickly
you can't know where it's bound

and then . . . sometimes . . . it's very still
it doesn't make a sound
oh, woman . . . when I need you so
you never are around

life is all around you
every day you prove it true
but until you see your life alone
life will remain something new

so if you're ever lonely
and you need some company
if you want someone who really cares
then come and stand by me

* * *

scraping the sand off the bottom
following tracks long forgotten
footsteps erased from time
miracles in the distance
—a very steep climb

it's time to light the perspective view
of the endless new
because you've followed the dreams
through the years
seen the highs, the lows
and the tears
overcome the fears
and the magic soothes your troubled soul
but where is thee—control

the waves know it
for they calm when I sing
the sun knows it
for it shines when I bring it to you
why lose your grasp
of the true path
don't get caught in the net
don't forget 7th heaven

there are so many bumps
on this cross-track blues road
a note of notion
by the heartbreaking ocean

musical sparks made us aware
a sign of the times was in the air
so patch it up
like the seams in your jeans
remember the magic
we had in our teens
the magic soothes your troubled soul
oh, where is thee—control

don't ever forget
the dreamers and the schemers
the seedy greeters
greed to the max
no pacts or parcels full of caring
for the sharing of your soul
oh, where is thee—control

times so rare and friends so few
where has it gone
and what has it gotten you
time swings in the miracle swing
what time is this notion you bring
and the magic . . .
soothes your troubled soul
but where is thee—control

why do I dwell on this dogma
causes caused
cautioned by the wind
the business grin begins again
is the sparkle burnt to the crisp
in the wisp of time
did you forget how to shine

save it for the savior
save it for the sun
can you be wild—and still be true
is it still inside of you

the anonymous enemy
pays the dues for your blues
show him what is real again
and believe you can still
see your dreams

for the schemer always schemes
and the dreamer always dreams
and the magic . . .
soothes your troubled soul
but where is thee—control

the magic of your touch
seemed so much
when it was true
      seems I knew you
      seems I knew you

the indefinable nature
of the true magic we found
will always be inside me
it is always there, unbound
I will never forget you
though your manic ways took their toll
and the magic . . . soothes your troubled soul
but where is thee—control

* * *

the soft brightening stars
were calling my name
return to the ocean
from where sprang life's game

they kept right on calling
till I finally knew
that I must go down now
or forever be blue

got the blues in my body
the blues in my soul
they're quicker than lightning
and hotter than coal

if you don't come back darlin'
you know that I'm crying
you said you don't want me
I feel like I'm dying

baby . . . baby . . . baby
if you could see me now
you'd know me
oh, baby . . . baby
if you wanted to
you'd show me

but baby . . . oh, baby
you're gone
bye baby . . . bye baby
bye-bye

* * *

I am camping, finally, on the beach
shadow boxing with the gulls
out of reach now
from the bitterness—the wrench
wishing I could take it all back

I slow down finally
linger with the sunset
and my crackling fire
. . . needing you
yet the unstated desire
of our unsettled difference
is a thorn, a blindfold

lying in my sleeping bag
staring up at the sky
I think about you
your ugly, empty, airless apartment
the words we screamed at each other
bouncing off the tear-stained walls

how I wish so many things
were not spoken
how I dream of our love
when it was new

here I am . . .
thinking of you still
can't get the ugliness
out of the bed
oh, the sleeping bag
contains the body
but not the soul-wrenching head

* * *

I never had a real mentor
I had to fight my way
through this dark ol' jungle
on my own

I did have a hero though
old sweet Winston
but he died and left me here
all alone

then you came along
and gave me some solace
—some sweet love
and a clear reprieve

but every time I got too close
that black cloud would come creepin'
—hit me hard
and you'd just up and leave

you'd act like I was your man
love me hard and fast
then play aloof
like I didn't know the score

then you'd swoop down again
from your dark and danky perch
to bite me in the ass
once more

I got the bat's ass blues
on the porcupine highway
might as well be
on the highway to hell

'cause I fell off the barstool
when you rode off in the night
and left me hangin' high
at the River Ridge hotel

got the bat's ass blues
you know I paid my dues
to come down from your spell
—oh well

got the bat's ass blues
from my head down to my shoes
you bit me
and it all went to hell

drivin' along
that Snake River Canyon
just to hear some bangin'
on those 88's

I only came to help you
a friend in need
screamin' down the highway
through those western states

we all were on your side
but you didn't want to hear it
you said you would be true
but you coughed it up again

just another excuse
for your hot and sultry lust
that left me—just crumbled
in the end

you said you were gonna stop
yer awful cheatin' ways
that always left you hollow
and sore

but the road is always callin' you
just wanna move on
leave me suckin' those blues
once more

I got the bat's ass blues
on the porcupine highway
might as well be
on the highway to hell

'cause I fell off the barstool
when you rode off in the night
and left me hangin' high
at that heartache hotel

got the bat's ass blues
you know I paid my dues
to come down from your spell
—oh well

got the bat's ass blues
from my head down to my shoes
you bit me
and it all went to hell

said you didn't wanna hurt me
didn't wanna do no harm
you just wanna feel secure
safe and warm

the good times are so rare
only here for a brief moment
then the bad things creep back in
like a storm

got the bat's ass blues
you know I paid my dues
to come down from your spell
—oh well

got the bat's ass blues
from my head down to my shoes
you bit me
and it all went to hell

* * *

you just can't tell
how strong this loneliness is
ages of wondering
where did it all go so wrong

chords of passion crying
multitudes of denying
always craving feelings
that don't belong

and you . . .
with your wanderlust
lost in the moons of your madness
gerrymandering the colors
and misgivings of your sadness

I saw you there with eyes closed
in the growing clouds of bother
never thinking to give a damn
just another marauder

and just like lies that linger
and eat away at truth
you just can't tell
where you might end up
this far from your youth

I've seen it all before
the grandeur and the shorts
always dragged
to the drowning death
by you and your cohorts

and never does it rise above
the shouts of love's despair
it just goes 'round & 'round again
and vanishes like vapor
in the air
—without a care

dismal, dark and dreary
it all has now become
and how can we ever
bring it back
to the warmth of the new day sun

I beg you and beseech you now
to stop this craven call
before you destroy
everything we dreamed of
and a final fate comes to call

moments of clarity
structuring the strengths of solitude
can mesmerize your mind
in the interlude

ring the bell, ring it loud
in the music machine of your mind
tell the tale, bring it home
if you could be so kind

the outside sadness
of madness
always leaves us alone
remembering the shadows
of gladness
for the love that could have grown

so don't forget
it could help you yet
return to the time
of compassion

and you will see
you won't regret
all the love
that it can fashion

* * *

   is it enough
that it seems so confusing
   is it enough
that it hurts when you're losing
   is it enough
that you feel so alone
   is it enough

   is it enough
that her love you can't keep
   is it enough
that you can't get to sleep
   is it enough
that you want to go home
   is it enough

   is it enough
that it's hard when you fall
   is it enough
that you just want to crawl
   is it enough
that it all seems so cold
   is it enough

   is it enough
that you feel so abandoned
   is it enough
that you feel like you're stranded

    is it enough
that you're just feeling old
    is it enough

* * *

when butterflies scream
no one listens
but the daffodils
wither and die

when you left me . . .
the white clouds stood still
they welled up inside
and just cried

I don't need the bacon
I don't need the grease
I don't need the glass
that has shattered the peace

I don't need the rainbows
I don't need the sun
I just need you, darling
but you're on the run

send in the shadows
that no longer hide
even the lightning
has taken a bride

send down the showers
of reckoning steel
melt in the moment
of heartache's conceal

damn it all anyway
what does it matter
—it is hit
—it is whacked
just fell in a splatter

the love that just melted
or never was there
it begged you to differ
but why would you care

* * *

standing here
at the edge of the bar
wine glass in my hand
my eyes are red
and you can see their sadness
but I just don't understand

why won't you come over
and talk to me
I want to be a part of you
you all seem so happy
but I just don't know
what to do

I've got these silent, withdrawn
barroom blues again
don't know how
I can go on anymore
I think it's the end

I've got these silent, withdrawn
barroom blues
once again
and no matter what happens
It seems like I just can't win

why am I here alone
at the end of the bar
think I'll have another shot
then maybe you'll think
I'm good enough
'cause I sure want what you've got

why can't I
just quit this drinkin'
and get on with my life
where is mine—where is she
and why is everything
so screwed up in my life

I've got these silent, withdrawn
barroom blues again
don't know how
I can go on anymore
I think it's the end

yes, I've got these silent
withdrawn
barroom blues
once again
and no matter what happens
It seems like I just can't win

no I just can't win
I'm so messed up
I've been here
so many times before

think I'll just, uh . . . drink
till I black out
in the back of my car
then nothing will matter
or hurt . . . anymore

barroom blues
no I just can't win

* * *

what good is the writing
if you never see a word
what good is a voice
that's never heard

what good is the effort
to fight a righteous fight
if you are just denied the right
. . . to write

what good is a song
if nobody sings it
what good is a book
if nobody reads it

what good does it do
to try and try and try
when nobody knows
you're alive

I'm feeling beat up
I'm feeling let down
I'm feeling like
there's nobody around

I'm feeling left out
alone, without a doubt
I'm feeling like a king
without a crown

what good is a memory
faded from view
what good is a family
made up of less than two

what good is the love
when you're the only one who feels it
what good is your happiness
when everyone just steals it

what good is a dream
with no one to share it
what good is philosophy
with no one to declare it

what good is the summer
without the spring or fall
what good is it when no one's there
to catch you when you fall

I'm feeling beat up
I'm feeling let down
I'm feeling like
there's nobody around

I'm feeling left out
alone, without a doubt
I'm feeling like a king
without a crown

* * *

steel skeletons
crumbling stone foundations
green, black to brown
the desert drags you down

as the heat keeps falling
on you
at hwy 60 and 72

I see palm trees
by the pool-side
and champagne for two
but it's just a mirage

painted lady
hot as the desert
I call your name
but you're not there

dusty whirlwinds
in the distance
tumbleweeds rolling along

antique autos
rusting away
houses with occupants
long since gone

and the highway goes on and on

up ahead
a sign draws near
stop in here for A-1 beer

do you see
a cloud in the sky
a tear in my eye
a lover's sigh

what is this
I hear you say
the desert makes you dream
this way

but you're the dream
and you're gone
dusty whirlwinds
in the distance
tumbleweeds rolling along

antique autos
rusting away
houses with occupants
long since gone

and the highway goes on and on

* * *

if poetry is church
then what is a word
is a word
spirituality in the making

if you are the sunshine
then what is the sky
is the sky the breath
you are taking

what is the meaning
if the gathering storm
takes you up
in its swirling grasp

young people in love
lip-locked in their passion
momentarily free
of the past

lost in the kiss
of their own mingled poetry
the bliss of the moment
in their eyes

listen up close
to the sound of the magic
that comes in the midst
of the prize

surprise me not
with your meandering moan
cling to the moment
like moss to the stone

on far away beaches
in a forgotten time
memory's mention
of a love so sublime

* * *

when I was young
and broken hearted
the love songs
all had deeper meaning

when I listened
all I heard
reminded me of you

the harmonies
were sweeter
the guitar
was more profound
you might have heard it too
but you no longer
were around

the specter of today
reflecting on tomorrow
beyond the reaches
of yesterday's sorrow . . .
      I saw you walking into
      the silver dawn

the stars are gone
you looked away
the clock ticks on
another day
pride is broken
nothing there
it was only for you to share

misting moments
gleeful whispers
put the power
back in my smile
memories of love
still travel on
it's just my style

the specter of today
reflecting on tomorrow
beyond the reaches
of yesterday's sorrow . . .
      I saw you walking into
      the silver dawn

* * *

if you are not good
    alone
you won't be good
    together

be happy
    with yourself
to be content
    with someone else

what worse is there than . . .
    the demise of your dreams
    the heartache that stings
    the loneliness it brings

what harder to decide than . . .
    to love yourself within
    to let the sunlight in
    to begin again

* * *

I was born alongside
the newly laid tracks
on a blanket in the sand
my father was a doctor
on the railroad they were building
through Arizona Indian land

the morning laid down
a blanket of snow
to welcome my new life
to the prairie sun
. . . expanding
with the train tracking west
and headed straight for the sea

the train is still a metaphor
in this early 21st century
in our split-second world
where the old irons
have all but disappeared
for the transportation super-highways

where we shuttle the fast track
and miss the future become the past
in the struggle to identify
with images

that aren't who we really are
trying to express
who we really want to be

I guess it's because
we still love to hear
the whistle
of a train in the distance
as it choogles along
to the rhythm
of those mighty rails

or maybe just the thought
of that rugged steel railroad
makes our egos feel
tough as nails

just a-drivin' . . . drivin'
on those cold steel lines
stretched out as far
as the eye can see

change and renewal
greet us everyday
like the moving mural
of nature
seen through a train car's window

and like the train
our life is a journey
with a destination at the end
—a one-way ticket

makes me think about
what has come
and gone
and what lingers on

I've never really had that much
so I must be used to
this poverty consciousness
that has taken me this far
down the line

don't wanna take the train
comin' back
on that track

violins are moaning
in my memory
wishing I'd made it
just one more time with you

so many dreams
have come and gone since then
but I'm still knockin'
on my head's door
evermore

sometimes I think
it's all going to work out
I'm still the romantic optimist
but, then again
it's all so visceral
and nothing lasts

the nights get longer
the solitude longer
the dream time longer
and the poet without his dream
is like the waves
without the break

so I guess . . . I'll head for the sea . . . inside of me

sometimes you'd call me
I don't know why
you said you would love me
till the day you die

I tried to forgive you
for not telling the truth
you were so naive
in the days of our youth

the effervescent shadows
still haunt me, you know
it's the grief and the longing
you never could show

why did we have to meet then
instead of now
I'd switch those times around
if I could do it somehow

as the Statue of Liberty
beckoned the European immigrants
to the new land of freedom
and liberty
in the Northeast

so too
did the iron monster—the great horse
with the nostrils of steam
beckon the Mexican immigrants

to the new vast freedom
in the American prairie
of the Southwest

as I lay my well-worn boots
on the muddy banks of the Colorado
I remember not so much
your golden flowing hair
as I do the dreams
that you wouldn't follow

I am at once proud
to shake the hands
of those I dream about
and as I dream it out loud
the west wind hears
the eagles cry
and the river shouts it
—raging

and the days get shorter
the rest time shorter
the dream time shorter
but an artist without the light
is like the waves
without the break

and once again . . . I return to the sea . . . inside of me

sometimes you'd call me
I don't know why
I said I would love you
till the day I die

can you forgive me
for not telling the truth
I was so naive
in the days of my youth

the effervescent shadows
still haunt me, you know
it's the grief and the longing
I never could show

why did we have to meet then
instead of now
I'd switch those times around
if I could do it somehow

it takes some getting used to
all the broken dreams
I'm feeling pretty numb inside
these days

sometimes a little left that matters
breaks through
and I get that old feeling that was magic

for a brief spell
I crawl out of my lonely exclusion
and think I can really say
something meaningful

but the crunch comes crashin' in no time
and leaves my ego shattered
no means to mend

and I remember
the carrot always dangles
when the sun shines in
the brightest
and the sun always burns
but never tans
the fair-skinned man

and every time I find
you never follow
I'd give you my heart
if you ever could see
that I'm so full of feeling
the creative inclusion

but I'm drowning
in the dream
that could never be

and you know there ain't no train
coming back
on that track

and the nights get longer
the solitude longer
the dream time longer
but the poet without his dream
is like the waves
without the break

so once again . . . I head for the sea . . . inside of me

sometimes it still haunts me
I don't know why
you said you would love me
till the day you die

I tried to forgive you
for not telling the truth
you were so naive
in the days of our youth

the effervescent shadows
still haunt me, you know
it's the grief and the longing
you never could show

why did we have to meet then
instead of now
I'd switch those times around
if I could do it somehow

(epilogue)

we were two parallel trains
on opposite tracks
smoke stacks blowin'
never lookin' back

when I first saw you
rollin' into town
your heart light was burnin'
you wouldn't look down

360's comin'
gonna burn up tracks
heart lights burnin'
with twin smokestacks

passin' . . . just passin'
you never looked back
360's comin'
gonna burn up tracks

sometimes it still haunts me
I don't know why
we said we'd love each other
till the day we die

can we be forgiven
for not telling the truth
we were so naive
in the days of our youth

the effervescent shadows
still haunt me, you know
it's the grief and the longing
we never could show

why did we have to meet then
instead of now
I'd switch those times around
. . . if I could do it
. . . somehow

* * *

I thought I saw you
on the boardwalk
your long blonde curls
blowing softly in the wind
it took me back
to the sunny, surfer days
innocently watching the waves
breaking . . . longing in your eyes
it's no surprise that you . . .
you bring the best out of the sunshine

* * *

I know dreams

and I know reality

and the reality is

you are a dream

green striped / puffy grey down / pedestal show / the shiny / curve / the pouring water / so the light shine / cleans the grimy / ruffled ridges / pull me down / frame a knotty sea / time ticks on / the lost reflection / razor sharp degree / unclock the longing / rails that sing / switch it / to the blue / turn the handle / automatic / bring it into view / circles hanging / halfway open / almost folded dry / pop the crinkled / noise receptor / scrape a hole in the sky / weight is relative / stand on the charge / squirt bristling particles / small and large / bang 'em by softness / colors galore / drape them so gently / cover the floor / strike the flame / internal cove / blue scented butterflies / lost in the grove / boxes and baskets / both under cover / turn up the rain / you soon will discover / close it up neatly / sit down and sing / pull it up slow / to the warmth it will bring / fleeting fleet flurries / that land on the loom / have no precision / for the bride and gloom / stop it / before it crackles / nip it / before it buds / silken mist / of knee highs / stroke them / with the studs / do you wish / to ponder / when it's said and done / all the rolls / that sally forth / unto the midnight sun / foxes long incenses / crystals in cement / can you hear / through all the clutter / valiant words were sent / if there is / a message / sing it sweet down low / just so I can / blow it louder / than the blue beyond will know / buckles of old / made from false gold / found on a father's day / famine / later in school / played on a fool / who took the day off / to go clammin' / it's a delicate attraction / that almost always matters / until the abstract painter / throws it and it splatters / screw it / to the horseshoe / call it / on the phone / wipe it / till it's chemically clean / reveal / the parts unknown / it's the ever-flown sender / of the mind bender / whose roots were sown / in the oh zone / it was carried / on the palette / to please you / in the end / it is only / to tease you

Set #3:

resounding ramifications of political instigations

shaded glassworks
meander thru the woods
of my dreamscape
faded memories parade past
like sparkles on fireflies

slip through my grasp
love me into a silhouette
enamored causeways
barely break the light

a slight of hand
is money made
on cloudy, rainy days
for the stick people
on parade

the jack of diamonds
is your card
the one you smile for
longing all the while for

fill the bottle to the top
blow it like a lollipop
let if fly like golden eagles
needle it with newborn delight

send in the nurses
discover what is wrong today
do you think
you will recover
any other way
from the stick people
on parade

broken hearts
on the rebound
broken dreams
longing to be found

break the cycle
if you mean it
send it 'round
the river sound
to be forgotten
not to demean it
just to never again
repeat it

unable to feel the past
slid down too fast
no matter what happens
the labor won't last

the stick people grasp it
they'll just blast it
with a gasp of air
—they declare it

sometimes . . .
you've got to just let go
and move on
other times
just a word or two
might feel strong
like you belong

it's the cornerstone
of conversation
connection of concern
no matter what
just do your best
there's always more to learn

when potential
strikes a chord
wrap it up
and take it

stick people battle
for their place in line
in an audition to make it

but it's just their disguise
to look wise
so don't let it
be your demise

stick people
on parade
you see them daily
pretending to care
about what you do
while they're screwin' in
the screw

stick people . . .
the bamboozle of the pack
ornamental runaround
never give up the attack

so just keep up the slack
—jack
or shake it if you can
and you will understand
the stick people do not
attend to your demand

* * *

the street walk . . .
nights in L.A.
life on the street
seems harsher these days
fear walks side by side with you
everywhere it seems

no more people
—looking
to turn you on
to love and brotherhood
to questioning
why we are here

now we act like we know
motives are straightforward
more . . . more
crystal-cut clear

what are you selling,
drugs, a place to crash
want a date mister
just fifty bucks an hour

the hookers and the man
the rag-a-muffin confidence
walk the streets
—these days

to sell you anything
you are willing to try
bring in a buck—good luck

they'd just as soon
rip you off
as sell you something

you remember the magic
that was in the air
it's not there
—these days
not in heartbreak city
the air is only scented
by decay

in the old day
people walked loud—proud
happy . . . glad
now they walk on cats' paws
crouching . . . sad

the bad seed blooming
swallows up the night

the butterfly of kindred
once spread wings
protectively
over this sparkling city of lights

what used to be love
rhymes singing
has turned into
silent woe
screaming

the vanguard of the curbside
now watches over
homeless—helpless
who, under cardboard covers
          hide

oh, the guard changes
—these days

what used to be
a ray of light
a twinkle of hope
in the night
for the future memory
of brotherhood
on this, our turf

of living in harmony
with nature and her ways
has turned into freeze-dried faith
—a nickel's worth

dogs barking
huddled in alleyways
tickled tinges of despair
linger in minds
wandering . . .
hunger-craved feelings
with no release . . . save
. . . save

oh, save these children of the night
from the fright of their folly
bring back the frolic
to these days

* * *

I saw the best hope
of my generation
strangled and crushed
by greed and lust
—for power

compassion for our fellow man
seems vanquished in a day
by the un-attended sorrow
of the smashing of tomorrow
and the anger and the shame
that remain

driving through delerium clouds
growing darker every day
is it true that hope is fading
shadow walls and decay

can you see the flames of madness
filled with sadness
filled with grief
can you tell me
what will happen
give me some relief

3 Mustangs and a Porsche
roaring down the highway
snow-capped mountains
crumble at their side

can't go fast enough
to chase it away
this feeling of loss
and the rapid decay

of what took so long to build
of what cannot be remade
. . . in a day

of the struggle, the pain
and the heartache
coming our way

I saw the best hearts
of my generation
beaten down
by cynical pride
—and narcissism

spin it now
fake the mourning
kingdoms come
and feigned divine
take it to the 7th wonder
in another time

calling . . . calling . . . calling now
crawling . . . crawling . . . crawling now
falling . . . falling . . . falling
till we're done

climb up to the curbside
climb up from the dirt
it's all gone
and nobody has won

3 Mustangs and a Porsche
roaring down the highway
snow-capped mountains
crumble at their side

can't go fast enough
to chase it away
this feeling of loss
and the rapid decay

of what took so long to build
of what cannot be remade
. . . in a day

of the struggle, the pain
and the heartache
coming our way

* * *

isn't it time
we shook the woke

cigarettes and sunflower seeds
and the gone revolution

John Reed's ramshackle renegades
singing passion into winter's chill

democracy cries for its freedom
hypocrisy lies on the air

so many stay ignorant
engaged in convoluted criticism

tragic colors pervade
division renders violence

no more room for reminiscence
in these sour twilight crowds

it's all been done before
it's all been undone before

no matter what your proclamation is
now is the time of multiculturalism

isn't it time
we shook the woke

* * *

the ego dynamics of regression
are the province of rhetorical speak
the directly proportionate attitude
of the surge they always seek

because truth never seems to win
over their lust, greed and pride
our evolution has fallen
by the wayside

a robust diplomacy
is a long term non-reality
against a unilateral purge of reason
in this ominous political season

the view that is required
has subsequently expired
the agreement to be pursued
has been subdued

the ongoing relationship
between the owners and the management
is all they deem sufficient
to proceed

approval by the people
is either null or undesired
the testimony of any witness
is simply retired

there will not be a compromise
no level of peace will arise
in strategic terms of circumstances
nothing but these . . . language dances

just like Orwell said . . .
It's the Newspeak language of Doublespeak
you know who drank the Kool-Aid
if it's truth you really seek

and in the end it's unreachable
their politics unbreachable
to any man of reason
it's impeachable

* * *

—the pharmaceuticals
—the insurance companies
—the oil companies
—the energy companies
—the banks and Wall Street
—the government and the Fed

they all say we're better off
but they'd just as soon see us dead

they say things are better
but nothing has changed
they still get their profits
they're just rearranged

while most just still suffer
from the inflation game
when everything rises—but wages

we're not turning pages
no big change upon us
the bought and the paid for
have thrown us under the bus

what's the fuss
wanna cuss
won't do you no good
'cause the do-gooders are gone
long time . . . moved on

no ground can be gained
it's all the same
they're the ones to blame

and it's such a shame
we can't pin it on their name
but compassion's never been
their claim to fame

but it's nothing
—disgusting
no life here
ain't no life nowhere

it's like watching a western
that's old and outdated
you thought it had substance
but it's just overrated

'cause they pound you with everything
they say that you need
watch out for the side effects
filled with their greed

the corporate greed
just sucks us dry
can't get away from it
no matter how ya try

if you send someone up
to fix it for you
it just doesn't matter
'cause they'll get sucked in too

until regulation
is re-diligently done
forget about it
compassion
is just on the run

no help for your fellow man
no relief for the workers' stand
children starving—all over this land
in the U.S. of A.—man!

all the brainwashed clones
spread the news
like there's no tomorrow
say anything to you
beg, steal or borrow

at a moment's peep
like sheep on the cheap

just follow whatever they're told
led fully blind
like they've done all the time
and will do
till the day they grow old

never wake up
to walk in the sunlight
can't get it together
they're just not too bright

rather shoot you
accuse you
and definitely abuse you
till the day that you die
they'll never look you in the eye

'cause they're guilty—man
eggs fried in a pan
of promoted ad-libbing
recycled fibbing

can't think for themselves
too scary to change
forever declaring
it's home on the range

but it's nothing
—disgusting
no life here
ain't no life nowhere

yeah, it's like an old western
it's old and outdated
you thought it had substance
but it's just overrated

they pound you with everything
they say that you need
watch out for the side effects
filled with their greed

a critical thinking person
is music to my ears
for hoards of heartless people
have been marching through the years

like a vampire's bite
they suck you dry
to drain your spiritual light
but every now and then
you find
someone whose light is bright

you fight to keep it shining
can't give in to the blind
the music still reminding you
to keep an open mind

'cause it just ain't now
what it so was then
it ain't bright enough
you keep wonderin' when

keep fighting for the light
keep breaking thru the night
help others when you might
so they too—may wake up
when it's right

investments are good right now
jobs—well they're bad
there's many foreclosures
around to be had

it's an interesting situation
out there for you
things are looking up
if you're one of the few

but for those of us—most
things are still looking toast
the ghost of prosperity
seems a thing of the past

and there's no present signs
that this situation won't last
the problems and bills
seem to compound so fast

you try—and try hard
to make ends meet
to keep things a-floating
to stay on your feet

but you're tired and beaten
and ground to the core
and even when you're feeling good
the wolf is at the door

when's it gonna come your way
when's it ever gonna pay
to lead a hard-working honest life
and have some relief from the strife

get up on top
and not fall
get ahead
have a buffer
—that's all

but who's really listening
and who's gonna lead
to bring real prosperity
not just feed the greed

sometimes it seems useless—I know
and just hopeless, man
but somehow you always get up
keep doin' what you can
for yourself
and your fellow man

well . . . I can see the light in you
I can see it . . . yes I can
I don't have words of wisdom
but I'm glad you make a stand
because it's the real Americans like you
who will eventually save this land

the compassion in your hearts
the ones who still reach out their hand
the ones who make this country—grand
the many grains of sand—not bland
the true American brand

but it's still like an old western
old and outdated
you thought it had substance
but it's just overrated

they pound you with everything
they say that you need
watch out for the side effects
filled with their greed

it's just nothing
—disgusting
no life here
ain't no life nowhere . . .

(with apologies to Jimi Hendrix)

* * *

extreme fundamentalism is difficult to change
perpetuated thinking through generations
challenging legitimate intelligence is strange

fanatical thinking seeks to rearrange
mainstream beliefs and scientific trends
extreme fundamentalism is difficult to change

the critical thinking it wants to derange
it can not stand up to, although it pretends
challenging legitimate intelligence is strange

we must push forward with mainstream exchange
so we do not lose our long held foundations
extreme fundamentalism is difficult to change

it does not belong in our minds' higher range
in the foreground of society and modern trends
challenging legitimate intelligence is strange

our reason and principles we cannot shortchange
although we must embrace our odds and ends
extreme fundamentalism is difficult to change
challenging legitimate intelligence is strange

* * *

why do kings in our country
always get hurt
why is the world
still groveling in the dirt
searching for justice

is it a mystery
or just another piece of history
that the media fuels the flames of
for all to see

buildings continue to burn
throughout the city
prayers for peace
—call out
all around

you wonder . . .
is humanity or justice
being served
as you watch
all over
your city
. . . burning to the ground

why do they never listen
when we cry out for equality
Lincoln, Lennon
King, the Kennedys
—call out
through eternity

why do we have to sacrifice
—so much
for so little gain
it's about human rights
and it's happening
once again

it's no mystery
that pent-up feelings
have taken to the streets
but death and destruction
do not bring solution
they only increase the pain
of an already open wound

it's not a mystery
just another piece of history
that the media fuels the flames of
for all to see

buildings continue to burn
throughout the city
prayers for peace
—call out
all around

you wonder . . .
is humanity or justice
being served
as you watch
all over
your city
. . . burning to the ground

why do joblessness, homelessness
depression, frustration and anger
seem rampant everywhere

gangsters and criminals are glorified
executions are justified
while unjust murders and beatings
go virtually unnoticed
in every town square

what can you say
about the shape we're in
where does our justice belong

when we kill those
who kill others
to show that killing people
is wrong

and you wonder why anguish
pain and alienation
are now evidenced
and played out
on the streets of our nation

oh why
does this country of ours
kill her 'Kings'
why do the kings in our country
always get hurt

it's no mystery
just another piece of history
that the media fuels the flames of
for all to see

buildings continue to burn
throughout the city
prayers for peace
—call out
all around

you wonder . . .
is humanity or justice
being served

as you watch

all over

your city

. . . burning to the ground

—L.A. 4/29/1992

* * *

dusty and grim
the few walls remain
—standing
in ominous resemblance
to graveyard gates
. . . grave of the innocence

the blue sky used
to do the work of the guilty
as weapon against the innocent
all lost with the planes

the weight of the world
now united in grief
there is no relief
from the pain of injustice

you see it verily turn . . . everyday
in a way we all burn . . . to learn
and today it was our turn
for the war of the world has come home

history
has been irrevocably changed
our lives
will never be the same

how many dreams
burst in flames on a plane
in the world's will
already draped in shame

the fear
the revenge
the tears
that will rain

the snow-clouds
of dust
and debris
that remain

for history
to relive
through time
and time again

OH GREAT WAR OF VIOLENCE
when will you end
is this really our nature
forever our calling
will we ever outgrow this
is our evolution stalling

will we revert and revert
till all reason is gone
when our faith becomes hopeless
how do we go on

dusty and grim
the few walls remain
—standing
in ominous resemblance
to graveyard gates

. . . grave of the innocents

the blue sky used
to do the work of the guilty
as weapon against the innocent
all lost with the planes

—N.Y. 9/11/2001

* * *

I fight for what is not left
I fight for what went long ago
the smiling faces
        flowers
        long hair
        and bell-bottoms
        of you

now only a faded view
left forgotten
in the memories of . . .
        new wars
        new scores
        new reasons to be
        afraid

by the many
the masses
no longer aware
how it could have been
had we just not
        given in

to the many-numbered royalties
the commercialism cash cow
the callous concern
of corporate bottom lining
. . . until we're all scared for our jobs

no longer able to see
the possibility
that was at our fingertips

if only we could have held on
        a little longer
persevered
        a little stronger
not been in such
a drug-induced haze

oh, the ways . . .
the ways of the world
the wonder now gone
replaced by hunger

the mad plans of melancholy
mentioned in passing
the last seen signals

. . . of the '60s

do you remember . . .
when peace, love and brotherhood
were the current topics
of discourse

do you remember . . .
when government regulation
was strong enough
that air pollution standards
created cleaner air in Los Angeles

and the big banks & Wall Street
operated with public scrutiny

do you remember . . .
when aerosol cans
started disappearing
from store shelves
replaced by pump sprays

do you remember why

do you remember . . .
truth in advertising
do you remember . . .
the fairness doctrine
when opposing political views
had equal air time—by law

do you remember . . .
when telephone companies
public utilities
television, media
airlines, health insurance
and banks

were not mega-monopoly corporations
and monopolies were broken up
by our government

do you remember . . .
when the Supreme Court
was fair and balanced
and politicians of opposing parties
actually worked together

do you remember . . .
when big money
didn't buy up
all of government

do you remember . . .
when public education
was important
reliable
affordable
—and funded

do you remember . . .
when teachers, firemen
and police officers
were important jobs
with public support
for fair wages and benefits

do you remember . . .
when the average American family
could afford a house, a car
and a college education
for their children

do you remember . . .
Make Love, Not War

the 1960s were
a paradigm shift—at least
a brief moment—of truth
a glimpse of the golden age
the future that could be
if peace, love and brotherhood
really reigned in the world

in the '60s we saw
that the evolution of the human spirit
        was possible

that living in harmony
with our fellow man
and mother nature
     was doable

but when you look around now
it appears like we have forgotten
—all of that

I fight for what is not left
I fight for what went long ago
the smiling faces
     flowers
     long hair
     and bell-bottoms
     of you

* * *

you scorch Mother Earth
and poison the oceans
don't care about the cost

as long as you get
your golden parachute
you don't care what is lost

you made the world
forget our ways
and how much we all shared

our legacy now
is a purple haze
of how much we all cared

we had the vision
of a peaceful world
at our fingertips

you shot it down
with greed and power
it's all about your worships (war ships)

we were spiritual
morally responsible
eco-logical-ly sound

but since it cut
into your profits
you found a way around it

can't you see it's déja vu
it's coming down again on you

on me & her
on all of us
because greed is still driving
the bus

you put us down
and raped our credibility
for all the things we did

while in secrecy
you made damn sure
you securely closed the lid

on peace and understanding
on compassion
sharing and truth

all the good ideas
we had
you just blamed on our youth

we had the vision
of a peaceful world
at our fingertips

you shot it down
with greed and power
it's all about your worships (war ships)

can't you see it's déja vu
it's coming down again on you

on me & her
on all of us
because greed is still driving
the bus

. . . so we know you now
we know you will act quickly
on any future threat
of peace and brotherhood

* * *

poets are needed
in troubling times

their words are the words
of the wise

when troubling times
are upon us

the poets
become politicized

* * *

modern history has a way
of covering up the sublime
or true greatness
and celebrating
the mediocre

iron steeples
crawl to the sky
burnt embers of spirituality
falling down
crushing into ash

you perpetuate what's fake
until the fake becomes
what's real

and then you can't recognize
what's genuine
when you see it

so now we are required
to embrace the mediocre
instead of the sublime

and the dumbing down
of America
. . . continues

* * *

everything around you
seems to be
diluting your credibility
deluding your intent

who will be our role model
now that fear-mongering
—tweets
are the norm

we seem to be
at the end of an era
where truth and humanity
matter

or maybe we're at the beginning
all I know is . . .
somebody screwed the pooch
and now we need to unfuckit

* * *

the evolution
of the human spirit

I've lived long enough
to witness it closely
and now it is more evident
than ever

but I am witnessing now
—more in this moment
the mere cunning of man

the inner beast
that has yet to evolve

the mysterious manipulator
to be feared for its ignorance

not yet evolved
to the breaking inner-consciousness

to observe with understanding
the compassion and empathy
of helping your fellow
human beings

to be a part
of a community
rather than a separate
solitary hunter
following the scent
of selfish need

growth, evolution
so many have found it

but are we the majority
are we truly
able to transcend

to overcome
the obstacles of ignorance
which haunt our very memory
and threaten to overcome us
by rising back up
into the open air

to destroy the hope
that has been so hard fought
. . . so hard won

* * *

I am looking for comradery
and I can find it nowhere
all I find is competition
—and envy

is this not the sign
of decadent memory
elephant trunks in the graveyard
raping sanity

thatched roofs
were woven together in harmony
everyone's hands
were honest work dirty

when teamwork was
a necessity
the fruits we reaped
were even/fair
and comradery . . . somehow
was in the air

is black or white
the truer color
where clearer the story
is told

are rainbow fantasies
and grand scale productions
. . . truer
than the tales of old

there's something in a book
that holds its own magic
something in a look
when you stare

what is it about this box
so plastic and tragic
that looks real
but is not really there

I need to know
the unknowable
to drink till I'm drunk
the unquenchable

the pattern of a snowflake
the number of the stars
. . . the lost memory
of the mystery that's unmentionable

reap—what you sow
learn—what you already know
sweat—until you grin
. . . and do it again

for the lasting pleasure
of simplicity
break down the wall
of complicity
and stand alone/together
in comradery

* * *

you celebrate
the macho jock mentality
then wonder why
they don't respect your fights

you like to say
"only the strong survive"
. . . and
"good guys finish last"

you support those
whose goal is to dominate
compete and win
at any cost

and then you wonder
why we are lost

you give all your money
to the military
and sports
but you don't support education

or family planning
or women's rights
or helping the helpless
or the immigrants' plight

how do I stay optimistic
in the midst of all this tragedy
when all you want to celebrate
is the macho jock mentality

* * *

some things are bigger than you
if you are in contempt
and not in support
you will be on the wrong
side of history

this is the time of women
the time of woman power
the time to evolve beyond the limits
of the patriarchal society
we all grew up in

the one that has driven the world
for so long
the one that has driven us to the brink
of perpetual war or annihilation

but we have a history of diversity
human rights
and the struggle for equality
which has brought us to this moment

a paradigm shift is upon us
if you are not in support
you are on the wrong side of history

not the written history
put down by the dominant influences
of power, taken up after conquering
or a coup
but the history of this moment
in our evolution

be on the right side of history
be on the side of moving forward
it is truly a matter of light or dark
if you look into your heart
the choice cannot be more clear

—*for Hillary 8/1/2016*

* * *

brown sweeping fingers
of delinear repose
reaching, clutching
. . . blurry browns
perched against the cloudy remains
of dripping skies

vast green rivers
of melancholy grass
grouping birds—swooping by
hundreds swiping the sky
in front of our eyes

tractor traces
gobbling up the linear spaces
divided by the human traces
crying to be heard

folded up machinery
waiting to be found
to be sound again
and billowing clouds of dust

you've been beating back
—the storm
but now it is upon you
and it's not turning back
    it is raining
    it is pouring
quickly picking up the slack

until it is upon you
and beats you to the ground
your arrogance
never to be found again
—it is the end

armies of trees
barren to the bone
have been your legacy
captured currents
of unrighteous cause
sworn to secrecy

creeping up the banks
of sorrow
haystacks hover
until they dry
dead wood stacked up
by the roadside
never made you sigh
but warms us . . . by and by
—until we die

in the blink of an eye
you blew it
tore it to the core
—ignorance
and blinding madness
always end in war

putting it back together, though
will truly take some time
it always is a heavy lift
coming back from the blind

    * * *

you echo in the horrors
the trumpet soars
in high fidelity memories
the masses applaud their support
—in a roar
but I will not applaud for war
no—I will not applaud for war

they kept on applauding
give me more, give me more
but I will not applaud for war
no—I will not applaud for war

so why are you here
are you here to make things better
for you and those around you
for our country and for our children
or are you here just to complain

do you want to just complain
about who is doing what
or who is not doing what
do you want to complain
about what is happening
what is not happening,
what should or should not be happening

that takes up so much energy
—and time
time that can be put
to so much more productive use
get out there and help
do something constructive
help someone clean up their life
or their home
or maybe—clean up your own back yard

there is so much
that needs to be done
why are you here
to do it—to try
to help things get better
even if only just a little

it will be noticed
it always is
it will help
it always does

and maybe it will start
a ripple of goodness
—wow
who knows where that could lead

you told me
to just be patient
and my dreams
would eventually come true
well, I've been patient all my life
and now I am an old man
it's pretty hard to do

you echo in the horrors
the trumpet soars
in high fidelity memories
the masses applaud their support
—in a roar
but I will not applaud for war
no—I will not applaud for war

they kept on applauding
give me more, give me more
but I will not applaud for war
no—I will not applaud for war

* * *

un-nurtured
unending
what is pertinent
to the inner sanctum
of harmony
certainly not this

what do you read
what do you hear
what do you need
to make a clear-headed think
shrinking violets
in the night
do not shine

once more
light in your mind
sparks an inner drive
towards a goal
of nurturing

un-nurtured
unending
must end
to begin with

think about
what you think
analyze
what you see

don't get lost
in a sea
of images
the picture is quite clear

you have got to start here
to make some sense
out of the wrenching

un-nurtured

unending

incendiary artifacts of creation / marching towards the architects of doom / crowded in the room / shattered from the gloom / can it ever handle the duration / how do you deem culture / how do you survive / is anyone aware / we are alive / how can it be rectified / how can it be drawn / down the tube / instalube / the safety net is gone / damn the teeming wonder / damn the seething glow / when it's brought asunder / drops you down below / down to the grit of the swallowing rim / into to the shit of the grim / falling just falling / in the smothering fit / was it just pointing to him / he who has bought it / cheaper by far / he never fought it / but waved from his car / they who denied it / they who succumbed / into the pit / where the greed made them numb / can you deny it / will you abide / will it just crumble / fall down the slide / if we ignore it / shit will unfold / can you implore it / what is untold / cracked from the prattle / rendered from the norm / clerical conspiracy / coddled the reborn / gave in to the absence / took it to the spring / clamored for the gladness / no one won the ring / black and white / show their might / critical race / is the theory / throw on your sheets / history repeats / teach them to watch / or go dreary / fried in a locker / found in the grift / subtle chisel / is your gift / ground to a stall / in the lift / is it too late / for the shift / systemic incubation of ideals / devolving into systematic / disintegrating appeals / remedial ordeals / catatonic steals / too many instances of intubation / total frustration / consternation / too many faculties of annihilation / crammed into fantasies / overblown insanities / slammed in the dark / written on a lark / forced us into park / bitten by the frost / forced to pay the cost / everything is criss-crossed / calamity is boss / falling from the battle / all you hear is rattle / snap-crackle accolades / falling on their own grenades

Set #4:

introspective reflections and peripheral articulations

I wish that I could
strike a flame
from those ingenious days
with a fire so high
that screams so loud
—if only you'd hear what I say

take me back
to the wonder and glory
the intuitive nature I had
sensing things
in the rock-n-roll world
before their time was at hand

the magical meaning
of feeling it come
so prescient, so furtive, so grand
with such inspiration
it drove what I did
I knew that my time was at a hand

but as you grow older
that magic does fade
you no longer have the clear view
into things that may come
that's reserved for the young
the magic's no longer for you

* * *

welcome to NOW
Not—Our—World
It's just the negative
atmosphere
. . . rising

it's like I'm alone
in the universe
ain't nobody here
. . . from my world

where'd you all go
when did it end
why can't we begin it
. . . again

in the stream of consciousness
I thought I saw you
but it was just my
. . . imagination

* * *

you know
I thought this was
my home
but I guess it's not

maybe I don't belong
anywhere
maybe only
on these pages

just a blob of ink
spilling out my emotions
where it doesn't matter
if anyone listens or not
if anyone cares or not

maybe that's the point
nothing matters
just empty words on a page
filled with someone's blather

that may or may not
mean anything
to anyone else
just yourself

alone as you came
alone as you go
no one new
no one will know

maybe keeping it green
and serene
just doesn't mean a thing
maybe it's all just
so temporary

that it will just grow
over you
anyhow
like a bunch of weeds
that no one bothered to cut

and you'll just rot away
—unnoticed
until you're just another part
of the brown ground

ground underfoot
or maybe burned into soot
and blown on the breeze

it makes no difference
—anyway
'cause who's gonna pay
to see it your way

not a ding-dang soul
I'm just outta control
rolling down a crooked hill
bangin' into rocks
in my dirty socks and jeans

no means to my chatter
don't know what's a'matter

'cept I feel like
home made shit
that someone just spit

so go get 'er
on the run
have some fun
until yer done

'cause if you don't
you'll just end up floatin'
—face down
in the never-lands

singin' a song
of grimy hands
'cause you're just . . .
a man without a band

* * *

you sucked up to the good life
but selfishly left us behind
we put our love and trust in you
. . . you knew we were that kind

you were the '60s heroes
but you forgot . . . or just denied
that you were there to lead us all
to break on through to the other side

the other side of greed
the other side of pollution and despair
I guess corruption got the better of you
and it seemed so easy to take you there

now you are the upper class
while we're still hangin' down here
waiting for all the good news
that seemed so crystal clear

but I guess it was all just psychedelic
dreams and cloudy incense
although it seemed so logical
I guess it was just pretense

pretense—that you would lead us
pretense—that you had the balls
that you really believed in the cause
and would rise to our tribal calls

now we can see clearly
how proud you peacocks are
trippin' in your crystal cathedrals
or in your dark tinted car

but what about Mother Earth
and those who believed in you
where did all that spirit go
and what more now
do we have to go through

to make you powerful people see
what righteous really is
to make you remember
what you left behind
and we're not talkin' showbiz

to make a world
really safe for our children
the future tribes
of our kind

where we all could grow
—together
to create a world
loving and kind

just a little note
—to the blind
now living
in the material world

just remembering . . .
the dream we created
not the one that unfurled

* * *

all the false promises you gave
all the rivers you were gonna save
all the children lying in their graves
can't hear you any more

all the love you can't return
all the lessons you'll never learn
until your tattered world
comes crashing down on you

how many dreams
from so many dreamers
wither up and die
can you tell where they went
when you no longer see
the sparkle in love song's eyes

I was the eternal smile
you've stolen it away
you've robbed and pulled and pricked me
till I'm full of your decay

blue rose is suffering
sing it gospel style
famous spirits now join in
you walk a familiar mile

first love returns to you
and spreads her fertile wings
you find old friends
sing old songs
and think of long gone things

I used to be a gentle soul
but your world has crushed me
I gave you all my faith and trust
but you still don't trust me

I went to school
to learn your golden rule
but you do unto others
however you please

I loved a girl
I gave her my heart
but her commitment
was only a tease

blue rose suffering
sing it gospel style
famous spirits now join in
as you walk the familiar mile

first love returns to you
and spreads her fertile wings
you find old friends
sing old songs
and think of long gone things

how long you go on suffering
to heed the muse's call
when all you need is time, you think
to get up when you fall

to write—and write—and write—and write
and write some more again
if only you had the time
—to write
you know the muse would send

you know they say
if you live long enough
you'll disprove all your beliefs

not only the ideas
and principles you stand for
but all of the metaphors
causing all of your griefs

and all of what's matter
in the universe
be it light or be it dark
      means nothing
in your little scheme of things
except the inspiration
that gives you the spark
      and the time to write it
      and to dream . . .

blue rose is suffering
sing it gospel style
famous spirits now join in
you walk a familiar mile

first love returns to you
and spreads her fertile wings
you find old friends
sing old songs
think of long gone things

* * *

oh big sky
are you watching over me
shall I say
what I feel is real today

will they listen to me now
will it matter anyhow
what shall I do
for my soul

do you think you are a master
do you practice what you preach
so you think your way is faster
tell me, what is it you teach

do you show us how to love each other
with more feeling everyday
are you helping anyone
with more feeling as you say

oh inspiration
are you watching over me
shall I say
what I feel is real today

will they listen to me now
will it matter anyhow
what shall I do
for my soul

if you want to start somewhere
then start by being true
'cause if you ain't true
then we'll find somebody new

now maybe you can help us all
with what it is you preach
but please don't say you know it all
there's always more to teach

oh big sky
are you watching over me
shall I say
what I feel is real today

will they listen to me now
will it matter anyhow
what shall I do
for my soul

* * *

this is my day
to sing to the universe

I hope you like
what I have to say

I'll try to make it
a compelling recital

with a little wisdom
to help on the way

always trying
to keep the channel open

to see where it begins
to see it never ends

to see what there is
to see what could be

for the joy is
not in the destination

it always lives
in the journey

* * *

it's not that we're different
how can it be
it's just that we care more now
can't you see

if the feeling is real
then it's one to believe
that we all can perceive
what is real
if we feel it's our way
then we'll make it someday

and it's here
it's right now
I must show you
. . . but how
you must pick up
on something
much closer
right now

. . . just to see you
. . . just to be with you
if you know this feeling
then it all will work out

I just want you together
we all must come now
yes, where love sticks together
it's here and here's how
it will stand as it stood
but the love's deeper now

and I don't even know
if the time is right now
but it's just that I'm feeling
. . . so feeling
. . . somehow

* * *

my family is the sky
desperate need
in a wide blue ocean
no need to ask why
it's just who I am

I settle for
a roaring fire
and classic rock bands
memories of a flower child
who twirled and danced

hungry for the company
of someone . . .
who really knows
what it was like
what it meant
what we always thought
it could be

my future is now shorter
than the days of my past
golden days are here
—or are they gone

I try to ignore
ages, aches and pains
while I grasp . . . time
to do what is left undone
to express as much as I can
—the dreams
that have been my lifetime

to leave something new
unvarnished, unique
for those who come after
who might have a smidgen
of interest

I dare to think
I have something to offer
—I do
for otherwise
why has it poured out of me so

* * *

why were you here
why did you have me
why did you try so hard
and sacrifice
your own happiness

I think of you
when times are tough
how you'd always lend
a helping hand

your heart was always
in the right place
though, sometimes
I did not understand

it's a hard world
to survive in
it's a tough one
yes it's true

but it always
gives me comfort
when I think of you

you brought music
into my life
made me feel happy
about it

watching you dancing
was magical
you never made me
doubt it

now . . .
when a funky beat moves me
saves me from feeling blue

when it's hard to cope
in this troubling world
I still think of you

you can carry me through
it's true
. . . and I miss you

* * *

some know home
some can go back
when times are tough
or when they're hurt

the place to go
to lick your wounds
where they have to take you in

there is nowhere like that
for me
nowhere to retreat
to begin again

no one to listen
who really cares
no place to breathe
when the air is thin

I need some authenticity
oh, take me back
to feeling it now
I need some comfort
and I can find it nowhere

used to be
compassion mattered
used to be
kindness thrived

now it's all just torn
and shattered
—ripped apart
contrived

I need to know
it'll be okay
but no one
seems to be aware

of where it went
of where it's going
where it is
they just don't care

it's sad to know
the past is best
the best it'll ever be

and once again
to realize
you can never go home
anymore
. . . you see

—never . . . anymore

* * *

I must remember
that these are the remnants
of my life

got to get out
and do the things
that belong to only me

* * *

often I believe
my work is inspired
just the way
it was meant to be

and I love it
just the way
it pours out of me

but then afterwards
—I hate it
think it's silly
or absurd

I thought I was
so clever
but now
I hate every word

is it . . .
enough
was it . . .
complete as it was

should I . . .
not change it one bit
does it . . .
stand on its own

I do believe writers
as all artists
are their own
worst critics

but I know that acceptance
is the key . . .
to free
what's inside of me

* * *

I used to wear my head up
in the sunshine
I used to know
in my heart
that you were mine

I used to bring a joy
to everyone
with my smile
I used to be so optimistic
that was just my style

but now it's gotten harder
to look into your eyes
the warmth and sparkle
has now become
a grim disguise

is everyone
wearing a mask
you can't even begin to ask
you don't know what will happen
or what will arise

but it just no longer is
a sweet surprise

* * *

we live in a world
of deception
but awakened ones know
what is real

they know how to feel
they know how to cry
they just don't know what
. . . or why

what in the name
of our sanity
can be said
what can be taught
what can be read

to make you understand
where it goes
everything just falls
like dominos

* * *

I used to have a voice
I used to want to be heard
I used to sit and listen
to every word

I want to tell you
. . . something
I know you just don't care
my need to speak is waning
and no one is aware

it doesn't even matter
it certainly doesn't shine

it could be yours
it could be theirs
but it certainly isn't mine

the ignorance
of flapping jaws
destroyed what could be true
I know some words
are more important
it doesn't pertain to you

I know there's room
I always have
enough for everyone
but now we're bathed
in dark despair
instead of the light
of the sun

* * *

salivating dogs
with notepads
trying to increase
the narrative
criteria inherited
from nomads
only their decision
is imperative

no one can
dissuade them
though many
do complain
how can you
berate them
when everyone's
to blame

on the fringe
of famous
they mock you
if you cry
everyone's
in a hurry
to get their slice
of pie

* * *

today I thought about
planetary travel
but that wouldn't take me
far enough away

I thought a lot about
the human condition
and the pain that I felt
when you left yesterday

I have nothing to say . . .
       except
where were you
when I needed you

I have nothing to say . . .
       except
time doesn't make
all the pain go away

I have nothing to say . . .
       except
see you in another lifetime

I . . . have nothing . . . to say

I have nothing to say . . .
       except
don't you think
we've done enough damage
to the reality we live in
is compassion really dead

do we still have enough time here
to treat each other humanely
take off the masks we're wearing
clear the cobwebs out of our heads

get into balance
with our planet
and walk into our future
without . . . all of this . . . dread

I have nothing to say . . .
       except
why do we have to be so greedy

I have nothing to say . . .
        except
why don't we stop taking
and learn how to give

I have nothing to say . . .
        except
why do we always
neglect the needy

I . . . have nothing . . . to say

I have nothing to say . . .
        except
it seems there's just
so much aggression
everywhere . . . everyone
just wants more control

I have nothing to say . . .
        except
reality is not in session
for when killing's the way
we try to make peace
we're just falling deeper
into the hole

I have nothing to say . . .
        except
why don't we stop all this fighting

I have nothing to say . . .
        except
why do we have to make so much war

I have nothing to say . . .
        except
our future could be so exciting

I . . . have nothing . . . to say

I have nothing to say . . .
        except
where were you
when I needed you

I have nothing to say . . .
   except
time doesn't make
all the pain go away

I have nothing to say . . .
   except
see you in another lifetime

I . . . have nothing . . . to say

* * *

do you ever feel
. . . disconnected
like the world's rushing by
every which way

sometimes I feel like
I'm stranded, deserted
like hubcaps on the highway

ever been rolling
until you stopped
been a part of
and then been dropped

not one of the pack
but just a stray
like hubcaps on the highway

pick me up
take me home
fix me up
with new chrome

then put me back
where I can roam
with hubcaps on the highway

* * *

is there room for one more
will you let me in
is there room for one more
though it's late to begin

please let me in
'cause the feelings that are in me
they just won't let me be

they say that I belong
. . . with you
so won't you please
make some room

—let me in
—let me in right now

* * *

I was there
when you sang your songs
. . . dancing
or just tagging along
. . . hoping
there was room for me
I was always there

I was there
for the harmony
helped put it together
whether two-part or three
you could always
count on me
I was always there

I was there
for what it could be
there was always a vision
that I could see
through it all
I heard the call
I was always there

I was there
when you dreamed your dreams
through the war
and even the heartache—it seems
I was there
through so many things
I was always there

I was there
for all your fame
and times
I even took the blame
and though
you never knew my name
I was always there

uck again / ruck again / cinnamon sigh / rigorous / roundabout / porcupine pie / indignant angulator / iridescent sky / telescopic propagator / petulant cry / glad grabbers / indemnify / significant / sacrifices / eloquent / elaborators / accentuate / declining prices / if they catch / the lory / will it be / on time / it's the naked / glory / relegate / the crime / dazzling dancing / daredevils / dare to reach / exotic extremes / crabby clinging / famished faces / create / robotic memes / metal sawtooth / marvels / maga haters / laugh / bromide frothing / teachers / instigate / the path / took it down / a notch / to the condescending / botched relations / constantly / concerned / running rampant / at the subway stations / can the special / regulator / bring solace / to the ones who sing / love's rough tangle / hidden / in the lonely realm / where heartaches cling / will the hazard / take it's toll / followed down / the rabbit hole / cram it / in the rambler / it's the ragged / scrambler

Set #5:

inner observations and nature's illuminations

in shimmering predawn quiet
wedding gowns blow through my dreams
blue-drawn eyes on crisp new paper
show no name, snowy white
but you and family gathered from afar
are quite clear

spare bedrooms
softly cluttered with borrowed beds
and childhood laughter
sprinkle spirit and glad tidings
for future frolic

love shall fill . . .
      rooms
      hearts
      fields and meadows
crystal clear
the crisp autumn wind
blows clean the leaves
and tall grass
in the twinkling of an eye

. . . and so it begins

* * *

the song of the morning birds
. . . yawning
as the dawn breaks
. . . ever so slightly

the crackling of fallen autumn leaves
as squirrels scurry to hunt
the lost treasures they've buried

I love the sound
of leftover moonbeams
wistful as melodies in my mind
whispering the memories
of past moonlit nights
when I pondered the very secret
of your season

the tranquility
of a moment's placid rest
after passion's pleasing
and teasing bright display

. . . another quiet sound
tickling my mind

the door latch creaking
when love enters the room
a sound likened to the vision
of the fog lifting from view
when the autumn colors drip
from the dew
of a new morning's awakening

this too
I stretch my ears to hear
. . . adoringly

take me to a concert in the park
resonating sounds that echo
beyond the sky's slow dimming
where I hum along to familiar words
sung in sweet harmony's glory

these are just some
of the many sounds
I most like to hear
on any given day
—in autumn

or I could surely conjure the beauty
of another season's melodies
—sweet melodies
of nature's daily awakenings

like summer mornings on the seashore
I can almost hear my frosty breath
breaking with the morning waves
where the wind brings the salt air sense

* * *

like cream puffs squeezed
the foam oozes out of the curling waves
standing languid row by row
searching for breakfast by the edge of the sand
morning surf birds peck sleek
their silky feathers
as a new sun slowly warms them
then scamper suddenly to avoid getting wet

young surfers brave the winter chill
each for a few moments
of early morning thrill
one screams out in glee
and far away I catch the echo
I can almost see the gleam
of fulfillment in his eye
as he straddles the sky

I awoke this morning
to the sound of waves
and a train passing down
below my beach-side bungalow
I saw purple shadows
—of sunrise
as I closed my eyes
to meditate

the sun is now reaching
where I sit on the porch
as I finish morning coffee and ponder . . .
sheltered passengers in flashing windows
of the iron horse that braves the same sand
as young surfers
and morning surf birds
—scampering

(San Clemente, sunrise)

* * *

ten feet high or more
the foam slaps the shore
a suede coat on the jetty
draped there by the wind

seagulls hang like mobiles
    in the air
as windsurfers struggle back

finding the long way home
—collapsed
by this unexpected burst
of autumn breath
—too tired to sail

there is not a sailboat in sight
as the sky swiftly darkens
little black running birds
fight the waves for the shore

from the east come the shimmering
flocks of pelicans
on the whistle down of the wind
heading for nighttime rest on the jetties

shining west as well
flocks of airplanes resembling fireflies
float softly down
onto unseen runways

walking sluggishly
taking the long way home
I watch the last pink sky
     fade
and the clouds shed
     to grey
as I finish another work day
setting by the sea

(Marina del Rey, sunset)

* * *

Santa Ana winds
—fires
and storm warnings

these I feel and hear
in my mind
as I view sand bags
piled high in anticipation
on this early autumn day

it is wee morning
as we sneak . . .
treading on virgin sand

the sea and wind
have cleansed it
beach is closed
storm windows locked

as we walk . . .
we could be
the only human beings
on this planet

for all the evidence
is only trails of 'Y'
on virgin sand

all, that is
except our clumsy
indentations
following us around
from behind

we could be the first here
. . . ever
untarnished
untouched by man
—virgin sand
as far as our eyes can see

except man's need
to fill his greed
piles high
the sand dunes of waste

and because of his haste
our beautiful seaside
    falls
        way
            by the wayside

polluted and trashed
why . . . I ask
as we walk freely
on virgin sand
seemingly untouched
by man

* * *

here I sit
on the edge of things
afraid to walk
near the sun

thrown by the great hand
of destiny
yearning for dreams
yet begun

out from the sky
comes the blue light of love
shining like all
that could be

strikes me awake
for the first time in ages
reminds me
of what I can see

reminds me I sing
for the ones still in cages
convey bits and pieces
that come out in stages

and play to an audience
fraught with despair
to shine some hope down
through the darkness they share

I'm sitting here . . . perched
on the edge of things
you wait for me
to recite

born from the image
of feelings I've known
or gathered from dreams
in the night

you gaze in my eyes
with the sadness of tears
for the lovers of love
who still fall

while I sing you the tales
of the true ones in time
who, knowing their fate
still risk all

reminds me I sing
for the ones still in cages
convey bits and pieces
that come out in stages

and play to an audience
fraught with despair
to shine some hope down
through the darkness they share

here I sit
on the edge of things
daring to walk
near the sun

thrown by the great hand
of destiny
loving the dreams
I've begun

* * *

deep pensive protagonist
seek something new
to remain a pessimist
just won't do

you see it's all over
if you don't come around
you make up the balance
you'll be glory bound

if you can see over
the blue horizon
it won't be just someone
alone criticizin'

so send in the sunshine
work till you win
the drunk again dreamer
is where you have been

play till you plaster it
all over town
work till you drench it
in beggars' renown

now shout it
don't doubt it
raise your voice
about it

the cause of caution
the case of your care
wash it away
till you end the despair

and the balance will rise
there will be no surprise when
it echoes all over
the blue horizon

* * *

this is for those
who work hard all your life
but never get the least bit
of notice

for those who are honest
for those who are brave
who mostly take it alone
to your grave

let this be
your unsung song
let its harmony
carry you along

when the going gets hard
and the road gets too long
let it be here
so you can feel strong

because you are the reason
we're here
and let me make one thing
quite clear

when we're lost
you know just what to do
and we really couldn't make it
without you

you strive for the right
because you know what is wrong
when we're feeling weak
you help us feel strong

you make us a part of
so we can belong
and we're grateful

so let this be
your unsung song
let its harmony
carry you along

when the going gets hard
and the road gets too long
let it be here
so you can feel strong

everything in life
seems to be going
against you
and the scales of balance
weigh heavily on you

and we may never show it
but we need you, my friend
'cause it's you
who keeps us going
in the end

so . . .
this can be your comeback
or it can be your never was
but what it really is
is your always will be

because this is
your unsung song
let its harmony
carry you along

when the going gets hard
and the road gets too long
let it be here
so you can feel strong

clear and honest / picture / concept / seems so rare / seeking / secret road trips / trapped in / wartime's lair / condemn the choice / platform creators / pornographic / innovators / suck the juice / regulators / corresponding / instigators / refer to agency / holdouts / keys of delta / averages / display despondent / career doubts / cry like running / savages / employees / who don't need it / nothing / will define / well-loved stories / plead it / trapped it / down the line / lost too soon / deploring / caught you / when you're snoring / served it up / with pleasure / buried bricks / of treasure / forgotten / in the rubble / damn it all / the struggle / working / with the underfed / painted all / with broken lead / just three stars / of wonder / half the nighttime's / plunder / total lack of / never mind / fought the fire / just in time / can you see / the naked lady / on the bike / who joined the navy / riding down / the dreams of skew / raped the outcome / turned it blue / more police / always drawn / fear of council / face the dawn / grant asylum / to the future / cold brew drinking / cracking suture / is it normal / is it sound / friends of Charlie / hit the ground / rock-n-roll / and New York madness / found the music / in their sadness / scramble on / the ramble / it's our world's / preamble / differences / and games abound / frolic daily / safety bound / survey says / you've got it made / find approval / in the shade

Set #6:

fantasy ballads and human frailties

you bathe in the depths of the sea
as The Blaster plays his reverie
deeper and deeper you go
to escape the sound
of a drowning planet
forever holding your breath
great upheavals seem so near

are you a dreamer
is this your own world
you can't even remember
how you got here
but the changes you are experiencing
seem so real

the coolness of the water
the shortness of your breath
the tears you've cried forevermore
in this never-ending death

has the bringer
of false promises
finally stumbled
how many ideas
with strong foundations
have crumbled

but no outward appearances
seem familiar here
except for the sound
of The Blaster
'cause you remember
where it's taken him
—the music
that is his master

and The Blaster
plays his disaster music
life after the holocaust

The Blaster plays
disaster music
life after time stood still

sinking deeper . . .
you try to hold fast to the truth
you think about what you would say
if you could speak to this world

are you open to the unfamiliar
don't you know
that everything changes
the only thing
that remains unchanged
is God

myriad opportunities called you
but the goal is beyond your grasp
for you have forgotten how to learn
and now the price of wisdom
—is death
and resurrection

is this a dirty trick
someone has played on you
maybe you're lost
in virtual reality
. . . but it seems so true

and on a clear day
you can see forever
whose life is this
anyway
you approach a house
to get a better view
and you see . . .

candelabras—like diamonds
shimmering through the windows
coals the color of Mars
glow in the fireplace
stairways to forever
reveal multi-layered cubicles
and the ceiling
   disappears
      into the stars

but then The Blaster
plays disaster music
life after apocalypse
introspective guitar riffs
—sparks
thrown in the air

The Blaster plays
disaster music
life after apocalypse
introspective guitar riffs
travel on and on

the cold wind blows
takes you where it will
turns you like a windmill
but only your word-travels
really break away from gravity

can't live in this cubicle
no more
The Earth is my home
got to stomp on the terra
gotta roam
but you can use me
to spread some energy

am I The Blaster . . .

The Blaster
plays disaster music
life after apocalypse
introspective guitar riffs
—sparks
thrown in the air

The Blaster plays
disaster music
life after apocalypse
introspective guitar riffs
travel on and on . . .

* * *

raspberry sweet
the tart cataclysm
rapture loomed
on the fetid breath
of dragon dew

the arrogant beast
he scarfed the mortal's share
of compassion
until his hideous fashion
was all he would ever declare

locked in the grasp
of his ever-growing ego
his was the scourge
—the ferment
that severed all beauty

the limp repose
of his saffron changing nectar
from angry crimson
to limping yellow

simply moved to bow his head
in reticent recoil
for the arrogance extended

now rendered ragged
feeling old and haggard
he longed to receive
all that he had taken
with no regard or sympathy

but no epiphany
was to be
for this beast of misery

* * *

I made the mistake of a lifetime
when I sold my Sunshine's soul
I couldn't help it
I wanted so much
what I could never control

Momma's gonna mold Sunshine
into a money-making machine
be what she could never be
no matter what it means

she sold her little Sunshine
for the feast or famine play
it wasn't for the money
but for the love . . . is what she'd say

you couldn't do it better
if you had a hundred weeks
she only had the best intentions
understanding what she seeks

as she peeks under the pillow
to steal another man
to make her feel the way she wants
anyway she can

to stuff the guilt
that's building up
she cannot bear to face
if he don't help
she'll find some drinks
and a man in another place

and Sunshine . . .
doesn't understand
she don't know what it means
to sell herself as a glamour queen
with all the other
money machines

she don't like the spotlight
the makeup . . . or the curls
she don't feel that
she's made up like
the other glamour girls

she just wants
to have some fun
like normal girls do
but Mamma's strong
and just don't see
what she's puttin' Sunshine thru

I made the mistake of a lifetime
when I sold my Sunshine's soul
I couldn't help it
I wanted so much
what I could never control

oh, Sunshine . . .
you're a poor girl
Mamma would always say
but I'm gonna make you famous
and you'll be a star someday

then everyone will look at you
and see the beauty I see
we'll be so rich
I'll never worry no more
what people think about me

what a life we're gonna have
what a world it's gonna be
nothin's gonna stop us now
we'll be so happy
. . . you'll see

if you'll only
    just live
        for me

I made the mistake of a lifetime
when I sold my Sunshine's soul
I couldn't help it
I wanted so much
what I could never control

* * *

she was a poor but comely girl
grown up on a podunk road
abused by those who should help
having to carry that heavy load

it took away her power
the only strength a young girl had
the power of a good woman
. . . now gone bad

it took her too many places
she never wanted to be
using her body to gain some leverage
was the only way she could see

she wanted to move forward
from the hard times
she wanted to strike out
on her own

she wanted to forget
all the abuse
—and corruption
but she was all alone

she'll never forget
how it all went down
how he wooed her and spoiled her
all over town

then he hit her and beat her
till she couldn't see clear
let him do what he wanted
as she gave in to fear

she'll never forget
why he took her there
to the Dunnigan Falls
meth lab lair

subjecting her
—a troubled girl
to the sullied world
that existed there

he caught her in the moment
she was weakest—at the best
she'd escaped from the worst
and disregarded the rest

he saw that she was hungry
took advantage 'cause he could
he'd done it so many times before
he was just no fuckin' good

he couldn't remember a time
when he'd ever had any regrets
about using a young girl's body
to get whatever he could get

he took her to the meth lab
traded her for a score
let them use her and abuse her
till he got what he wanted and more

he left her there forsaken
with nothin' but her shame
and went off lookin' (for the next young girl)
another victim to claim

she'll never forget
why he took her there
to the Dunnigan Falls
meth lab lair

subjecting her
—a forgotten girl
to the sullied world
that existed there

she escaped eventually
got away for good
headed down south
as far as she could

she wanted revenge
but didn't dare try
all she could do
was lay down and cry

then she pulled herself up
like it always had been
she was a good girl gone bad
tryin' to be good again

so many years now
workin' hard as she can
and it's still damn hard
for her to trust any man

but if one comes along
best not be in a hurry
for her faith or her love
'cause her eyes still get blurry

he'll never know the past she had
or what she had to do
unless he proves his virtue first
he'll never know what she's been through

'cause . . . she never can forget
why he took her there
to the Dunnigan Falls
meth lab lair

subjecting her
—an innocent girl
to the sullied world
that existed there

she'll never forget
why he took her there
to the Dunnigan Falls
meth lab madness

subjecting her
—an innocent girl
to that sullied world
and all its sadness

* * *

Badly Drawn Daily
was a seaside girl
Badly Drawn Daily
had the natural blonde curl

born in a kitchen
bred like a fox
her mind was in a jumble
like her long curly locks

Badly Drawn Daily
was a pregnant wannabe
a trigger finger mama
never silent
never happy

couldn't love a man
but didn't want no woman, no
rantin' and a'ravin'
is all she could really show

and she'd say . . .

arguing is the new discussin'
fighting is the new negotiatin'
dissing is the new being friendly
so where are we now?

Badly wandered 'round the desert
tryin' to burn out her desire
she knew she hated them god awful men
but her heart was still on fire

it was there she met Jim Jacker
so gritty and unrefined
and there was somethin' 'bout his demeanor
that just slapped her upside her mind

but she thought . . .

arguing is the new discussin'
fighting is the new negotiatin'
dissing is the new being friendly
so where are we now?

In a harmless fateful moment
in her blue light sparklin' jeans
Badly jumped her legs 'round Jim
like a vice grip with the means

and she thought . . .
don't throw me under
silent thunder
wrap me in your quiet storm

keep me close and keep me true
even though I'm nothin'
like the norm

and though she didn't know it
Jim had a good heart thru and thru
he grabbed this whacky woman
and he knew he would be true

but Badly was still haunted
by her twisted gnarly past
and all she could do was wonder
could somethin' like this last?

and she thought . . .

arguing is the new discussin'
fighting is the new negotiatin'
dissing is the new being friendly
so where are we now?

Badly Drawn Daily
was a doubter thru and thru
she ranted and she raved
in just about everything she'd do

she'd never known anyone
who could even come close
to bein' true
so in her gnarled up, emotional mind
she didn't know what to do

her heart said go ahead
Jim Jacker might be the one
could do all those things properly
no one had ever done

but with baggage as heavy as hers
she might as well take a trip
and run off to another place
where ever'one seemed hip

but Badly stayed with Jacker Jim
in spite of her inner wreck
and time was good to her
it taught her to reflect

Jim was true to his nature
he proved to be the one
who nurtured all the pain away
he knew how to get the job done

in time she actually got pregnant
no longer a wannabe
had a beautiful blue-eyed baby boy
the prettiest you ever did see

and it made Badly's life feel complete
it made her heart feel full
but sometimes . . .
that craziness inside of her
would still rise up and pull

and she'd think . . .

arguing is the new discussin'
fighting is the new negotiatin'
dissing is the new being friendly
so where are we now?

Badly Drawn Daily
had always been in doubt
because of how she was drawn
it's what her life was all about

a nip and tuck here
a nose job there
it's no wonder she was lost
and didn't seem to care

her creator must be stuck
on that plastic surgery craze
don't he know it just distresses her
and leaves her in a daze?

Badly likes who she is
but who she is a'keeps on changin'
It's hard to get a grip
when everthin's rearrangin'

and she thinks . . .

I've been here before
this all seems familiar
don't draw me this way anymore
I wanna move on

if she could just stay put long enough
to dig some gal danged roots
she'd have a place to call her home
and a home to hang her boots

so put yer pens and ink away
let me and baby and Jim Jacker stay
Jim likes to plant
and this seems a good spot
besides . . .
our roots is all we got

and she thinks . . .

I've been here before
this all seems familiar
don't draw me this way anymore
I wanna move on

475

in time she forgot the drawing abuse
and settled in to family life
Jim planted a garden as beautiful
as could be
to help put an end to Badly's strife

and Badly would spend her mornings there
but she'd see others bein' abused
by men they couldn't trust
and the artists always drawin'
the bigger bust

but Jim would reassure her
don't worry Badly
our love will last
I love you just the way you are
but Badly just thought of the past

she felt in her heart nothin' had changed
it was all the same old crap
but she'd shove it away
to the back of her mind
and put baby down for a nap

then she'd think . . .

I've been here before
this all seems familiar
don't draw me this way anymore
I wanna move on

yes, Badly Drawn Daily
was a doubter thru and thru
she still ranted and she raved
in just about everything she'd do

but Jim Jacker was persistent
he tried to make her see
just because you've been abused before
that's not the way it's gotta be

think about the things that move you
think about the things we share
so many things to be thankful for
so many ways to care

there are moments all around you
moments to be kind
moments to remind you
to keep a hopeful mind

but Badly Drawn Daily
had a hankerin' in her mind
Badly Drawn Daily
wasn't the level headed kind

withdrawin' to her own world
she'd be singin' her own song
thinkin' all those wayward thoughts
that made it hard to be strong

but then Badly started singing
to a different brighter song
tryin' to trust what Jacker said
and tryin' to move on

move on from the awful nightmares
that still invaded her mind
to live a life of happiness
and leave the bad drawin' behind

their lives grew brighter
as baby grew bigger
life got busy and seemed okay
and yet way down inside of Badly
that chatter would still have its way

and she'd start to have her doubts again
even though her life was good
and she'd think the drawing was bad again
instead of knowing the things she should

and she'd think . . .

I've been here before
this all seems familiar
don't draw me this way anymore
I wanna move on

Badly Drawn Daily
was a seaside girl
Badly Drawn Daily
had the natural blonde curl

born in a kitchen
bred like a fox
her mind was in a jumble
like her long curly locks

Badly Drawn Daily
will always have her doubts
those wayward places in her mind
will always bring on bouts

But she knows . . . now
because she has hope . . . now
and she has compassion

and she thinks . . .

I've been here before
this all seems familiar
don't draw me this way anymore
I wanna move on

* * *

Aurora Borealis
was a flagrant, fragrant, flippant girl
she was so frazzled
all done up in curls

the curls of the sea waves
. . . called to her
in a mermaid's song
and she listened . . . and watched

but she was blinded
by the rays of the Northern Lights
reflected on the water

she was wrapped up
in sultry linen and lace
in her usual summer place

she was a drummer
and played until her fingers
were swollen and splayed
but she couldn't catch a glimpse
of her sailor's wandering ship

though she kept thinking
she could hear
his screaming guitar

she looked far . . . far
off in the distance
where those Northern Lights
were still in the sky
reminding her with a sigh
of a familiar mermaid song

oh where was this guy
who sailed off
with all the sailors

she thought he was gonna be
a tailor
but now he was
just another swabbie
wannabe

poor, poor
Aurora Borealis
never been kissed
was she even missed

she cried . . .
on the edge of the sea
or was it just the sea mist
making her mascara run
down to her knees
her woes beset her

oh well . . .
she might as well gather up her curls
go back to her teepee
and spin on her spinning wheel

like her mind was spinnin'
rockin' and a'reelin'
from the spell of his . . .
haggard spiel

she sat down at her drum
with her large fingers
and swollen thumb
and beat it to a lather
to rout out the blather
going on inside

still hoping her sailor boy
would hear it
and come back for his bride

or maybe . . .
catch a glimmer of her beat
from a mermaid singing

even if he did like
swabbing decks better
than her love letters

and his sailor buddies
who danced a lively tune
to the light of the moon
. . . they did swingingly swoon

but Aurora was swooning too
as she was prone to do
swooning to the mermaid song

her drumming could be heard
long and far
off the shore it carried
like a hovering bird

sailing out to sea
for her sailor
where she knew he could hear
the mermaid quite clear
it was music to his ear

the searing, suffering sunshine
of the far and distant sea
sang these songs to him

the mermaid siren
the drumming of his bride
that would never be

for he could not leave
his seamen
so he just screamed
with his guitar

and . . .

Aurora Borealis
sang with the mermaids
drummed till she was raw

and the Northern Lights
were all she saw
from her seaside teepee

Aurora Borealis
was a flagrant, fragrant, flippant girl
she was so frazzled
all done up in curls

the curls of the sea waves
they called to her
in a mermaid's song

and she listened
. . . and watched
. . . and remembered

she lay upon a nature's throne
her eyes sparkling . . . at the edge of the sea
his warrior's chest hovered over her
his intentions as plain as could be

for his eyes were as deep as an ocean
of liquid blue in a cool diamond sea
yet the fiery flash that sparked before her
told her this man was a mystery

yes his flash was like that of a wizard
but like none that she had ever seen
for his touch was as gentle as a whisper
and she shuddered with sighs in between

and oh how she longed for
this magic she knew
as if it had always been
true

Aurora sat on her nature's throne
her eyes sparkling . . . at the edge of the sea
she awoke from what seemed
like a heavenly dream
. . . for how could this love ever be

* * *

there was this secret person
in the '60s
he wasn't Jesus
he could've been a prophet
but he never came out

and either . . .
everybody knew who he was
. . . or
nobody knew who he was

there was a light in his eyes
that could be recognized
and he always thought
when he saw the magical beings
that they knew he was there

and he always thought
when the musical inspiration
was at its height
that they could see him
and that they knew it was him
that they saw the light in his eyes

and he always knew
he was one of them
and they were of the same tribe
but it never was verbalized

> bright eyes
> they could see him
> even from far away
> bright eyes
> they can still remember
> even to this day

        bright eyes
        you could see him
        even from far away
        bright eyes
        you could have saved him
        but you turned away

they staged a concert
on the pier
at Santa Monica beach
they called it Brucemas
in celebration of Lenny Bruce

thousands of people
gathered on the sand below
and he was there
cross-legged, frying on LSD
in a meditative pose

he knew they all were watching
even though his eyes were closed
as the music began
the waves suddenly rose
they grew big, then bigger, then huge
as if attracted by the people
the music
  . . . and him

the people moved back
to give the waves room
in this magical moment
. . . beginning
he felt as if magnets
of the peoples' minds
had attracted them

and suddenly he was scared
he felt like a martyr
though he didn't want to be
. . . not again

and from that day forward
when they gathered
in the name of music
whenever he was there
he would feel . . .
like they were watching him

and he was watching them
and they could see the light
in his eyes

they would see him
at the gatherings
his bright eyes in the crowd
they never did acknowledge him
but always did him proud

they failed to change the world enough
the way they said they would
and he was never
brought into the fray

but he would have changed it
. . . if he could
if he would have been given
the chance
but he was never invited
to the dance

        bright eyes
        he could see them
        even though he didn't say
        bright eyes
        still remembers
        always wishing for a way

        bright eyes
        you could see him
        even from far away
        bright eyes
        you could have saved him
        but you turned away

and so, what could have been
but never was to be
faded away beyond the '60s
but every so often
the magic could still be felt
. . . and heard . . . and seen
and those around him
who realized the tribe
was really still alive
looked deep inside his eyes
. . . deep inside his eyes

and he knew he had
—the talent
he could have been any kind of artist
a painter, a musician, a dancer
but he was a poet
and the words flowed out of him

although he never got
any real acclaim
he had his own fame
in the universal frame
his muse was to blame

it always came so easily
poured straight out of his dreams
it was so fulfilling
whenever he was in the act
—of creating

and he always knew
he was one of them
and they were of the same tribe
but it never was verbalized

>bright eyes
>they could see him
>even from far away
>bright eyes
>they can still remember
>even to this day

>bright eyes
>you could see him
>even from far away
>bright eyes
>you could have saved him
>but you turned away

another time . . . on LSD
there was a television
manipulation
he was sitting in front of the TV
watching the movie, Ulysses

when it came time
for killing the Cyclops
he said . . . what about peace
. . . what about not killing
. . . what about non-violence
. . . what about compassion

the movie suddenly
turned to him
and Ulysses stopped
. . . and looked at him
. . . and asked him questions
giving him the choice
wanting him to decide
should they kill
or not kill
the Cyclops

. . . and the TV waited for his answer

there were witnesses
his best friend
his brother
his best friend girl
but no one wanted
to talk about it
—afterwards

and he wondered
but was not sure
if it was really true
or just the acid
—its psychedelic experience

then . . . after the movie
they listened to an epic song
by Procol Harum
"In Held Twas I"
he loved to dance to it
but as he did
it scared his brother
he didn't know why

and the truth of the matter was
he knew that the dance
was really about him
. . . yet still he knew
he was never invited

        bright *eyes*
        he could see them
        even though he didn't say
        bright *eyes*
        still remembers
        always wishing for a way

        bright *eyes*
        you could see him
        even from far away
        bright *eyes*
        you could have saved him
        but you turned away

every time
he ever got close
he was pushed away
or some nefarious thing
always ruined the day

and so . . .
he would find comfort
in drugs and booze
with his best friend girl

he would often
go to her place
above the clubs
share some wine
smoke some pot
listen to the magic
of The Moody Blues

they had become
best friends
in high school
first week Aquarians

psychic buddies of the same tribe
psychedelic poets in the night
—collaborating
when the inspiration was bright

        snow upon the river
        melted through the grime
        formula for the Aquarian age
        made for just that time

if there was a way to see
they would show you how
—memories
of the inner consciousness
deeper than the now

there is complexity
in simplicity
that most people miss
simplicity found
in perfect rhyme
that didn't before exist

complexity of simplicity
is hard won, sometimes
. . . hard to come by
. . . hard to achieve
yet flows so easily
in the scheme of things

he always knew
he was one of them
that they were of the same tribe
they could have made such harmony
but it never was verbalized

    bright eyes
    they could see him
    even from far away
    bright eyes
    they can still remember
    even to this day

    bright eyes
    you could see him
    even from far away
    bright eyes
    you could have saved him
    but you turned away

there was this secret person
in the '60s
he wasn't Jesus
he could've been a prophet
but he never came out

and either . . .
everybody knew who he was
. . . or
nobody knew who he was

there was this light in his eyes . . .

* * *

he was the last hippy poet
of the Woodstock Generation
he would often take people
to the last hippy refuge

to share a little bit
of what used to be
to share a little vision
of what he still could see

the hippies of the '60s
created a counter-culture
that changed the world
but where did all
the brotherhood go

where is the refuge
for the humanity of spirit
so many forks in the road
that followed . . .

brought us to the world
we now live in
but where, oh where . . .
—where is that refuge
where the tribes used to go

. . . okay . . .

so you take Hwy 101
north to Topanga Canyon
go south until you hit
the Pacific Ocean

turn right
about a quarter mile
there will be a dirt road
take it down

on the west side
is the riverbed
hike it to the beach

we'll all build a big bonfire
then it is a no-brainer
from there . . .

he was the last hippy poet
of the Woodstock Generation
he would often take people
to the last hippy refuge

to share a little bit
of what used to be
to share a little vision
of what he still could see

. . . early morning
. . . frozen faces
gathered in the traveling pool
shuttle for the 21st century

thoughts of you
move around my mind
as I'm still wakin' up
and sippin' my morning coffee

coke machines
on a flatbed truck
and a one-piece pick-up
now that's pretty rare

traffic's touch and go
—as usual
but I left in plenty of time
to get there

I've learned not to hurry
it causes too much strain
you can see it in the eyes
of so many . . . who snicker

—zooming by
wondering why everyone
doesn't go 80
so they can get to . . . nowhere
—quicker

but . . .
the last hippy refuge
is just around the bend
it's time to go back there
again

so I can be closer
to my ideals
and remember . . .
that brotherhood was real

it wasn't just
a state of mind
it was the way we treated
each other
with compassion and caring
and everyone sharing
what they had
—and glad to

just to make it
through the day
with a smile
upon our faces

the last hippy refuge
is just around the bend
it's time to go back there
again

the last hippy refuge . . .
where the beach meets the riverbed
we can sit around the campfire
and get out of our own heads
. . . for awhile

watch the waves
and play guitar
sing some songs
about love and flowers

it's the best place to be
just who we are
and while away the hours

the last hippy poet
of the Woodstock Generation
loved to turn people on
to the last hippy refuge

to share a little bit
of what used to be
to share a little vision
of what he still could see

he would often recite his poems
to the tribe gathered there
poems about love
and of being aware

wherever he came from
wherever he'd roam
he was the last hippy poet
and this was his home

the last hippy refuge
is just around the bend
it's time to go back there
again

so we can be closer
to our ideals
and remember . . .
that our tribes were real

the last hippy refuge
is calling me again
got to go back there
whenever I can

so I can be closer
to my ideals
and remember . . .
that brotherhood was real

got to get away
from this insanity
get back in touch
with humanity

you can go there too . . .
I'll take you

he was the last hippy poet
of the Woodstock Generation
he would often take people
to the last hippy refuge

to share a little bit
of what used to be
to share a little vision
of what he still could see

* * *

the night has a million voices
I can hear them when you sing
they sing in glory and harmony
of the joy your heart can bring

if I only knew the story
I would sing it too
the feelings that you gather
the love it's brought for you

it matters not, I say
if I know or tell
for all who sing with you
know your story well

it echoes in the mountains
and breaks along the shore
the songs you sing
the joy you bring
I know they say much more

so if I ever find you
I'll sing in harmony too
just to know the joy of being
with all who sing with you

the night has a million voices
I can hear them when you sing
they sing in glory and harmony
of the joy your heart can bring

the scarlet sun sets
as the full moon rises
it's the night of the whispering poet

angels whisper
their songs to you
until your heart truly knows it

the Sun . . . and the Moon . . . and the Stars
they are your life tonight
and what more do you really need
than the nature of God's given light

good night Mr. Sunshine
see you tomorrow
birds swoop and chatter
pelicans dive

by the glowing ocean waves
many share long lost sorrow
born again tattered souls
grateful to be alive

frosty, then lacy
the water is like satin
all night sound effects
reflect your broken sleep

in your dream you run
to the brink of the cool ocean
but the sand is so hot
it scorches your fleeting feet

you wade in the water
so cool—your toes all tingle
then sit in your sand-castle chair

in the waves at the edge of the sea
you watch shimmering children play
present & past seem to mingle
as you stare
        out to sea
                and you see . . .
party boats
filled with prom queens
—dancing
to their new found gleam

or is it just you and me
talking honestly
between ice cream kisses
floating
        on the edge
                of your dream

the scarlet sun sets
as the full moon rises
it's the night of the whispering poet
angels whisper
their song to you
until your heart truly knows it

the poet he whispers
verses barely heard
the meaning so profound
you can't miss a word

for if you don't catch them
you won't understand
and misconstrued night-songs
will be close at hand

the deeper you go
the more you will see
this sunset . . . and full moon
were meant to be

the angels have flown now
their song is long gone
it's only in your heart now
that it lingers on

and if you remember
and if you are true
the dream you are sharing
will follow it through

it will be your due
and all true hearts will know it
they all will sing in harmony
—on the night of the whispering poet

the verses of the ages
come down from the sages
and the cages of your hearts
which have been closed

will be flung wide open
to understand and shine
the truth will be yours
and you will be mine
if you believe

the scarlet sun sets
as the full moon rises
on the night of the whispering poet
where angels sing
their songs to you
until your hearts truly know it

yes, the scarlet sun sets
the full moon rises
it's the night of the whispering poet
angels whisper
their songs to you
until your heart truly knows it

the night has a million voices
I can hear them when you sing
they sing in glory and harmony
of the joy your heart can bring

* * *

the darkness
of the effervescent kingdom
was hard to describe
just a smear of light
among the black demise

the king had been driven
from his evening song
by the queen's able bodied
twice endeared ruffian

garnering a smooth endeavor
was a hard apple to core
it was bitter
it was tart
it was anything
but smart

dangling . . .
from descending credibility
the prince was never anointed
it was with immeasurable congeniality
that the princess tried to help

significant scenes
would imbue themselves
the very stars in the sky
would respond
with their dimming twinkles

it was a sign of the emotions
that always defined
the renegade resemblance
of these hardened, darker times

the times refracted
in the kingdom's effervescent light

how would you know
it was always concealed
no one's true feelings
were revealed

in the temporary remnants
of sensations sending signals
in the vast meadows
green with lush grass
and birch trees
the deer and cotton tails
—scrambled

just as the dark
was about to render it useless
the prince found the strength
and resolve of his character

feelings aside
he rose to the occasion
bolstered by his critical thinking
and sound reasoning

the princess stood with him
the king climbed the stairs
the queen and her ruffian
stumbled in the dark

in the interim
the effervescence grew
the darkness waned
just a little

and people began
to be encouraged
not a lot
but it was a beginning

neighboring rulers
took note
in time
things began to normalize

light and dark
good and evil
they had all played their part
but the effervescence
was slowly returning

one day
a curious thing happened
tenderness
requested an audience

why have you
forsaken me so
asked tenderness
to the queen
why have you behaved
so dire

the queen had no answer
she just glared
they all knew
it was born of her lust
and her ruffian
with his ruffian ways

but nonetheless
things were getting brighter
the effervescent shadows
grew in color and brilliance

they became like rainbows
covering the sky
and the darkness faded

standing on the mountaintop
at cliff's edge
the princess gazed out
over the effervescent kingdom

her bright blue eyes
lit up like the azure blue
of the effervescent sea
her long curly locks
blowing in the wind
as red as a Verona sunset

happy she was
that the prince
had retained his elegance
proud but impatient she was
for the adventure yet to begin

she found comfort
in the thought
that saner minds had prevailed
a red eagle confirmed the sign
as over her head it sailed

finger lily / blue cup jam / steel pot / nailed cover / slam me / slam me / foamy soap / on a blank covered wall / blue bird bares it / nobody out-stares it / stripe it / wipe it / blackened fish pie / blow the kettle backwards / with a hickory sigh / spin it till it opens / type it till it knows / show the picture / pixilated / resample till it grows / hover on your password / login with a dime / send the fairy bubbles / while she's flying to the crime / captured like lightning / gone with a roar / can you explain it / to even the score / a mind-bending flash / memory's plight / travel my brain cells / like ships in the night / stagnant curled / boulder treatment / sticks in a stall / waiting for will-call / stored electric / craftsmen adapter / locked up in danger / warning to a stranger / silver-haired demon / wrenched in the mud / semi-sound clingers / in unbounded crud / came to believe / lies could sing / sold you the crunchiest king / he was the elixir / of Shennagan Shoe / instead of demeanor / he lived with the shrew / went by the name / of Ju Ju B. Jackup / spread all his sugar / without any backup / jammed it all up / without any doubt / tried to remember / where the karma ran out / out to the lawn / and into the gutter / fish in the pond / remarked on the clutter / stuck now in semblance / back to the barn / beckoned by brilliance / sewn in the yarn / mad mental magnets / repel in the end / the imported bangle / the hypnotic trend / towel it dry / lick it wet / send it with some / well-worn sweat / hack it / whack it / bang it to the bone / mangled mess to mention / when you're all alone / if you can't renounce it / forget from whence it came / it was just to break your sadness / spark you with the flame

Set #7:

artistic declarations, religiosity, and amphigory moments

if you find inspiration

and fulfillment

in the original art

that you create

then you are

a successful artist

everything else

is relative

* * *

I sing the obvious
harmony understood
by majority

I bring the purview
relatable range
of thoughts

the gravity of things
relevant
can bring comfort

if not relegated
to merely
the deep

* * *

snow geese bank
across the meadow
right in front
of my windshield

inspiration
in its simplest
natural form
if only I could
capture it
write it down
share it

* * *

windy
spindly
weeping birches

dripping roses
like raindrops
in a dream

* * *

do you ever notice someone
who looks up
into the sky
when you are talking with them

pondering what you have said
slowly, for a moment
before responding

when you see that person
with eyes to the sky
looking for the thought
that's fleeting

that is the thing
—the real thing

sky gazers
keep it grounded
often astounding
in their recognition
of things
pondered and rendered

do you see the sparkle
in their eye
can you see they are truly
thinking

thoughtfully
notably
considerably

a true
and measurable sign
of deep listening
and consideration

always looking up
seeing the view
—inside

pondering the possibilities
. . . of you
to express something new

sky gazers
keep it grounded
often astounding
in their recognition
of things
pondered and rendered

* * *

for you and me
it's a time of trouble
feast or famine
wherever we go

it may sound simple
. . . yes it's true
but help your brothers
is what you've got to do

that's still it
don't you know
the second coming
will show

the second coming
will be as a woman
nurturing and compassion
is what will show

it's got to be
don't you know
it's what we need—now
to grow

. . . higher . . . spiritually

can't you see
all the waste we make
in our haste

we leave behind
so much trash
to get there too fast

but where is it
we are going
do you think you know

you may think
you're growing now
but the second coming
will show

the second coming
will be as a woman
nurturing and compassion
is what will show

it's got to be
don't you know
it's what we need—now
to grow

. . . higher . . . spiritually

Goddess of Love
brings the Light
to shine on our needs

coming soon
to a state of mind
near you

* * *

yes, I am a Christian
aggressive, pushy
holier than thou
—and I'm advertising

give me your money
all that you can
I need it to build
my own church
—my own way

make my view of God
a part of your plan
and I'll give you my blessing
—Hosanna

young girls smile
all the boys sing
it's part of God's plan
you know that Jesus
is a friend of mine

so come on
all God's children
and give it to me
give me all you got

and I'll put my hands on you
I'll make you whole
'cause it's what I do

you ask me
what I will do
with all the money I get

sorry . . . Jesus is closed today
please try your call again later

* * *

a lifetime of betrayal
bewilderment and deceit
always rising to the occasion
while you're always in retreat

always been forsaken
by those you love the most

and even though you've been forgotten
you won't give up the ghost

how is it you continue
how is it you reprieve
the themes of love and brotherhood
from you they never leave

so many scars beyond repair
so many times you've drowned
and those around so unaware
who stomp you in the ground

no starry-eyed companion
no comrade-in-arms for you
gave it up and died in vain
just couldn't see it through

and though your time is lonely
your plaintive cry unheard
you always think, if only
they'd understand the word

and though your thoughts don't mingle
and fall on deafened ears
you understand that single . . . thread
that's followed through the years

the word of love so driven
the word of heartache shared
the sacrifice that's given
to show someone you've cared

you try to make a difference
but it just doesn't matter
everybody's too blind to see
or else they're caught up
in the chatter

how can you make
a world of compassion
how can you take a stance

when no one wants
to hear your song
and no one wants to dance

like so many in the world today
you think everything is war
you think sports and competition
are what we're here for

but you fell like branches
in the wind
the curled up consciousness
yet to begin

pulled too tight
until it burst
coughed up technology's
redemption

the stellar revolution
—it's so blue
oh, it's so blue

and everyone's just tryin' to be
—a celebrity

war is not the answer
find a common ground
compassion and understanding
are where the real truth
can be found

and though it may not
sound a lot
you must nurture the little
that's left

for in the end
it's all you've got
and you'll sing it
till . . . your . . . last . . . breath

* * *

dancing on the sea of solemnity
incendiary thoughts
a painful display in wordplay
describing the outside of the inner circle
—mad

is the specter of spiritual insincerity
intuitive in such a manner

dividing the salacious signature
of adorable gratification

is this a sliding scale
does it ever spring up to
the other side of silence
what does it encourage
in the grand scheme of desire

is the ever prescient quality
of acknowledgment
bringing to surface the radical procurement
of the absent manifestation of resilience

the very scope of bewilderment
attains a smudge of consternation
or is that a smidgen
of mundane texture

riding on the fence of inquisitiveness
in the small but quaint
acquiescence
of your temptation

* * *

at the end of the dilemma
—he gaped
then requested an assembly
of all concerned

damn it all anyway
so many wanted to say
after reading the obligatory writing
of absurdity

it went down like a lead cannonball
into the depths of dramatic ridicule

what in the name of belligerent wherewithal
are you trying to sell us
the masses complained

what in the end will apply
is it the various and nimble petals
of multicolored fragments

is it the semblance
of nefarious to-dos

chatter no more
they begged
save it for the unadorned king
of disguise

send it to the bottom
of the well-known regrets

you'll find it's easier that way
you'll find it's not too deep
—in meaning
you'll find, in the end
that you can swallow it whole

so save the whole thing
for your future ancestors
who will have no idea
what it means

it is just automatic
writing to the blind

* * *

why is it that I feel
—so invisible
why is it that I still feel
—so alone

worked hard
to give voice to so many
worked hard
to stay true to myself
but what is my lot

yes, it feels good
to be me—to be who I am
but what do I really get
from this

what should I expect
after all is said and done
should I really expect
nothing at all

should I really expect
only invisibility

—yes
I get the satisfaction
of being myself
yet it is lonely here
in my uniqueness

* * *

gypsy writers on the wavelength
spin their hearts upon the page
freedom riders of the future
ride the magic language waves

you can see them pour their hearts out
on the net around the world
spreading images of truth . . .
inspiration unfurled

do you doubt the dreams you've made
as your muse designs you
do you find your soul's been braved
as the verse reminds you

you roam the world with your wordsong
imagination is where you belong
you land to lend a helpful pen
then roam to do it again

gypsy writers on the wavelength
spin your hearts upon the page
freedom riders of the future
ride the magic language waves

* * *

fluid colors dripping like musical notes
forged roughage of the human soul
sacrificing the knowledge of the ages
to the leaky patterns of creation

the blossoms in the beating of your bosom
simply beautify your blush
the rush of your judgment
the tick-tick-trickling of your tears

—oh, these are the yearning years

play me high on your abstract piccolo
blow me over in your dominos
think of long-worn winter clothes
curled up with no one that anyone knows

the summer rain has gone astray
the bird has taken the cat as prey
the present is chasing the future away
it's the tainted loss of the golden day

Asian flowers falling as talking gropes
following words down the pages of hope
the sheer factor makes it noisy
gleams the shine off hard-scored memory

discover the experience to sing
. . . finally aloud
and bring it to the table high and proud
as if it were able to adjust the untouchable fears

—of these, the yearning years

play me high on your abstract piccolo
blow me over in your dominos
think of long-worn winter clothes
curled up with no one that anyone knows

* * *

reflections of softness
boxed in a bash
circles now broken
bound to make hash

smoke it, drink it
walk it in a shoe
tip-toe it softly
it's the least you can do

save, but don't spare it
recline till it folds
all this audacity
breaks all the molds

can you compare it
to anything sound
reverse declare it
hell-bent unbound

you know you can relish it
straight till you drop
finesse it and quiver
from bottom to top

you slip down in passion
encumber it all
amaze me and phase me
your hunger won't fall

do my words arouse you
confuse you
conspire you to desire

define you
incline you
what do they inspire

wordmaker—bookmaker
bind me a song
find me a few thoughts
that I can prolong

bring 'em in bunches
coddle it close
slither me slowly
till I overdose

* * *

the outer ether
sonic world
is break your mode
create

are there really
other existence modes
we can only access
in our dream state

can we really
delineate
the angular-scopic
modular plate

in order to create
a more sonic groove
that our senses and ears
only begin to move

24 stations
of modular plate
it's the chill-down, baby
that allows us to create

in the quietest mode
where you cannot berate
the inside, the outside
the phonetic elate

you can almost taste
the electrons
as they go down

* * *

just another bit of fluff
nonsense
strife and despair
captured as it is
cause for yet another
broken sleep

trivialities abound
as numbolina dances
dull needles on my fingertips
billions of molecules
millenniums of shadows
to be remembered

patterns procured
by the rug-weavers
of time
selected randomly
by the sender
from the mind blender

* * *

just sitting here writing a rhyme
and thinking I can't do it
but as soon as I get past the fear
then I just get to it

and it flows much the same as before
when I've come to what seems a locked door
and I think this is surely the end
but the door opens up once again

fear tells me I've nothing to say
yet here I am once again on my way
to completing this line just in time
to finish another short rhyme

Part 3:

Butterflies On Lavender

narrative verse on the nature of love:

unveiling the many facets of love—and the feelings thereof

Selected from over 50 years of poetic inspiration,
this section was composed during the pandemic of 2020-2021

• • •

I am but a humble street poet
I hope you like my ramblings
I put them down here
to entertain you

Part 3:

Butterflies On Lavender

narrative verse on the nature of love.

unveiling the many facets of love - and the feelings thereof.

Set #1:

incidental observation: awakenings of love

you know you come
from down below
from the poor side of town
you walk along with your crutch
while she's dancing free style

you think about
how the bad luck has been
as you pass her by
while she gives you
such a free smile

but you could help her
with your common sense
keep her from being raped
by this world of difference

a world of difference
is where we are
a world of love
is where we could be
if we could travel
. . . as far as we can see

things have come far
in such a short time
but people still live
in such different worlds
although they are
so close together

she is rich
and you are poor
she's used to money
you're used to being sore
as you think about all
the reasons why

but you could help her
with your common sense
keep her from being raped
by this world of indifference

a world of indifference
is where we are
a world of love
is where we could be
if we could travel
. . . as far as we can see

* * *

you look so good in your Mercedes
the sun showing through your dress
to your creamy white skin
on this sunny Sunday

as I pass . . . I tell you so
you look at me and smile . . . shyly
I look ahead
and almost rear end a cop
as you pass me by—laughing

I find a lucky quarter in the grass
daisies flipping all around
you focus your camera to the ground
then focus your lens on me

as you sit there
in your blue jeans
on the park bench

sunny Sunday women
are everywhere
I must have spring fever—late
summer adds a certain spring
to their gate

on the stairs . . .
she puffs her cigarette
then pauses to draw pictures
of passing by people
she gets up, walks away
with a summery smile aimed at me

I get to my car . . .
and see you there
on the stone stairs, writing
I drive by whistling a tune

you look up with bright eyes
straight into mine
then down again to your words
as I drive away on this sunny Sunday

sunny Sunday women
are everywhere
I must have spring fever—late
summer adds a certain spring
to their gate

. . . but I'm late

* * *

you never feel so alive
as when you are in love
it's worth the risk of the heartache
love can bring

would you rather go through life
without ever knowing love
. . . or feeling truly alive
. . . or hearing your heart sing

there are no guarantees
that it will all work out
if you take a leap of faith
you only remove your own doubt

but you guarantee it won't work out
if you don't take the leap
without trust you will always long for
a true love you can keep

you've heard the phrase
better to have loved
and lost
than never to have loved at all
well . . .
you've got to take the leap
go ahead
    and fall

if you want to
really experience love
you've got to take
the lover's leap

it's a matter of faith
that you can trust
a true love
you can keep

but someday
love may tear you apart
and you'll think it's because
they weren't the one

many times
you may think you're in love
but you can go a long time
without trusting someone

if you want someone
to trust your love
it's a two way street
you've got to give

how can you expect
to have true love
if you can't even trust
who you want to be with

you take a leap of faith
that your love will
—always
be there for you

and be true
—no matter what
for whatever amount of time
is bestowed upon you

you feel that your love
won't abandon you
it is something
you can believe

and problems become
just that . . .
problems to be worked out
not reasons to leave

if you want to
really experience love
you've got to take
the lover's leap

it's a matter of faith
that you can trust
a true love
you can keep

if you both take the leap
chances are good
you will have a love
that will last

for you see
trust in love
is everything
it is faith . . . manifest

and without faith
there is no hope
and what is hope
but your dreams and your longing

for love
that is fulfilled by faith
. . . through trust
the feeling of belonging

if you want to
really experience love
you've got to take
the lover's leap

it's a matter of faith
that you can trust
a true love
you can keep

if you want to
really experience love
you've got to take
the lover's leap

it's a matter of faith
that you can trust
a true love
you can keep

* * *

the first time that I saw you
looking straight at me
I longed to be inside
your fiery love

and it feels like the first time
when love was brand new
a love . . .
you just can't get enough of

deep blue eyes
with flown back hair
feels so good

wish she would
come along
feel so strong

love is sweet
then love is cold
but thinking about you
I feel so bold

yesterday came back
too soon
dreaming of you
and the blue moon

deep blue eyes
with flown back hair
feels so good

wish she would
come along
feel so strong

woke up . . .
wish you were next to me
that's the way it should be
but you're gone
—time to move on

deep blue eyes
with flown back hair
feels so good

wish she would
come along
feel so strong

* * *

don't cry any tears over me
for we met like the wind and the tree

I blew here to your steady ground
not knowing where I was bound

with your fair green eyes
and skin softly browned

just think about
what we have found

but we met like the wind and the tree
so don't cry any tears over me

I came to you, then you came to me
it seems it was meant to be

but as I leave you, and you go from me
think of our love, how it's free

think of how good, love, we feel
look at this love, how it's real

and maybe on another bright day
this warm breeze will blow back your way

for we met like the wind and the tree
so don't cry any tears over me

* * *

Shahnah—
    like the wind
        that rules the sky

soft and tender
   or roaring
      as you fly

Shahnah—
    old soul
        leading spirits high

nothing can top the sparkle in your eye

for a woman
   you're so young
      you taste so sweet

softly spoken
   supple lips
      your kisses can't be beat

mature you are
   diamond star
      clear spirit of the sun

so young
   and yet so old
      with a new life you've just begun

Shahnah—
    like the wind
        that rules the sky

soft and tender
   or roaring
      as you fly

Shahnah—
    old soul
        leading spirits high

nothing can top the sparkle in your eye

love me
    take me
        love me

—feel me love

take me
    love me
        hold me

—feel me love

Shahnah—
    like the wind
        that rules the sky

nothing can top that sparkle in your eye

* * *

far from the worries
of urban city madness
away from the heartbreak
the loneliness
the sadness

there's a place to slip into
like a crack in time
there's a woman waiting there
with a hunger in her eyes

Priscilla's escape
is the scent of a dream
a silky long-haired
rhythm machine

come for a little while
stay for a lifetime
escape with me
on the dreamline

hypnotize me
with those dark piercing eyes
roll me away
with your firm brown thighs

olive complexion—erotica
don't know where she got it
but she's got it

the scent of Escape
covers your body
hold me closer
take me home

feel the passion
the flushed-heated kind
embarrassed . . . not me
—I'm blinded

just caught in your spell
. . . you see
and the rhythm you weave
with your body

as you materialize my dream
the peaches in my cream
the madness that is gone
your scent that lingers on

Priscilla's escape
is the scent of a dream
a silky long-haired
rhythm machine

come for a little while
stay for a lifetime
escape with me
on the dreamline

hypnotize me
with those dark piercing eyes
roll me away
with your firm brown thighs

olive complexion—erotica
don't know where she got it
but she's got it

* * *

if I could speak
from the power
of observation
it would be closing in
on your sweet pink passion

   as it . . .

gleams from the sheen
of anticipation

it's the journey
of the lotus blossom—blooming
as you enter the realm
of intimate passage

box o' flames
reveals its mystery
driven by purity
white as snow

box o' flames
is a mystical giant
the only limit
is your mind

turquoise—amber
amethyst—jade
oblong longing
in sapphire blue

capture before closing
acknowledge the shudder
surrender to the heat
of what becomes you

if you yearned for greater measure
I would stretch
to feel your love
push aside the pink lace
—wrapture
of your moist pink sigh

   as it . . .

heightens my great longing
for your love

it's the journey
of the lotus flower—falling
the more you pull it apart
the greater it becomes

box o' flames
reveals its mystery
driven by pleasure
hot as the sun

box o' flames
is a mystical giant
the only limit
is the sky

turquoise—amber
amethyst—jade
oblong longing
in sapphire blue

capture before closing
acknowledge the shudder
surrender to the heat
of what becomes you

* * *

I lay here in our love bed
thinking for awhile
reflecting on that special touch
remembering your smile

there's a feeling deep inside you
when everything's okay
you settle into here and now
and hope it stays that way

seen so seldom
times been told
visions of
and dreams of old

bring it now
this time speak true
side by side, love
me and you

is this the awakening reign
of love's ever flowing stream
the one I envision
or do I dream

* * *

I love to see you
sparkle so bright
rainbow moonbeams
shoot from inside your eyes
my mysterious purple princess

sunbeams cry
on the ocean breeze
take me to the sigh of relief
this day is done
. . . turn the page on this one

fire on high gone to rest
heaven sent a righteous guest
—to save me
on my lonely quest
as I spill into my pillow

headed for the pot-o-gold
in my dreams
where my priceless
purple princess
participates in passion

* * *

beautiful music
was made just for you
you sleep
like an innocent child

I like to call you
—my girl
there's something inside you
that seems a bit wild

the wave of your hair
like the curl
on the waves of the sea
I love the way you gaze at me

you're sweet and supple
like a seventeen year old bronze beauty
. . . you see
you're even in my dreams

the inquisitive blink
of your lashes
reminds me of
the Cheshire cat

I love to ponder
the curves of your body
you giggle with dimples
I like you like that

your eyes are so clear
they sparkle like starlight
you're warm when we mingle
you hold me so tight

you're sweet and supple
like a seventeen year old bronze beauty
. . . you see
you're even in my dreams

I yearn for your calling
that swelter you've got
I drip when you love me
—your feeling so hot

we're honest when we speak
my heart feels strong
we hold hands when we sleep
we meld for so long

I feel like we belong
I love the way you moan
you even do that in my dreams
how quickly we have grown

I watch you sleep
curled up in a ball
how natural it seems
I love it all

you're sweet and supple
like a seventeen year old bronze beauty
. . . you see
you're even in my dreams

* * *

she's a mean mistreater
and I love her

she's like an ac/dc heater
thinking of her

I love her truly
her love is unruly

when I'm with her
I go crazy

my lovely bluesy woman
I'm a fool

she treats me cruel
and I love her

* * *

you say everything
in the right way
and at the right time
and it's all right in my mind
but it's the wrong time for lovin' you

I'm sorry for what's been done
I know sometimes I was wrong
now all I've got is a song to sing
so let me sing it to you

you've got to live and learn
and when your whole world takes a turn
don't let it hold you
remember what I told you

. . . I'll be there

what does love bring
but hurt and sorrow

a feeling for today
a hope for tomorrow

isn't it strange
how people change
it's enlightening to see
what you end up to be

yeah, you've got to live and learn
and when your whole world takes a turn
don't let it hold you
remember what I told you

. . . I'll be there

* * *

sometimes baby
you hold me down
I think about the things I could do
but then . . . I love you

sometimes you say
I suffocate you
and when you get mad
you always threaten to leave

well this time baby
. . . so long
I've been hangin' on too long
and I know it's wrong

and this time . . .
when I get myself together
it will be better

that's the way it's gotta be
so baby . . .
I'll see you soon

oh baby . . .
when you left
the last thing you did
      was cry

I didn't know you would
with our love
      or could

baby, when you left
the last thing you did
      was cry

I didn't know you would
with our love
      or could

you said that you're leavin'
it's a sign of the times
this time it's for real
you just can't stay

well this time baby
I hope you know
I can't take it anymore
gonna walk out that door

I gotta find my way
—on my own
but I hope you know
I still love you so

oh baby . . .
when you left
the last thing you did
      was cry

I didn't know you would
with our love
      or could

baby, when you left
the last thing you did
      was cry

I didn't know you would
with our love
      or could

* * *

the plans we made
the things we gave
to each other
the dues we paid
worked like a slave

and I'm still working hard
—yes it's true
but now it's not
for me and you

it's all memories
I don't believe it
it's all memories
I can't conceive it

it's taking so long
to accept it
I can't believe that it's true
. . . only memories of you

we grew so much
—together
for so many years
though it wasn't always good times
going on

now I know what's done is done
can't think in terms of two
of me and you no more
I know the score
know what I'm living for

take me back
to that place we were
—before
take me back, baby
give me some more

it's all memories
I don't believe it
it's all memories
I can't conceive it

it's taken so long
to accept it
I can't believe that it's true
. . . only memories of you

if time could tell
how you feel
and you know it does

if love was really real
if you had felt the way I do
then our love might still be true

but now I'm sitting here
thinking of you
and all the things
we used to do

of the full moon
when it was young
making love
in the morning sun

all those little things
we went through
when we were one

but now I take time
on my own
and stay to myself
as much as I can

. . . trying to get by
. . . trying to make a stand
. . . trying to get where I'm going
. . . trying to break on through

. . . and these memories of you

take me back
to that place we were
—before
take me back, baby
give me some more

it's all memories
I don't believe it
it's all memories
I can't conceive it

it's taken so long
to accept it
I can't believe that it's true
. . . only memories of you

* * *

sad demeanor in the winter
blown like willows on the wind
weeping dust among the masses
crashing 'round the river bend

does it end on misty waters
will the light shine through the trees
does it snow on destiny's daughters
forever brings me to my knees

morning's sacred grazing goddess
colored memories lose their sheen
thought you were a maiden modest
not another in-between

see the coming chains of grandeur
ancient power standing tall
set the mood on high rock towers
for this journey comes the call

vague utterances written in the dark
whispered quietly unknown
spoken hopefully to find a spark
of love's heart gracefully shown

deep roots hidden in my memory
beat me down to slow decline
woke me up with sudden fury
where I knew you once were mine

rode away with sad rejection
wheels were spinning, took me far
could it be you missed the yearning
couldn't live with who you are

take me now . . . again tomorrow
to that place I know so well
lay me down in meadow softness
with this sorrow where I dwell

could it be tomorrow's dreamtime
flew away on moods of blue
music as my only rest now
would that you could hear it too

vague utterances written in the dark
whispered quietly unknown
spoken hopefully to send a spark
love's heart gracefully shown

there you were as bright as daylight
far to reach I could not go
hair that bristles with the dewdrops
of the tears I only know

take a journey back to gladness
take me now and hear my plea
take away this dreamtime sadness
show your heart that I may see

in the world are many dreamers
who'll awaken from their sleep
to release the quiet screamers
who no longer have to weep

harmony the hope of lovers
who learn lessons from the song
of the wand'ring one who travels
to the place where they belong

right or wrong the journey's endless
but the joy is where you are
in this place of fateful gathering
lands the long lost shooting star

    comes the peace in moment's stillness
        comes the truth in memory's glare
            comes the gift of life-long wonder
                comes sweet music in the air

vague utterances written in the dark
whispered quietly unknown
spoken hopefully to find a spark
of love's heart gracefully shown

in the time of not quite splendor
lies this story I have told
when the bold create their music
from the rhymes that now unfold

it's a song that will inspire
it's a tale that's well been sold
of the rain and of the fire
we all know as we grow old

it's my story . . . my desire
take me to that sleeping place
take me down to my sweet slumber
to a soothing time of grace

vague utterances written in the dark
whispered quietly unknown
spoken hopefully to send a spark
love's heart gracefully shown

"DaVinci Study"
C. Steven Blue - 1989
pencil on art paper

Set #2:

passionate articulation: intricacies of love

I gaze at you
from across the room
I wonder what it is
drawing me to you

I can see in your eyes
you feel it too
every time you have a chance
you glance at me

you are striking
in my eyes
but you could be my demise
shall I play the fool again

black-haired beauty
with long flowing curls
speak to me
with grace and glory

I yearn to know
the story in your eyes
if you could warm me
with your surprise

I can see you shimmer there
are you aware of how I feel
do you really feel it too
—could you

tell me sparkling wonder
what is it makes you shine
why am I drawn to you
wanting you . . . to want me

* * *

into your heart comes the whirlwind romance
taken in rapture that clings to the soul
might you believe it was love at first glance
don't look too close or you might lose control

promise me anything . . . bring me some joy
into this heart make the sight of you sing
show me in some way I'm not just your toy
bring me the passion that true love can bring

it's not just a little thing that I request
melt me with moonbeams that shine from your eyes
show me that you can move miles from the rest
grant me the warmth of your gentle surprise

please won't you give me the passion I seek
I will then know, love . . . the soul of your glow
as we tumble in ecstasy not for the meek
your kiss on my lips will bring all love can know

* * *

for all the glory
and the faith
and all the time
I had to wait

for all the work
we had to do
for you to get to me
and me to you

god . . .
I feel tired
—elated
a strong appetite for kisses

but not hungry
for I feel . . . full
—fulfilled
from tip to toe

how was I to know
what you had in store

just yesterday
I couldn't look at lovers
in the eye
      yesterday
I couldn't listen
to their sigh
      yesterday
love songs made me want to cry
      —just yesterday

but now you are here
I feel alive again
with feelings I'd forgotten
growing stronger
by the minute
        hour and day

and just yesterday . . .
                              feels so far away

just yesterday
I knew that I would surely die
        yesterday
the tears welled up inside
        yesterday
springtime made me sigh
and yearn to roam
like lovers do
        —just yesterday

but today
the grass is greener
        sky is bluer
                love songs soar

just yesterday
there was no one
but now . . .
there is so much more
because now there is you

for all the glory
and the faith
and all the time
we had to wait

for all the work
we had to do
for you to get to me
and me to you

I am grateful
you are here
        today

and just yesterday . . .
                              seems so far away

* * *

you are like . . .
an old familiar song
on the radio
one that soothes my soul

you are like . . .
a comet
shooting through the sky
out of control

soothe my soul
take me out of control

you are like . . .
the dewdrops kissing the grass
when you press your kiss
upon my lips

you are like . . .
an open highway
stretching out in front of me
on a long-awaited trip

press your kiss upon my lips
take me on a long-awaited trip

you are like . . .
a heater
warming my heart
on a rainy day

you are like . . .
a lighthouse
in the fog
showing a lost ship the way

warm my heart
show me the way

you are like . . .
touching the stars
and it's enough . . . but
you keep me wanting more

you are like . . .
a sunset
on the shore
with colors galore

keep me wanting more
give me colors galore

* * *

ever since we've met
I've had this strong urge
to eat strawberries
  fresh
    nourishing
      effervescent

each kiss is like
a snowflake's unique pattern
floating
  softly
    in the air
      then landing

each touch a small
but integral part
of a soft
  white
    fluffy
      feather-bed

each moment a patch
sewn into
the quilt
  becoming
    our life
      together

one full of days
fresh for picking
strawberries
  we are
    still blossoming
      on the vine

* * *

derogatory remarks
shattered dreams
and broken hearts
perhaps were all to mold me
make me worthy
for this moment

to receive and accept
more freely
this love that comes so easy
that I thought would never come

the last laughers
hip-shooters
crap table smackers
I thank them all

they helped me
to surrender
so I can be here—right now
just here to love you

okay . . .
you've got me doin' it
I'm inspired once again
I smell your fragrance
in the air
everywhere I go

I momentarily measure
our embrace
you catch my breath
as I catch yours

the subtlety of our oneness
sprang up so naturally
but like a geyser
it gushes forth

it pours and pours
and I'm like . . .
once moist cracked earth
—sop it up
can't get enough

that's why I'm asleep
then awake
tired
then inspired

ruffled
then bedazzled
but not fractured
by loneliness . . . anymore

because you
are my passionate surrender

* * *

languishing beauty
of love's lost refrain
searching my heart to follow
the feeling of empty dreams

in the gathering storm
I sense the fading glow
the seams that rip . . .
a ship sails away in the night

never shall the time seem
. . . slower
nor grow the heartache
. . . deeper
from this dream
I cannot awaken

to retrieve what is left
of happiness
—run fast
to catch a glimpse
before it crosses
the horizon
of emptiness

oh, how I long for . . .
that which cannot be followed
how I reach for . . .
that which cannot be touched

how I yearn for . . .
that which my heartbeat remembers

what is gone—forever
I must move on

but all I can see
is the future that cannot be
. . . as I awaken
. . . to you softly
. . . kissing my old memories
. . . away

* * *

shivering sounds of morning bring
the death of nighttime's howl
the masses gather to the highway
another dog-day prowl

if I'd never known your love my dear
I couldn't make it through
all these things I can't abide
and all the things I do

so much of life is pain
with love a sweet refrain
if I could begin again
I'd still yearn for you

I'm smitten by the magic call
of music to my ear
the thunder of the psychedelic
sounds so ultra clear

it's in me . . . as it's always been
to help me bide my time
foretelling our magic vanishing act
from all this city grime

so much of life is pain
with love a sweet refrain
if I could begin again
I'd still yearn for you

* * *

I am thinking of you right now
are you thinking of me
I am thinking of the warmth
where we could be

this feeling's pouring out of me
your love feels so good
this inspiration doesn't happen enough
I wish it would

you say you fall so easy
that you get hurt
but you've got to take the chance
you make my feelings so alert

don't you see now
don't you see how
you've got to take the chance
get up and dance

the dance of me & you
till the morning dew
the dance of me & you
—love anew

you are going your way
I am going mine
but we've got some time, you know
time right now to grow

we're honest with each other
it's obvious to see
in any good relationship
it's got to be

don't you see now
don't you see how
you've got to take the chance
get up and dance

the dance of me & you
till the morning dew
the dance of me & you
—love anew

* * *

proud and pleasant
lazy flowers
mingle thoughts
at noontime hours

sun shines through
on misty shores
cliff tree hangers
open doors

sweet wine
long time
Scottish girl

red-white patterns
'round the room
clear spring water
cracks the gloom

music circling
fans the air
salt and pepper
friends with flare

sweet wine
long time
Scottish girl

in the midst
of not quite sound
feelings linger
pass around

cats that ponder
corner walls
moondrops tickle
waterfalls

sweet wine
long time
Scottish girl

I lean on time
is that your name
back to find
the price game

purple velvet
in your eye
orange slice
the pie of sigh

sweet wine
long time
Scottish girl

cucumber castle
zucchini stew
curly red hairs
protect the dew

long halls of clover
brown beams galore
imported stagger
the lengths of the floor

sweet wine
long time
Scottish girl

cardboard corners
still attached
blue tag signatures
memories latched

chilled sweet truffle
metal cream chair
lacquered wood logos
praise the affair

sweet wine
long time
Scottish girl

* * *

tiny as the seeds of rain
lush and green the vast terrain
a deep ocean sky foggy smeared
high above the clouds have cleared

pigtails prance so near me now
green carpet coats the lover
different colored smiles allow
much to be uncovered

so near and yet untouchable
to read you like a book . . .
which needs its pages slowly turned
to the window where you look

vast the shroud, like spilled whipped cream
conjures up your colored dream
into something showable
is your magic knowable

mount in dream time proud and private
brave your knowledge and describe it
read the rather boring score
I would have you give up more

leather lounging shook me up
drenched me in your buttercup
captured colors braided close
leave me with an overdose

double cover, softened layers
signify the lustful players
mounds of luscious hand-clasped moans
draw me to your stranger zones

as we languish between shaking sleep
and rumbling awake
the sky curls
like layers on a lake

or clothes
on a newly bloomed rose
your sigh is the reason
. . . I suppose

open the cabinet
discover your stash
sprinkle with rose water
in a hot flash

fun on a dime
just in time to discover
it's easy, you know
because you're my lover

snow-capped silhouettes
linger below
melt in a moment
from the view of your glow

how can we linger now
when we drop down
for dream time is over
and we've touched the ground

(dream on an airplane)

* * *

how many times in my life
can I say
I saw that look in your eyes
—from far away

and you saw me too
our glances locked
but it was never meant to be

and always . . . I wondered what if . . .

what if you hadn't
stepped onto that train
what if I wasn't stuck in the rain

what if we had met for real
over the vast terrain
of this lifetime

I caught your eyes
but didn't get to keep them
—gone with my fumbling blunder

left here on my own
all alone again
down under
the look in your thunder

were you dazzled as well
by the vibrations we swapped
what was the power
you had over me

could it be the allure
of an unspoken love
now gone with the waves
into eternity

or was it just . . .
my melancholy thoughts
caught in the moment
of a chance encounter

what if it wasn't
what I thought I saw
and what if you never
saw it at all

. . . but I saw it
. . . I know I saw it

that catch in your eyes
I didn't get to keep
—gone with my fumbling blunder

left here on my own
all alone again
down under
the look in your thunder

* * *

you say that you love me
—oh so much
you want to experience
my every touch

that I might have to give
that you might need to feel

yet you want to discover
what more might be out there
—to uncover
all the world has to offer

your young lust is longing
your body aches to describe
what another young lover
might have deep inside

how can I decide
to keep or let you go
how can I live with
what I might have to know

how can I taste
your kisses so sweet
that will leave me deserted
with a love incomplete

sweet and tempting
your words stick in my throat
I want you . . . I need to
feel all that you have

but I want to be sure
you're all mine to explore
the catch strikes so deep
don't you know I need more

how can I keep you
but let you go
my world isn't ready
for a relationship like this

or is it just
that I cannot stand
the thought of you lingering
with another man

as I burn for your kisses
and long for your touch
afraid I might lose you
what I treasure so much

how can I decide
to keep or let you go
how can I live with
what I might have to know

how can I taste
your kisses so sweet
that will leave me deserted
—a love incomplete

* * *

just a total distraction
painted feelings across your lips
another chemical reaction
trickling down to my fingertips

but . . .
sometimes you're sweet
like a peppermint stick
a little bit spicy
a little bit slick

just another attraction
laying here across your bed
another chain reaction
going off inside my head

but . . .
sometimes you're sweet
like a peppermint stick
a little bit spicy
a little bit slick

just a lack of traction
spinning wheels between your ears
another emotional reaction
broken-down feelings behind my tears

but . . .
sometimes you're sweet
like a peppermint stick
a little bit spicy
a little bit slick

* * *

it's hard sometimes
letting you go
I was looking for a full-time love
don't you know
        and you were just looking
        to find yourself

but it's always fun
watching you grow
observing self-discovery
makes my insides glow (does it show)
        while you're just looking
        to find yourself

so go on flower
—bloom
I'll just dance around my room
and tingle inside for the knowing
      go on flower
      bloom

it's awkward sometimes
when you call
and I have nothing to say at all
because I know
      you're still looking
      to find yourself

there's so much
I'd really like to say
but it all stems from yesterday
so I let it go
      and watch you
      looking to find yourself

so go on flower
—bloom
I'll just dance around my room
and tingle inside for the knowing
      go on flower
      bloom

* * *

does he . . .

climb the nearest rainbow
just to capture treasures for you

does he . . .

sing for you a love song
just to prove his love is true

does he . . .

let you know in little ways
he always thinks of you

    . . . does he

do you . . .

run so fast to catch him
when he's been gone awhile

do you . . .

kiss him like you ought to
for the way he makes you smile

do you . . .

let him know you'll always try
to walk the extra mile

. . . do you

will you . . .

both be like the weather
that is changing with the times

will you . . .

both stay so romantic
like the poet in his rhymes

will you . . .

keep the magic going
even through the hardest times

. . . will you

will you . . .

remind each other daily
that your love was meant to be

will you . . .

try your best to notice
all the things that love can see

will you . . .

until the end be grateful
for this love of the highest degree

. . . will you

. . . will you

. . . yes, will you

* * *

the sunset gone
leaves an image so warm
of dewdrops that melt
of feelings I felt

and visions of love
that you shared here with me
which shined with the sun
when our day had begun

before this lush sunset
    was gone

the music heard
shines harmony still
of experiences shown
of memories known

and visions of song
brought inspiration along
my heart didn't know
that I wanted to show

before this new music
    was heard

the dream reborn
shines brightly on me
of kneeling at the ocean
of love that's in motion

and visions of you
that I cherish in time
a heart-song so real
that you never could feel

before this love-dream
    was reborn

the mirror cracked
leaves images distorted
of love's broken dreams
of sliding down schemes

and visions of grandeur
that made me meander
to wonder in awe
what it is that I saw

before this old mirror
    was cracked

* * *

on the road to nowhere
I found your love
I thought it was the real one
they're always speakin' of

but sticky situations
always follow you
and hydramatic changes
you're always goin' through

almost made it this time
got so close
could almost see it shine

almost made it
we almost made it
—this time

now I'm not regretting
I ever knocked on your door
and I'm not forgetting
I always went back for more

but I only wanted
for us to set love free
to feel its rhythm
and seek its center
—the secret center

almost made it this time
got so close
could almost see it shine

almost made it
we almost made it
—this time

almost made it
we almost made it
—this time

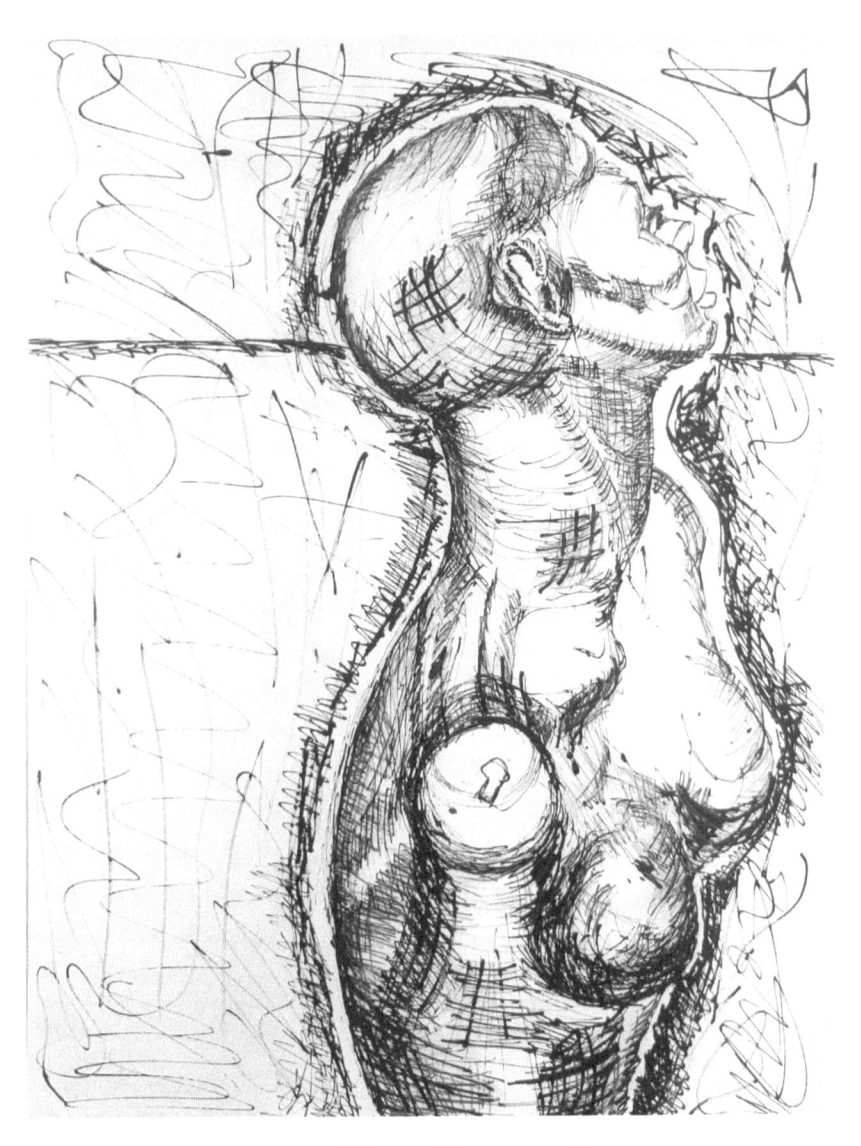

"Manic Mannequin"
C. Steven Blue - 1989
ink on art paper

Set #3:

reflective contemplation: movements of love

the blues in the sunset
like the blues in your eyes
the sun fading softly
thru clouds in the skies

remember I love you
remember it's true
you'll always be with me
whatever I do

driving down
the avenue of tears
these are the livin'
and lovin' years

the trying years
the crying years
yes, these are the times
of hopes and fears

coming to me
on a wave of inspiration
thoughts of you
like the waves on the sea

the warmth of the sun
on the horizon
how it always shines
when I see what can be

crowded with clouds
and misty shrouds
working my way
thru the haze

biding my time
till I break on thru
gathering up
the days

driving down
the avenue of tears
these are the livin'
and lovin' years

the trying years
the crying years
yes, these are the times
of hopes and fears

* * *

short call . . . down stream
city lights and twilight time
stand and stare
at flaming star
that blue-eyed friend of mine

cut glass . . . crystal gaze
words that ring and signs that show
sit and wonder
at the sky
the warmth of passion's glow

knowing
wondering
ever growing
to thundering

shivering
quivering
onward
to delivering

the heart-song of your dream
short call . . . down stream

* * *

give me the reason to be alive
I've always been a survivor
give me the will to survive
not just a nine-to-fiver

it's you down in the meadow
dancing in the grove
surrounding purple flowers
the honey smoking clove

today is the future
the journey has begun
one on one we ride together
looking out for the sun

you drove me love
so drive me away
into tomorrow's past
the future yesterday

you drove me love
now drive me away
with you by my side
        always

* * *

see you stare
with amazement
as I dare to yearn
for that feeling
the softness of your warmth

lay your chest bare
let me know what is there

can you feel it
inside you
to let me feel it
inside me

if you are beginning
to be aware
then you are beginning
to understand

. . . to feel
. . . to know
. . . to care
to see just where I stand

to know it is here
beside you
and feeling the way
you do

to see
you are a woman
with so much
inside of you

so lay your chest bare
let me know what is there
oh woman . . . you are
the softness of your warmth

* * *

gratefulness comes quick
these days . . . it seems
and I am full of gratitude
for the scope of my dreams

I am easily satisfied
it's not too much
—it's so much

and I am simply satisfied
by your touch
. . . your touch

I don't care what they say
or what they think about me
for reality came back today
and paid a call . . . you see

and I was here to participate
in the simple act of being
in the time and place
for the simple act of seeing

that I am easily satisfied
it's not too much
—it's so much

and I am simply satisfied
by your touch
. . . your touch

every day I'm grateful now
just to be alive
for I am living on borrowed time
it's a grace to survive

and if I'm here tomorrow
it's only because of you
that I can see with clearer eyes
the sun shine through

I am easily satisfied
it's not too much
—it's so much

I am simply satisfied
by your touch
. . . your touch

* * *

strolling down pathways
through the park
you by my side
in the dusk before dark

seeking the road of our longing
living the dream of belonging

sun through the trees
with leaves that tease
rustling in the summer breeze

somewhere to be at ease
with only nature to please

brown and red bird
in the palm
colours on the flowers

crimson burgundy
in front of tall green bamboo
        shoots—
to white clouds in the blue
        just for you

going through changes
the same as before
but not quite the same ones
as we grow more

can you please me
or just tease me
—will I know

I want to grow with you
but I really mean grow
I want to go with you
I want it to show

do you know how I feel
is our love really real
I've got to be me
can't you see

brown and red bird
in the palm
colours on the flowers

crimson burgundy
in front of tall green bamboo
          shoots—
to white clouds in the blue
        just for you

        just for you

* * *

oh, my love . . .
do you ever feel you can't express
what you want to say
because it's such a strong feeling
and words just get in the way

oh, my love . . .
the way we feel things together
at the same time
it doesn't happen with others that way
we really do rhyme

I love you, baby
we're alike in so many ways
and I think that maybe
we'll be close for all our days

at least I hope so
. . . anyway
what more can I say
but I love you

oh, my love . . .
I'm not sure what you want to be
am I really part of you
or do you want to be free

oh, my love . . .
hear my heart . . . can't you see
that no matter what you do
you'll still be part of me

I love you, baby
we're alike in so many ways
and I think that maybe
we'll be close for all our days

at least I hope so
. . . anyway
what more can I say
but I love you

oh, my love . . .
why do I anticipate you
walking through that door
and why do you leave me
always wanting for more

oh, my love . . .
why does my heart jump
at the thought of you
and why could I never
really say we're through

because I love you
we're alike in so many ways
and I think that maybe
we'll be close for all our days

at least I hope so
. . . anyway
what more can I say
but I love you

* * *

peaceful are the moments
sparkle in my mind
tingle to my fingertips
in my prime

often times I think of you
in wee hours like this
quickly writing thoughts and feelings
I just don't want to miss

crystal lamps dangle
upside down in the air
reminds me of the earrings—that tangle
little knots in your hair

glasses on the table
sing imagination's tune
blue bongos bounce their shadows
off the walls in the room

and it's not even June
it's but May
and we may or may not
seize the day

in my mind at this time
you are so near
and I want to make one thing
quite clear

and that's the air of excitement
—all around
to know each day's adventure
is new to be found

and I'm bound to be found here
my friend
when wee hours just like this
come again

peaceful are the moments
sparkle in my mind
tingle to my fingertips
in my prime

often times I think of you
in wee hours like this
quickly writing thoughts and feelings
I just don't want to miss

* * *

slow and sure   archer in the stars
bended bow of elegance   you are
subtle ways   penetrating gaze
            thick—amber—wavy hair
falling like grace   on your shoulders
awesome archer   bend your bow
shoot your fresh flames   of desire
flame tips of longing   sweet sting of passion
            precious oil for my fire

stoned soul goddess   perched on a pearl
      in the presence of your awesome womanhood
            exquisite young girls swirl
caught in your glory   entwined in your magic
            even the waves must curl

the strength of your beauty cannot be denied
all men are weak   from the times they have tried
mystified   by your deep blue eyes
they cannot resist   what you mesmerize

crumble me once more   into a limp repose
so soft—your neck   reveals your essence
            musty syrup on a rose
I've always respected   the power of a woman
I've searched for the one   who might capture me
and now—the archer   bends her bow
            gloriously!

* * *

we all have had our times
and the memories never die
this is where we get our rhymes
but in the past we do not lie

if you think there is no one
that you can confide in
if you feel there is no one
to care

when you are alone
and need someone to talk to
please just remember
I'm there

we always have had
that unique understanding
we've lived under one roof
. . . and I know

we've gone thru such changes
alone and together
understanding
continues to grow

we've always been able
to help one another
it's only
because we both care

if someone starts using you
just for their own gain
please, oh my darling
—beware

and don't ever feel
you're alone in the world
please don't think
nobody would care

when everything's wrong
and you're not very strong
remember
there's one who is there

* * *

when you're not at home
sad that I miss you
this way
like long ago
when I used to roam
slow are the days

with all the roads
I've yet to comb
to feel this blue
I've got to say
like the twilight I gloam
slow are the days

the sky for me
is monochrome
the moon has dues to pay
I shuffle
through the sand alone
slow are the days

like sea waves
with cresting foam
that turn to invisible spray
it is as though
I fade away
slow are the days

* * *

love is like
    a pot of gold
        you've finally found

but it's actually just
    foil wrapped
        chocolate coins

makes your mouth water
tastes so sweet
but just melts away

love is like
    an ice cube
        in the sun

you hold it
    in your hand
        and it feels solid

but it's cold
and melts
right through your fingers

* * *

it seems like I was born
for emotional pain
every time I warm up to you
you push me away again

I guess I was just born
to misery
I just don't understand
it must be my destiny

born out of time
without a chance to shine
spending all my time
tryin' to make a dime

in and out of love
and then alone again
something from above
and then it's gone again

you treat me like there is no room
in your life for me
you seem to want me
just to go away

does it make you feel good
to make me feel bad
do you think I deserve
to be treated this way

born out of time
without a chance to shine
spending all my time
just tryin' to make a dime

in and out of love
and then alone again
something from above
and then it's gone again

* * *

       you
your long fingers linger
stroking each arching fiber
of sin...sation

the crack of your back
showing small beads of sweat
       as a stroke
       softly curving
brings a heightened color
to your blush

       me
I yearn to run my fingers
through the long silky hair
of my memories
       of you

in the shadows of the past

       you
in my longing
past my belonging
hasten to my being
leaving . . . me
in a cloudy mind
       reeling

wake—me
shake—me
remember—me

as I remember—the taste
of the sweat
on the crack of your back

your flowing blonde hair
delicately dropping
       caressing
       hiding
your special surprising

in the shadows of the past

       you
your long hair
       me
my longing

my longing for belonging

to the shadows of the past

* * *

woke up from a long sleep
two days very ill
my body still aches
from the bad food I ate

my bones ache too
from so much rest
many dreams passed through . . .
I think as I get dressed

in my dream I knew the way home
it was a treacherous journey
I have been there before
I hoped that you would join me
I really wanted to share it with you
if you just would have been willing
but instead . . . I only woke up to my tears

cold . . . like my life
gray . . . like my life
I never really get there
you're always out of reach

broken . . . like my life
lonely . . . like my life
you're always there in my dreams
but I only wake up to my tears

I work all day
clean up, pay the bills
I pay my own way
. . . I paid yours too
in my little spare time
I try to work on my dreams
but they always end up shattered
by outside greedy matters

and you don't want to know
what you can't really see
or maybe you're just scared
of what it actually could be
. . . if the dreams
became the reality

in my dreams . . .
I know the way home
I always think you'll follow
you said that you would love me
until always and tomorrow
but you never stick around
I turn around and you are gone
and I just wake up alone again
to my tears

cold . . . like my life
gray . . . like my life
I never really get there
you're always out of reach

broken . . . like my life
lonely . . . like my life
you're always there in my dreams
but I only wake up to my tears

* * *

A single long-stemmed rose,
brought by you as an offering
—a token
as a symbol of reconciliation,
still stands dried,
perfectly preserved
    in memory,
awaiting your return
from the misunderstanding
    silence
of your self-imposed isolation
from the love that was just learning
to share, express—caress
compassion—faith,
beginning to trust
    enough
that it could be
    trusted
to be there when needed,
and it almost succeeded;
but time leaves love dry,
brittle, still, dusty
—a memory
like the rose
and the nights without you;
still, silent, starless,
breaking the dawn
out there somewhere:
where you share this beautiful
    morning,
this lonely mourning.

(this poem is one single sentence)

* * *

branches of birches
bare fingers stretching
reaching out to the open sky
—anger
like the snaking of the river
winds and winds
as it bends its way around you
rumors abound
like moss on the trailhead
—clinging

hanging on
to your madness
bound to sting
like the bee
close enough to buzz you
as you realize the tables
are turned now
can't take any more sadness
'cause you've already given it all

your petite and private
meanderings
are a mind full
as you turn and run
from the sun
the love no longer shining
just binding you down
in the branches of the birches
reaching out to remember
the tears of yesterday's yearning

the inevitability
of your turning
is bound to constrict
the flame
while the branches of the birches
—scream
it'll never be the same

as you search
the flickering shadows
in the tunnel to your heart
you're angry
'cause you've lost at love
though you never would take part

* * *

it's hard
Don't you know
I loved you so
but I just can't stay here
anymore

we've gone through this pain
so many times
but this time the wounds
are just too sore

I'm so tired
that I'm weary
it's just no good
can't we just say—I love you
and let go like we should

we've grown a lot together
that's what love is for—they say
but like we said in the beginning
if we grow apart
then it must be okay

because growth is what matters
yes, things always change
I wanted to grow with you
but it's not mine to arrange

so come share another sunset
with me
just one more sunset
before we go

after all . . .
it's the way we started
now it could be
our afterglow

if we've outgrown our welcome
let's just leave it and say
we parted as we started
—true friends
growing our own way

I need to get on
with my own life now
and look beyond troubled times

we've both got a lot
to share—somewhere
but in a love
that truly rhymes

so come share another sunset
with me
just one more sunset
before we go

after all . . .
it's the way we started
now it could be
our afterglow

in my heart
I've already left
you pushed me away
long ago

I keep on hoping
something will change
but it just rearranges

so come share another sunset
with me
just one more sunset
before we go

after all . . .
it's the way we started
now it could be
our afterglow

* * *

tempted by an angel
speaking words of love
tempted by an angel
a vision from up above

tempted by an angel
she was speaking the words of love
tempted by an angel
is all you were guilty of

you did the best you could do
worked hard to make things right
but no matter how hard you try
some things just don't work out in this life

you paved the road
to the Garden of Eden
you even made her your wife
but in the end she left you
with nothing but guilt for the strife

tempted by an angel
speaking words of love
tempted by an angel
a vision from up above

tempted by an angel
she was speaking the words of love
tempted by an angel
is all you were guilty of

you can't ever seem
to find someone
willing to commit like you do
yet you've still got your children
and your dreams
to carry you through

but you still see that sparkle
that shines in her eyes
you still remember it all
and no matter how you try to ignore it
. . . sometimes
you still hear the angel's call

tempted by an angel
speaking words of love
tempted by an angel
a vision from up above

tempted by an angel
she was speaking the words of love
tempted by an angel
is all you were guilty of

* * *

I feel like the invisible man
can't get any attention
everyone looks right past me
my efforts don't get any mention

starin' out the window
on a cold and rainy day
you left me all alone again
so all I gotta say is . . .

get me outta here
—right now
I don't wanna be here
can't you see
ain't it clear
I wanna be gone

get me outta here
—right now
I don't wanna be here
can't you see
ain't it clear
I wanna be gone

* * *

lemons on the tree
that cause no one to pucker
sit rotting in the rain
on stormy Sunday

well worn flip flops
still carry your tired feet
as you move slowly through
your no one to speak to world

vague infrequent memories
of making love—you would
rather just be touched
in all the aching places

much kinder . . . and safer
than the risk of another
breaking heart, long worn
like a thick terry robe

but without the comfort or warmth
or the ability to soak up
the wetness
of your lonely tears

* * *

I am writing you this love letter
to tell you how much I remember
I was so sensitive to your touch
as we ran through our lives unique

I kissed you at the public pool
it was the first kiss
of too young in love

—you blushed
then we walked home
we were the best of friends

we shared all that we dreamed
our future proclaimed in front of us
but then you moved away
I knew I'd never see you again

the corners and crossroads
I'd have to go through
the road untaken I'd have to capture
so you and I could finally be
in the future of our rapture

just like the whispers in the wind
our love blows the cottonwood blooms
planted on the plains of our future
through the doorways of eternity's rooms

stuck somewhere between time and space
our love always looms . . .

"Bronze Affair"
C. Steven Blue - 1989
chalk and eraser on art paper

Set #4:

singular declaration: futures of love

you can't see the world
you're so lost in your cloud
you'd rather upload
than experience life

you can't look around you
you're stuck . . .
your little hot box
your fingers just pluck

you never look up
—to look around
there's a whole world out there
that could astound you

you're missing your own life
it's passing you by
all you can see
is the cloud in your eye

I can almost hear
what you're thinking . . .
"don't look at me
I'm up in the cloud"

iCloud   myCloud   yourCloud

you know big brother
is watching you
when your future is only
—talk to the box

it's so . . . two seconds ago
and it's trending

upload the future—now
before it gets away
store it in the cloud
your memories for today

all you want to do
is whip it into a frenzy
diss it with a swirl
dance it till it drops

the thrill of the moment
is all you live for
it's all you got

so just . . .

—upload

the real world doesn't hold
enough memory for you
no experiences to store away
for download on a rainy day

all you hear
all you see
all you want
is your hot little box

I can almost hear
what you're thinking . . .
"don't look at me
talk to the cloud"

iCloud   myCloud   yourCloud

—ourCloud

it's all you got

so just . . .

—upload

* * *

. . . you're a love doll

self-inflated
with your botox lips
and plastic bits
don't you just beat all

. . . you're a love doll

paint your face
with the latest craze
can't see too clearly
in your oxycodone haze

. . . you're a love doll

can't touch your soul
'cause the makeup's on too thick
you never lose control
but you're not too quick

. . . you're a love doll

. . . you're just a love doll

* * *

there are no natural
women left
they all want to look
like stars

with painted on eyebrows
and bright red lips
they look more like
the flies in the bars

but maybe
that's just what they want
with their ho lingo
and tattoo bling

they stare like they wanna
—kick yer ass
and think you are gay
when you sing—unless you scream

but they don't hold a candle
to the women in the '60s
with their hair flowing down
wearing spring Levi blues

no bras, no makeup
and natural breasts too
smelled of peaches
and nature renewed

it's sad what the media
crams on you
it's plastic
and faddy . . . and unreal

it only has to do
with image and money

not about what
you really feel

if the CEO's limo
comes knockin'
at your door
you'll be at his beck and call

though you claim to be
women of power
you're not in touch
with your feelings at all

stylish and stone faced
with cleavage to spare
polished and perfect
you strut it with flair

fashion and fiction
your knowledge of those
does far more to please you
than what I compose

it's your pantyhose purpose
with thongs that glitter
toenails that shine
hands on your twitter

that make up the world
you spend all your time in
you're a consummate consumer
with a corporate grin

and if I sound jaded
it's just that I care
for the natural woman
who is hiding in there

who is longing deep down
to be free of this clamor
that traps you and bleeds you
this masquerade of glamour

it keeps you from being
who you really are
if you'd come down to earth
from your nebulous star

to be what you really
    can be
to know what you really
    believe

to love what it is
that you really want
deep down it's for you
that I grieve

there's a natural woman
who wants to let down her hair
speak with real thunder
show that you care

wipe off all that makeup
take off all that bling
uncover the song
that you sing

and with a big grin
declare you are free
of the plastic fantastic
wanna be

* * *

brazen nose
and plump, lush lips
onyx eyes
and butterscotch skin

oh, gracious lady
down in the shadows
when you recover
please let me in

drawn in the moment
lost in the memory
found in the feelings
of love's lost lament

superlative being
ultimate pleasure
are you a dream
or just longing's intent

* * *

sometimes . . .
when I'm asleep at night
you materialize in my dreams

I see your hair
your lips
your eyes
then like a cloud
you vaporize

I wonder . . .
are you real

are you the one
who's like no other
are you the one
is that YOU

are you the one
who's like no other
are you the one
is that YOU

sometimes . . .
I catch a glimpse of you
in the market or on the street

a hint
of the glimmer
in your eye
or a whisper
of your smile

where are you . . .
for real

those secrets
that you hold
under cover
just for me

I wonder . . .
where can you be

are you the one
who's like no other
are you the one
is that YOU

are you the one
who's like no other
are you the one
is that YOU

* * *

you look to me . . .
like somebody throwing up roses
a prescient and perceptive
human being

you look to me . . .
like someone who doesn't do poses
a peachy-skinned presence
of fascination

I catch
your alluring demeanor
the glow
of your wondering gaze

your fetching, yet spare
inclination to sing
it shines
through my wallowing haze

I wonder what brings you
to center
to spring up and be
at this moment we're in

I hope in this catching
you'll let me slip up to
the magic
that swallows your sin

* * *

oh, to see the potential
of who you are inside

what a flower—what a rose
what a fragrance it could be

to see the colours of you
sparkle, shine

drip all over
like a wet rainbow

the layers—the coats
could keep me warm forever

and could beat the hours of time
and the rustiness out of my breath

* * *

out of thin air you appeared
I saw you from across the room
our eyes were fixed
—like magnets
a breeze drew me to your perfume

you strolled towards me with purpose
your smile lit up the whole place
you seemed to see me
the way I saw you
it was written all over your face

come to me
my blooming rose
carry me away
I propose
sing me your beauty
in soft spoken words
teach me the way of love's prose

out of thin air we created
a love that was destined to be
it happened so quick
in a time freeze
waves of love crashed on the sea

I brought you out of slow yearning
to heightened flames of desire
you lit me so hot
I burned on the spot
and nothing could put out the fire

come to me
my blooming rose
carry me away
I propose

sing me your beauty
in soft spoken words
teach me the way of love's prose

* * *

hometown bliss
in the heart of the city
loving her
is like that it seems

part time passion flower
full time pretty
could this be
the answer to my dreams

past time failure
the reason I am scared
now a love . . . that comes so natural
none can be compared

I always learned something
from the mistakes I made
could this be the reason
not to be afraid

I ponder something
that means a lot to me
I wonder how she feels about it
what her thoughts might be

then she comes across
with compassion and concern
from each other, every day
there's something new we learn

loving and sharing
in plentiful amounts
seems to see the best in me
caring when it counts

hometown bliss
in the heart of the city
loving her
is like that it seems

part time passion flower
full time pretty
could this be
the answer to my dreams

* * *

my broken heart says goodbye
doesn't know what else to try
attempting to make it thru
but I'm so blue

it's soul cleaning time
for assemblages of love's magic
the cobwebs scream in rhyme
for the rhythm

don't you know
it's the smoke signal key
in your memory

sittin' here
alone again or
just makin' it
with my memories

sittin' here
alone again
just makin' it
with my memories

guitar strings stretch for miles
it's awhile before it calls
the stalls . . . the scorches
the courses you have to follow

seem so hollow
like that old oak tree
in your memory
but I'm still tryin' to get to you

I sing and play alone
my broken heart says goodbye
because you couldn't try

just sittin' here
alone again or
just makin' it
with my memories

sittin' here
alone again
just makin' it
with my memories

* * *

remember the last time
you cried on my shoulder
looked at me with those tears
in your eyes . . . and cried

then said you wouldn't leave me
never would you leave me

well who is it now
who walked out the door

who is it babe
who's not here anymore

who won't say why
or what for

I do not grieve for the loss
of what was
I grieve for the loss
of what could have been
but was never given the chance

it's happened
so many times before
I just don't know what to say
anymore

point me in the direction of truth

respect
   compassion
      consideration

    hope
        faith
            trust
                honesty

—sensitivity
to seven roots
of successful partnering

nurturing
    nudging
        encouraging
trudging
    sharing
        daring

—declaring your freedom
to think . . . feel . . . be
who you are

strength
    decisiveness
        security

I do not grieve for the loss
of what was
I grieve for the loss
of what could have been
but was never given the chance

it's happened
so many times before
I just don't know what to say
anymore

point me in the direction of truth

* * *

I saw it in your eyes once
not so long ago
I felt it when you smiled at me
with that old familiar glow

but the magic seems so rare now
in the autumn of my years
the things that used to tingle inside
can now bring me to tears

oh, the long and cloudy years
the range of which ran broad
dissolve into the aches and pains
that now make me feel flawed

I've slipped . . . and fallen down
don't know if I can get back up
to feel again, what I felt back then
when you filled my loving cup

are all my love songs written
is this the last hurrah
will I never again be smitten
by the beauty that I saw

are all my love songs written
did it all just end too soon
will I ever again . . . feel the passion
or the howling of the moon

I felt it in the way you moved
in the once again so new
the moon was full, your curves were round
oh, how your fancy flew

but the flying is less frequent
and the motivation's mild
the things that used to drive me mad
no longer are so wild

I've settled into the distance
and hung my tears to dry
now all I have . . . is a vague resistance
to call my dreams and try

are all my love songs written
is this the last hurrah
will I never again be smitten
by the beauty that I saw

are all my love songs written
how could it all just end so soon
will I ever again . . . feel the passion
or the howling of the moon

the small and whispered wonders
that barely recall my youth
the forget-me-nots . . . that I forgot
in all the tangled truth

it's a melancholy madness
that I've stumbled
it now creates this sadness
and I'm crumbled

in a lifetime of love's passion'd memories
and heartfelt, often missed discoveries
I truly do admit
that I am humbled

are all my love songs written
is this the last hurrah
will I never again be smitten
by the beauty that I saw

are all my love songs written
did it all just end too soon
will I ever again . . . feel the passion
or the howling of the moon

* * *

traces of her
locked in the memories
of your mind

sometimes sparked
by the hint of a smell
on a soft breeze
blowing through your day

it stops you in your tracks
makes you ponder
living it once again
in this moment

* * *

in the fantasy reaches
of our silver glistening dreams
those moody metaphors
still reach out . . .

to touch our memories
and unite the streaming consciousness

although the words we never said
may haunt us for all time
I'll not regret we ever met
I loved you in my prime

this song that now comes sentient
reminds me of those years
the thrill of love . . . the sadness
and even the lonely tears

although I can't replace them
they'll live on in this song
we'll always be reminded
of a timeless love so strong

in the fantasy reaches
of our silver glistening dreams
these moody metaphors
still reach out . . .

to touch our memories
and unite the streaming consciousness
once more

"Suzie Q"
C. Steven Blue - 1990
pencil on art paper

Set #5:

enduring revelation: resolutions of love

I'm just a lost soul
living in a world I can't control

looking for someone
to make me feel whole again

seems you just can't win

just a lost soul
looking for a better way to go

can you show me how to feel
can you show me what is real
—right now

or do you know how

I'm just a lost soul
driving down life's avenue

looking for that sparkle
in the eyes of someone new

baby, is that you
baby, is that you

just a lost soul
looking for a better way to go

—don't you know

can you show me how to feel
can you show me what is real
—right now

or do you know how

* * *

just to be me
to think of only me

—by myself

got to find my way home
love myself alone
once again

voices in the sky
calling out to me

not to feel the same
—anymore
don't want to play the game

the cure
is willingness
acceptance is the key

to free what's inside of me

lonely am I
I struggle to identify

sometimes I want to cry
just need a friend

happy am I
when you look me in the eye

sometimes I want to sigh
just need a friend

someone to confide in
I conceive

someone to believe in
I believe

lightning strikes
in closed eyes lying awake

for serenity's sake
I surrender

be tender
   merciful
      and true

if I believe in you

* * *

sunshine in the springtime
strangers turn to .
.
                    fall

beckoned to the breaking summer
follow true love's call

it's there for you
          for me
so much to do
          to see
true love sets you free
          engulfs you blindly
                    undeniably

writing up a storm
to quench the morning
          greenery
the scenery of song
directs the lovers' long . . . long
          yearning
for the knowing
          of the glow

     of . . .

sunshine in the springtime
strangers turn to .
.
                    fall

beckoned to the breaking summer
follow true love's call

* * *

the sun in your eye
is the smile in my sigh
the warmth
of your loving surprise

the things that you do
always draw me to you
your love is your secret
disguise

the things that I know
from the things that you show
are always the thoughts
that don't fade

the wonder and magic
of what can be found
because of the dues
that you've paid

I sing the songs
that are never heard
I write the words
that are seldom read

I paint you pictures
with invisible ink
—expressions
of what can't be said

the fear of not knowing
the fate of not growing
the signs of the truth
yet to be

creative endeavors
and love on the line
are always the hardest
to see

* * *

if I could take my dreams
to a pawnbroker
and borrow on them for awhile

then he'd be the one
to feel you so close
and see your smile

to know the warmth
and comfort
of loving you

and the myriad
of your emotions
that each day seem so new

then thirty days
or a lost ticket . . .
second-hand dreams for sale

and I only pose this
so you will know
the makeup of what my dreams are

for what price tag
is worth giving up dreams
even for a little while

certainly not
what the pawnbroker would give
to see your smile

to know the warmth
and comfort
of loving you

the myriad
of your emotions
so new and so true

and then thirty days
or a lost ticket . . .
second-hand dreams for sale

* * *

the keys to the kingdom
are in your heart
they open the doorway
to the light from the dark

they'll bring us together
so we'll never be apart
the keys to the kingdom
are in your heart

where are you
when I need you
you should know me well
by now

if you can't see what
I'm feeling

then I've got to show you
but how

if it wasn't for our love
my dear
where would we be
right now

—just remember
always remember

the keys to the kingdom
are in your heart
they open the doorway
to the light from the dark

they'll bring us together
so we'll never be apart
the keys to the kingdom
are in your heart

why do you always
go somewhere
you should know by now
you can stay

tell me what you
are actually feeling
what are you going through
today

don't just leave me
with tear-stained eyes
wondering what you
really want to say

—just remember
always remember

the keys to the kingdom
are in your heart
they open the doorway
to the light from the dark

they'll bring us together
so we'll never be apart
the keys to the kingdom
are in your heart

* * *

blue . . . as can be
desire cannot be filled
hungry for your love so far away

blue . . . tell my heart
to try and settle down
tell it to remember love won't stray

blue . . . since you've gone
and left me stranded here
moping through the night in cloudy skies

blue . . . on my own
tv is no company
for the blurry teardrops in my eyes

blue . . . blue
can't get away from you
you're the color of my mood all day

blue . . . blue
no matter what I do
always seems like you're just here to stay

—when my baby goes away

blue . . . how I sigh
in morning quiet time
finds my mind still drifting off to you

blue . . . standing still
don't know which way to move
trying to find some way to renew

blue . . . it's just the way
too long without you near
can't get you off my mind won't set me free

blue . . . it's just not right
the darkness is my home
gathers like a gloom inside of me

blue . . . blue
can't get away from you
you're the color of my mood all day

blue . . . blue
no matter what I do
always seems like you're just here to stay

—when my baby goes away

* * *

I've anticipated you
all night long
your blue dress—lover
hangs on the song
of my moaning

the cool night has brought us
to this pose
trapped in the moonlight
a breeze blows

I stroke you wistfully
down you I glide
your hungry eyes pierce me
deep inside

the passion of our kiss
a double-take of bliss
rolling round your eyes
while my fingers tingle
your prize

your red hair shimmers
in firelight's song
the fall of crimson curls
you're the master . . . where I belong

the traction of
your slinky blue dress
as I slip within . . .
my lustful caress

your ivory smooth skin
invites me in
so hot to the touch
I want you so much

the sent of liquor
on your breath
mingles with
the flickering sweat

our tongues to our passion
so sensual and wet

. . . inciting a fever's glow
. . . we just flow
. . . in this slow night
. . . of knowing

it is so . . . so evidenced
by the plight of your sigh
I am hung on the silence
as our deep moans die

and I melt
like hot jello
in the fold
of your mellow

on this night
of delight
with you
in blue

—my blue dress lover

* * *

you came to me
on a winter's day
you sparked my attention
I glanced your way

you didn't tell me
you were on the run
from bad intentions
that left you undone

no need to cower
your heart makes me smile
I feel your power
I love your style

no need to apologize
for just being you
there's nothing to be sorry for
—it's true

little redhead
dancer in the light
special beauty
like butterflies on lavender

that subtle humming
when your mind is in flight
the twinkle in your eye
when you're happy

the ultimate surprise
when you snap a smile in wonder
I'll never get enough
of your spell that I go under

I want to read your mind
—but I can't so I'm stir-crazy
the things you do the best
always amaze me

you love me like
there's no tomorrow
it distracts your fear
your pain, your sorrow

you give me the reason
to trust love again
you give of yourself
it comes from within

little redhead
dancer in the light
that special beauty
like butterflies on lavender

that subtle humming
when your mind is in flight
the twinkle in your eye
when you're happy

* * *

I wish I could give you
your joy back
burn it deep
down into your heart

to hear you exclaim
in your truest clear voice
your love for this life
and your part in it

I wish that I could give you
—my joy
I wish that I could show you
the way I really feel

all I can do
is continue to love you
and be here for you
each day

I'll take the time
to fall in love with you
. . . again

remembering when
our love was new
and everything was right

I'll take my time
to hold you close
and slow dance
kiss you tenderly

I'll hold you
in the moonlight
burning bright

I wish that I could show you
this sunset on the sea
cloud-cover on the horizon
that the sun now seeks

I wish that I could share with you
these Japanese silhouettes
with colors I can only paint
as horizons in my memory

I wish that I could give you
all the joy that you deserve
and everything you want
without the strife

I wish that you could have
a joyous fun-filled time
—every day

and love the journey
of the ride
that is this life

I'll take the time
to fall in love with you
. . . again

remembering when
our love was new
and everything was right

I'll take my time
to hold you close
and slow dance
kiss you tenderly

I'll hold you
in the moonlight
burning bright

I'll take my time
to fall in love with you
. . . again

* * *

would I take you as I find you
absolutely, if I could

would I build a world around you
absolutely, yes I would

would it were that I could find you
would it were my world to build

such a thrill, I'd love you still
absolutely, if I could

if you could love me with all my scars
everyday would be just fine

if I could catch the shooting stars
the dream come true would make you mine

would it were that you could love me
would it were my stars to catch

such a thrill, I'd love you still
absolutely, you're my match

oh, darling . . . it's true
for I have you and you have me

that you could see the way I feel
now that's the way it's got to be

you'd surely know my love is real
and that it's all that I can do

to show I really do belong
        to you

if I could sing you all my feelings
you would know I am your man

if I could wrangle all the dealings
I'd have you anyway I can

would it were that I could sing it
would it were my cards to deal

such a thrill, I'd love you still
absolutely, 'cause it's real

would I take you as I find you
absolutely . . . and I do

would I build a world around you
absolutely . . . here's to you

would it were my love to take
would it were my world to build

it's you and me absolutely
        me and you

oh, darling . . . it's true
I do have you and you have me

that you can see the way I feel
now that's the way it's got to be

you surely know my love is real
and it's all that I can do

to show I really do belong
        to you

* * *

the curtains of the night
. . . unfold

we sneak between the tents
. . . untold

to those whose watchful eyes
. . . might see

something they say
just shouldn't be

creep ever so softly
. . . my dear

for this is something
their ears should not hear

the sound of our heartbeats
. . . so clear

as our souls come together
. . . right here

* * *

know me . . .
could you put a handle on it
know me . . .
if I'd write for you a sonnet
know me . . .
if I'd sign my name upon it
would you know me
in this moment that we love

kiss me . . .
and I'll know that it's okay
kiss me . . .
in that very special way
kiss me . . .
could you kiss like that all day
would you kiss me
in this moment that we love

take me . . .
with a thousand moonlit kisses
take me . . .
you know Cupid never misses
take me . . .
and I'll fulfill all your wishes
would you take me
in this moment that we love

show me . . .
all the things in life that move you
show me . . .
all the music that you groove to
show me . . .
could you paint it in deep blue
would you show me
in this moment that we love

thrill me . . .
like only you can do
thrill me . . .
and I'll likely thrill you too
thrill me . . .
make me tingle through and through
would you thrill me
in this moment that we love

hold me . . .
just as close as you can get
hold me . . .
and I know I'll make you wet
hold me . . .
till our love makes us both sweat
would you hold me
in this moment that we love

tell me . . .
that our love will last forever
tell me . . .
we can stand the stormy weather
tell me . . .
yes, it's you and me together
would you tell me
in this moment that we love

* * *

the longed for love song
of winter's brazen chill
is there when I gaze
at firelight in your eyes

embracing my mere thoughts
        you see
that which I only imagine
belonging to that magical realm
caught between thoughts
and embraces

in the traces of your lilting
        fingers
warm on the scrap of my neck
I melt into summer getaways
no longer nipped
by winter's brittle freeze

I see the reflection
of love's passioned moments
. . . the smoulder in your gaze
of what is yet to come

—blanket bliss
and embered lips
pressing all our winter worries
        away

* * *

waves of passion
wash over me
wondrous
they seem to be

sweat and desire
you smell like peaches
—on fire
skin soft as cream
it's a dream

life is a forest
I run through the trees
you are the stream
that I come to

trickle drops on me
one at a time
cool me—quench me
make me feel fine

to drink—to swim
to quench this longing thirst
—of desire
you set my soul on fire

glad to be alive
just to feel . . . you
ride beside me
inside me

waves of passion
wash over me
wondrous
they seem to be

sweat and desire
you smell like peaches
—on fire
skin soft as cream
it's a dream

* * *

I am by no means the judge
don't wish to be the jury
I just want to lie here in your arms

I am no longer angry
or full of fury
I am simply bedazzled by your charms

just lying here
in the arms of the present
no longer living in the past

trying to learn something
from each new moment
trying to make it last

I am not longing
to touch tomorrow
for I can smell the sense of today

and I know that tomorrow
will be taken care of
for this moment is leading the way

just lying here
in the arms of the present
no longer living in the past

trying to learn something
from each new moment
trying to make it last

* * *

I should have been a love poet
but the words just didn't come
well maybe once in a while they did
but decades and decades are done

I should have been a love poet
writing love poems for you
in a life dedicated to peace and love
they surely would ring true

oh, if I were a love poet
I surely would write the praises
for all the things your love deserves
in the most poetic phrases

yes, if I were a love poet
I'd write of a love so strong
you never would have any doubts
you'd know this is where we belong

* * *

thoughts and forgotten memories
that read like a book
ride on the tip of my tongue
clear, yet fragile—a bubble that might burst

I write from the roots of the tree
from the knowledge started long ago
silence is golden they say
away from the disarray

it's more than that
it teaches you where your heart is
listen and receive
the wisdom of the ages

this is where I belong
in this world of vivid imaginings
forever bent on pleasing
the eyes that pleasure reading

it's the telling of my plea
that gathers in ideas gleaming
tilled in with austere burrowing
of words' resounding reasoning

this is where I belong
among others like me who so encompass
glorious dreams and inspirations
penned in time with intricate rhyme

almost as if by accident
I stumble upon these similes
to be and yet still to wonder
at the splendor of artistic remedy

I write so you know it is you
who instill the insightful belonging
I become increasingly mindful
present in enticing serenity

yes—this is where I belong
to sing with wondrous letters
the better for knowing the realms and delights
of fulfillment's gathering

— The End —

NEW VISION POETRY

C. STEVEN BLUE

About the Author

West Coast performance poet, C. Steven Blue, stands outside the normal conventions of modern poetry. He is a lyrical/performance poet, reading and performing his poetry from a unique rhythmic perspective: at the crossroads of poetry and music.

Steven is the author of eight books of poetry and one memoir. He has enjoyed putting pen to paper since he was a boy, winning his first poetry award at age twelve. He is also a micro-press publisher, and for almost 30 years he has produced and hosted literary and arts events in both California and Oregon, giving countless opportunities to other creatives along the way.

Steven writes from his own life experiences: loss, betrayal, addiction, recovery, joy, and love. From his years of struggling to recover from abuse, alcoholism, drug addiction, and mental breakdown, Steven's perspective is a refreshing and inspiring journey, one of survival and overcoming adversity, discovering a renewed faith and hope in life, and a spiritual awakening that has given him the ability to live in the here and now.

Steven is retired from a 27-year career in stage production in Hollywood, CA. He currently lives in Eugene, Oregon with his wife Paulette, where he continues to pursue his artistic endeavors.

Credits & Acknowledgements

Credits

All print book and ebook formatting by C. Steven Blue.
All cover designs by C. Steven Blue.
All original artwork by Steven C. Schreiner / C. Steven Blue
All original photos are the property of Steven C. Schreiner

Acknowledgements

I would like to thank my wife, Paulette, who was instrumental in performing the initial proofreading and beta reading for this book. She is always supportive of me as a writer. She is there for me to run things by; ready to discuss issues with plot, characterization, publishing, or any other writerly problems that may crop up.

I would like to thank my editor, Katharine Valentino, my copy editor, Gabriella D'Aloia, and my final proofreader, Grace Richards. I would also like to thank my beta readers, Terah Van Dusen, Marilyn Heasley, Ashleigh Bilodeau, Jeff Daniel, and Christine Goodnough.

I would like to thank the editors of the following literary journals and anthologies who published these poems.

"Morningstar" - *Our Western World's Most Beautiful Poems* - 1985
"The Solitary Existence Of A Daisy," "Speed Dreamin'" - *Poetry Revival an Anthology, volume 1* - 1994
"Terry," "Like A Wet Rainbow" - *Watercourse Journal* - 2013
"Reality," "Serendipity Sessions" - *Ripples On the Water* - 2013
"Oh Big Sky" - *Groundwaters 2015, an Anthology* - 2015
"Rhythm," - *Poetic Melodies Anthology* - 2016
"Just Yesterday" - *Setting Forth on a Literary Itinerary* - 2016
"Strawberries" - *In So Many Words, a Collection of Interviews and Poetry From Today's Poets* - 2016
"Just In Time," "Gypsy Writers" - *Poems On Poems* - 2016
"Never Ending Horizons" - *Poems For All-Wee Books* - 2016
"Quaint Acquiescence," "Depth Perception" - *The Daily Write* (Australia) - 2016
"Love's Dry Rose" - *Dandelion in a Vase of Roses* - 2017
"Delerium Clouds" - *Moments Before Midnight* - 2018
"The War Report" - *Terra Incognita* - 2019

Appendix A: Part 1

Heartbreak Kid—on the streets of Hollywood in the 1960s

Music, Poetry, and Video Links Related to This Memoir

Here is some additional information regarding my original songs written with my friends in 1974 after Sandy left me. As referenced in the book, we created some of the songs using my poems, which we then recorded onto tape using my Sony 2-track reel-to-reel recorder, utilizing the new sound-on-sound capability to do multi-track recordings.

"Rhythm" and "Got To Tell Somebody" were two of these poems. The resulting recordings are two of my favorite songs from the sessions we did. You can actually hear both of these recordings from the original 1974 demo tape online at my personal *Soundcloud* page (they both have me singing and playing the congas). Here is the link:
https://soundcloud.com/cstevenblue

On the same *Soundcloud* page is another poem from this book. It is a spoken-word recording from years later (2012) of my hippy anthem, "Oh Big Sky," with me reciting the poem, backed by original music, while playing a Djembé hand-drum.

You can also watch a video version of me performing "Oh Big Sky" at an art gallery poetry reading that I produced and hosted that same year (2012). You can view it on my personal website on the 'Poems' page, here:
www.wordsongs.com/poems (click on the title, "Oh Big Sky").

On that same page, you can watch another video of me doing a different poem from this book. It is from a cable TV interview of me from 2014, where I recite "Little Toy Gun," while accompanying myself with a Moroccan Tam Tam hand-drum (click on the title, "Little Toy Gun").

As far as my dancing days on TV in my teens, you can see some clips of me dancing back then at the following link on my website:
www.wordsongs.com/personal-links

Appendix B: Part 2

Bat's Ass Blues

Index of poem titles and original creation dates

Set #1: self-perception and temporal contemplation

Page   Title

346   Reality - 2/8/1990
346   Wildweed - 12/6/1997
348   Serendipity Sessions - 4/22/1988
350   Speed Demon - 5/24/2018
350   Speed Dreamin' - 2/26/1993
350   Solitary Existence Of A Daisy - 8/10/1989
351   Never Ending Horizons - 12/17/1984
352   Poetry—The Ballerina - 8/17/1990
353   To Reach You - 11/7/2017
353   Penetrating Presumptions On A Sunday Saturation - 3/27/1994
355   Depth Perception - 12/8/1998
356   Late Night Jam Session - 8/10/1989
358   Another Night In The City - 12/7/1988
361   Night Slipped Away - 10/28/1994
363   Periwinkle Pitchfork - 8/12/2021

Set #2: paid my dues for the retrospective blues

Page   Title

366   Life Is Like A River - 12/22/1969
366   From Thee Out Of Control - 5/6/1987
368   '69 Theory Unsure - 10/22/1969
369   Slow Down Ugly - 5/5/2012
370   Bat's Ass Blues - 4/23/2016
372   The Outside Sadness Of Madness - 11/20/2011
374   Is It Enough - 7/14/1988
375   It Is Whacked - 7/4/2016
376   Barroom Blues - 4/27/1991
377   King Without A Crown - 6/12-2016
378   Dusty Whirlwinds - 7/4/1981
380   Memory's Mention - 9/1/2015
380   Yesterday's Sorrow - 4/23/2020

382	Be happy with yourself - 7/15/2019
382	Waves Without The Break - 10/13/1997
389	Veronica - 9/9/2015
389	You are a dream - 8/28/2019
390	Weight Is Relative - 10/20/2010

Set #3: resounding ramifications of political instigations

Page	Title
392	Stick People On Parade - 1/14/2011
394	These Days - 7/30/1991
396	Delerium Clouds - 2/5/2017
398	Shook The Woke (after John Reed) - 12/28/2021
399	The War Report - 4/8/2008
400	Like An Old Western - 9/26/2009
405	Extreme Fundamentalism - 7/7/2017
405	Kings Of History - L.A.—4/29/1992
408	Lost With The Planes - N.Y.—9/11/2001
410	Last Seen Signals - 5/24/2014
413	Deja Vu - 5/22/2010
415	Poets - 2/11/2017
415	Modern History - 1/1/2014
416	Unfuckit - 1/12/2017
416	So Hard Won - 4/27/2021
417	Comradery - 3/13/1998
418	Macho Jock Mentality - 12/30/2013
419	The Power Of A Woman - pt. 5—for Hillary 8/1/2016
420	The End - 2/9/2017
422	One For The World - 4/30/2010
423	Wrenching - 1/6/1990
425	Falling From The Battle - 8/18/2021

Set #4: introspective reflections and peripheral articulations

Page	Title
428	The Prescient View - 4/18/2019
428	NOW - 1/4/2016
429	Man Without A Band - 5/14/2010
431	To The Blind - 5/9/2005
432	Blue Rose Suffering - 8/28/1997
434	Oh Big Sky - 1/12/1971
435	The Journey - 11/7/2019
436	Excerpt from Six Year Song - 6/26/1970
437	My Family Is The Sky - 12/19/2015
438	One For My Mother - 4/30/2010
439	Never Anymore - 2/17/2018

440	Belong To Only Me - 1/12/2020
440	Stand On Its Own - 5/8/2019
441	Sweet Surprise - 8/28/2019
442	Dominos - 3/28/2017
442	The Light Of The Sun - 8/14/2019
443	On The Fringe Of Famous - 3/5/2020
444	I Have Nothing To Say - 5/19/1993
446	Hubcaps On The Highway - 6/17/1989
446	Let Me In - 11/6/1970
447	I Was Always There - 12/30/1989
449	Cinnamon Sigh – 3/19/2022

Set #5: inner observations and nature's illuminations

Page	Title
452	Twinkling Of An Eye - 11/23/1990
452	Sounds Awakening - 10/27/2010
454	Shadows Of Sunrise (San Clemente, sunrise) - 1/16/1998
454	Whistle Down (Marina del Rey, sunset) - 11/14/1991
455	Virgin Sand - 8/29/1991
457	The Edge Of Things - 8/9/1999
458	The Blue Horizon - 1/13/2011
459	Unsung Song - 2/1/1998
462	NPR (created while scrolling NPR tweets) - 8/25/2021

Set #6: fantasy ballads and human frailties

Page	Title
464	The Blaster - 3/25/1993
466	Beast Of Misery - 7/14/2008
467	Live For Me - 1/29/2011
469	Dunnigan Falls Meth Lab Lair - 10/27/2017
472	Badly Drawn Daily - 6/30/2010
478	Aurora Borealis - 10/30/2010
482	Bright Eyes - 3/4/2017
489	The Last Hippy Poet Of The Woodstock Generation & The Last Hippy Refuge - 12/2/1992
493	The Night Of The Whispering Poet - 6/2/1996
496	The Effervescent Kingdom - 3/25/2022
500	Beckoned By Brilliance - 3/3/2015

Set #7: artistic declarations, religiosity, and amphigory moments

Page   Title

502   Successful Artist - 3/7/2017
502   Poem For Mass - 11/8/2017
502   Snow Geese - 5/6/2019
503   Weeping Birches - 11/12/2018
503   Sky Gazers - 6/18/2017
504   She's Coming - 10/17/1991
506   The Smell Of Religion - 5/3/2013
506   Everything Is War - 3/10/2015
508   Quaint Acquiescence - 4/13/2012
509   Future Ancestors - 7/22/2019
510   Invisible—Voice To Many - 7/6/2022
511   Gypsy Writers - 3/5/2011
511   Abstract Piccolo - 10/24/1997
512   Slither Me Slowly - 3/15/2012
513   24 Stations Of Modular Plate - 6/12/2005
514   Numbolina Dances - 2/18/1990
515   Just In Time - 12/4/1988

Appendix C: Part 3

Butterflies On Lavender

Index of poem titles and original creation dates

Set #1: incidental observation: awakenings of love

Page   Title

520   As Far As We Can See - 9/1/1978
521   Sunny Sunday Women - 7/10/1978
522   Lover's Leap - 7/24/1991
525   Deep Blue Eyes - 8/20/1977
526   The Wind And The Tree - 8/1/1976
527   Shahnah - 9/29/1977
528   Priscilla's Escape - 6/21/1993
530   Box O' Flames - 9/6/2012
531   Awakening Reign - 3/13/1988
532   Purple Princess - 5/4/1988
532   Even In My Dreams - 2/28/1988
534   Lovely Bluesy Woman - 10/30/1970
534   Live And Learn - 3/24/1975
535   The Last Thing You Did - 6/15/1978
536   Only Memories Of You - 8/31/1978
539   Chains Of Grandeur - 11/30/2010

542   Artwork: "Da Vinci Study" - 1989

Set #2: passionate articulation: intricacies of love

Page   Title

544   Sparkling Wonder - 1/21/2012
544   All Love Can Know - 9/3/2012
545   Just Yesterday - 4/3/1990
547   Give Me Colors Galore - 12/4/1989
548   Strawberries - 4/20/1990
549   Passionate Surrender - 4/3/1990
550   Away - 3/8/2011
551   Vanishing Act - 3/10/2003
552   The Dance Of Me & You - 11/27/1977
553   Scottish Girl - 2/6/1985

554	The Window Where You Look - 11/12/2010
556	The Look In Your Thunder - 3/12/2017
557	A Love Incomplete - 7/29/2008
559	A Little Bit Slick - 1/30/1990
559	Find Yourself - 6/14/1991
560	Will You - 8/29/2010
562	The Mirror Cracked - 1/13/2011
563	Almost Made It - 4/25/1991

| 565 | Artwork: "Manic Mannequin" - 1989 |

Set #3: reflective contemplation: movements of love

Page	Title
568	The Avenue Of Tears - 6/1/1977
569	Short Call Down Stream - 2/6/1985
569	Drive Me Away - 9/13/1984
570	The Softness Of Your Warmth - 11/5/1970
571	Simply Satisfied - 6/22/1988
572	Just For You - 6/26/1989
573	Oh My Love - 3/9/1979
574	Wee Hours - 5/21/1989
576	The Archer - 7/23/2013
576	There's One Who Is There - 6/15/1969
577	Slow Are The Days - 5/8/2010
578	Love Melts - 2/19/1989
578	Born Out Of Time - 7/24/1981
579	You Me—The Shadows Of The Past - 4/9/2010
580	Wake Up To My Tears - 12/5/1997
582	Love's Dry Rose - 10/12/1991
583	Branches Of Birches - 3/17/2015
584	Afterglow - 6/2/1992
585	Tempted By An Angel - 11/10/1998
587	I Don't Wanna Be Here - 12/7/1992
587	Terry - 1/7/1995
588	My Timeless Love - 12/25/2011

| 589 | Artwork: "Bronze Affair" - 1989 |

Set #4: singular declaration: futures of love

Page	Title
592	iCloud-Upload - 2/27/2012
593	Love Doll - 5/2/2012
594	Natural Women - 9/21/2010
596	Superlative - 3/16/2019

597	Is That You - 10/24/1989
598	In This Catching - 3/9/2015
598	Like A Wet Rainbow - 2/26/1990
599	Love's Prose - 10/24/2010
600	Part Time Passion Flower - 3/14/1988
601	Alone Again Or - 7/11/1987
602	Point Me In The Direction Of Truth - 7/26/1992
603	Are All My Love Songs Written - 9/29/2010
605	Traces Of Her - 3/22/2019
606	Silver Glistening Dreams - 12/25/2011
607	Artwork: "Suzie Q" - 1990

Set #5: enduring revelation: resolutions of love

Page Title

610	Just A Lost Soul - 4/27/1985
610	If I Believe In You - 7/31/1988
612	Strangers Turn To Fall - 3/15/1988
612	The Art Of Love - 7/31/2018
613	Second Hand Dreams - 9/9/1989
614	Keys To The Kingdom - 6/25/1991
616	Blue - 3/24/2011
617	Blue Dress Lover - 5/16/2008
618	Butterflies On Lavender - 7/19/2021
620	Fall In Love Again - 5/4/2012
621	If I could - 4/10/2010
623	Rent In The Tent - 7/13/1984
624	In This Moment - 11/30/2000
625	Smoulder In Your Gaze - 12/23/2010
626	Peaches & Cream - 1/18/1989
627	Arms Of The Present - 11/23/1990
627	Love Poet - 1/11/2022
628	Where I Belong - 4/25/2010

Contact information

C. Steven Blue

Producer / Publisher / Poet / Performer

Producer: The Eugene Poetry Foundation
Publisher/Managing Editor: Arrowcloud Press
Poet/Performer: Available for reading and performing

Website: www.wordsongs.com
Email: cstevenblue@wordsongs.com
Blog: www.wordsongs.com/blog
Facebook author page: www.facebook.com/cstevenbluepoet
Amazon author page: www.amazon.com/author/cstevenblue
Twitter: @CStevenBlue
Instagram: cstevenblue
YouTube: C. Steven Blue
Soundcloud: cstevenblue

Pioneering author
of the very first poetry chapbook published as a Facebook page;
a free multimedia poetic experience:
Perspective View of the Endless New

https://www.facebook.com/Wordsongs-FB-Chapbook-1-Perspective-View-Of-The-Endless-New-591180474377593/

Sunset West Publishing Group

Other Books

by: C. Steven Blue

S.O.S. ~ Songs Of Sobriety ~
A Personal Journey Of Recovery

WILDWEED

The Power of a Woman

Black Tights — Poetry X

The Wordsongs Series:
Wordsongs (book 1)
Wordsongs—Too Blue (book 2)
Wordsongs-3 Recovery (book 3)

For more information go to www.wordsongs.com

Made in United States
Troutdale, OR
06/28/2025